LIBRARY
MURRAY STATE UNIVERSITY

Fiscal Federalism and the Taxation of Natural Resources

Books from
The Lincoln Institute of Land Policy

The Lincoln Institute of Land Policy is a school that offers intensive courses of instruction in the field of land economics and property taxation. The Institute provides a stimulating learning environment for students, policy-makers, and administrators with challenging opportunities for research and publication. The goal of the Institute is to improve theory and practice in those fundamental areas of land policy that have significant impact on the lives and livelihood of all people.

Constitutions, Taxation, and Land Policy   Michael M. Bernard

Constitutions, Taxation, and Land Policy—Volume II
    Michael M. Bernard

Federal Tax Aspects of Open-Space Preservation   Kingsbury Browne

Taxation of Nonrenewable Resources   Albert M. Church

Conflicts over Resource Ownership   Albert M. Church

Taxation of Mineral Resources   Robert F. Conrad and R. Bryce Hool

World Congress on Land Policy, 1980   Edited by Matthew Cullen and
    Sharon Woolery

Land Readjustment   William A. Doebele

The Rate of Return   Edited by Daniel M. Holland

Incentive Zoning   Jerold S. Kayden

Building for Women   Edited by Suzanne Keller

Urban Land Policy for the 1980s   George Lefcoe

Fiscal Federalism and the Taxation of Natural Resources   Edited by
    Charles E. McLure, Jr., and Peter Mieszkowski

State Land-Use Planning and Regulation   Thomas G. Pelham

The Role of the State in Property Taxation   Edited by H. Clyde Reeves

Land-Office Business   Gary Sands

The Art of Valuation   Edited by Arlo Woolery

Fiscal Federalism and the Taxation of Natural Resources

Edited by
Charles E. McLure, Jr.
Hoover Institution,
Stanford University
Peter Mieszkowski
Rice University

LexingtonBooks
D.C. Heath and Company
Lexington, Massachusetts
Toronto

HJ
275
F557
1983

Library of Congress Cataloging in Publication Data

Main entry under title:
  Fiscal federalism and the taxation of natural resources.

  Proceedings of a symposium sponsored by the Committee on Taxation, Resources, and Economic Development, held at the Lincoln Institute, Cambridge, Mass., Sept. 10-12, 1981.
  Includes Index.
  1. Revenue sharing—United States—Congresses. 2. Revenue sharing—Canada—Congresses. 3. Natural resources—Taxation—United States—Congresses. 4. Natural resources—Taxation—Canada—Congresses.
I. McLure, Charles E., Jr. II. Mieszkowski, Peter M.
III. Committee on Taxation, Resources, and Economic Development.
HJ275.F557 1982   336.2′783337′0973   82-48581
ISBN 0-669-05436-4

Copyright © 1983 by D.C. Heath and Company

All rights reserved. No part of this publication may be reproduced or transmitted in any form or by any means, electronic or mechanical, including photocopy, recording, or any information storage or retrieval system, without permission in writing from the publisher. Permission will be granted for royalty-free use of chapters 1 and 2 of this book.

Published simultaneously in Canada

Printed in the United States of America

International Standard Book Number: 0-669-05436-4

Library of Congress Catalog Card Number: 82-48581

Contents

350940

LIBRARY
MURRAY STATE UNIVERSITY

Figures and Tables

Introduction: Taxation of Mineral Wealth and Interregional Conflicts

Charles E. McLure, Jr.
and
Peter Mieszkowski

Disparities in the fiscal capacity of states and provinces have long been a fact of life in Canada and the United States. Similarly, states have long collected royalties, severance taxes, and other levies on natural resources. But during the last decade, following the actions of the Organization of Petroleum Exporting Countries (OPEC), which have increased prices of energy, fiscal disparities have grown or at least their geographic pattern has changed, reflecting large increases in taxes received by a handful of resource-rich states.

The price shocks of the 1970s induced by OPEC have resulted in enormous windfall gains to the private and public owners of energy resources at the expense of consumers. The price increases have resulted in considerable strains on intergovernmental relations in Canada. Federal price regulations, not lifted until very recently, deprived the producing province of Alberta of substantial amounts of royalties and taxes. But even with Canadian prices at one half of world levels, this province collected petroleum revenues of $2,000 per capita in 1980 and has accumulated a Heritage Savings Trust Fund of more than $5 billion.

Because of the mechanics of Canada's fiscal-equalization program, the increase in petroleum revenues received by Alberta has put severe strains on federal-government finances: when Alberta gains additional revenues, Ottawa makes increased equalization payments to have-not provinces from general revenues. This fiscal strain led the federal government to suspend the deduction of provincial oil royalties from the base of federal corporate-income tax, further straining federal-provincial relations.

Canadian writers have been prominent in discussions of the implications of natural-resource revenues in a federal system. For example, a book edited by Anthony Scott (1976) and a special issue of *Canadian Public Policy* edited by Roger Smith (1980) are devoted to questions of the assignment

This introduction draws heavily on comments made by Charles E. McLure, Jr. to the Southern Governors' Association on 29 September 1981 and before the Subcommittee on Fossil and Synthetic Fuels of the House Committee on Energy and Commerce on 29 March 1982 and published as "Severance Taxes and Interstate Fiscal Conflicts," *Texas Business Review* 56 (July/August 1982):175-178. Reprinted with permission.

of taxing authority between federal and provincial governments and the efficiency and other implications of unequal access to natural-resource revenues.

The discussion of similar issues in the United States is of more recent origin. Although oil prices were also regulated in the United States until early 1981, regulation generated less tension between producing states and either consuming states or the federal government than in Canada, perhaps because oil production in the United States (outside of Alaska) is less concentrated geographically; royalty payments to subnational governments are less important in the United States than in Canada; and large-scale Alaskan production did not begin until the late 1970s. Texas, the largest oil-producing state, appears less greedy than its Canadian counterpart, since it imposes a relatively low rate of severance tax and does not have a corporate-profits tax.

Provision for gradual decontrol of the price of oil in the passage of the windfall-profits tax and increases in the energy prices of 1979-1980 stimulated discussion of the magnitude of the resulting fiscal transfer accruing to mineral-producing states. Two prominent court challenges—one to Louisiana's first-use tax on natural gas produced on the federally controlled Outer Continental Shelf and the other to the 30-percent Montana severance tax on coal—have quickened legal and economic interest in analysis of state and local taxes on energy production in the United States.

In September 1981 we organized a conference of the Committee on Taxation, Resources, and Economic Development (TRED) under the auspices of the Lincoln Institute of Land Policy to examine intergovernment aspects of the taxation of natural resources. Of the seven papers presented, six are chapters in this book.[1] Two of the chapters have a Canadian orientation and the others emphasize U.S. data and institutions. One of the chapters on each country focuses on legal and constitutional issues in state and provincial taxation of natural resources.

The Fiscal Landscape

Collections from severance taxes have risen enormously in recent years. From under $800 million in 1972, the year before the Arab oil boycott, they increased eight-fold to $6.4 billion in 1981. Between 1980 and 1981 severance-tax collections increased by over 50 percent. As a result, the percentage of total state tax revenue accounted for by severance taxes has doubled since the early 1970s. To a large degree these increases in revenues reflect increases in the value of output rather than in the volume.

Severance-tax collections are, of course, quite concentrated geographically. Texas has historically received the largest share of severance-tax revenues in the nation; in 1981 it accounted for just under 35 percent. Louisiana at 13 percent and Oklahoma at 8 percent have also outdistanced other states. The most dramatic increase in severance-tax revenues has occurred in Alaska. Severance-tax collections in the state increased ten-fold between 1978 and 1981, to $1.2 billion or nearly $3,000 per capita. By comparison, the severance taxes that have drawn the most public attention, litigation, and legislative proposals for limitations—those levied on coal by Montana, Wyoming, and North Dakota—amounted to a relatively modest 5 percent of national severance-tax revenues in 1981.

Important as they are, severance taxes are only one way in which governments in producing states benefit directly from higher energy prices. The state of Alaska owns all the lands in the state currently producing oil. In addition to bonus payments of almost $1 billion received when land was leased, Alaska collects over $1.1 billion annually in royalties on production on its public lands. In all, Alaska collected $3.3 billion in petroleum revenue in 1981, or about $8,000 per capita. Texas also receives royalties on land owned directly by the state or by the University of Texas, to the tune of over $500 million in fiscal 1981. A few other states also receive important amounts of royalties from production on either state or federal lands.

Local governments in several states also collect property taxes on deposits of natural resources. The data on this source of revenue are more scarce, but it appears that local property taxes on deposits of energy reserves are significant only in Texas, Montana, and Wyoming.

Finally, some state governments also use corporation-income taxes to siphon off part of increased profits from natural resources. Of particular note is Alaska, which seems to have followed a pattern of modifying the way its tax is imposed to maximize revenues. In 1978 Alaska passed a special corporate-income tax on oil companies requiring the use of separate accounting to calculate oil profits originating in the state. In response to court challenges, Alaska recently modified the tax, but the allocation formula in the new law ensures that Alaska will continue to collect corporate tax at a high level.

Consuming states have also attempted to garner increased revenues from natural resources. They have done this in essentially two ways. First, New York and Connecticut both imposed gross-receipts taxes on the major oil companies operating within their boundaries, combined with prohibition of price increases intended to prevent the tax from being shifted forward to consumers in the states. The price controls, however, have been found to violate federal energy policy and therefore are unlawful. Similar plans considered by other states seem, thus, to be in abeyance.

Second, several states are considering enactment of the unitary approach to the taxation of corporate income, at least for oil companies. States generally use a formula based on the state's share in a company's nationwide sales, payroll, and property to apportion the nationwide income of the firm among the states. Most states do this on a company-by-company basis, even in the case of groups of affiliated firms. But California, Oregon, and Alaska have followed an approach under which both the income and the factors in the apportionment formula are combined for groups of affiliated firms deemed to be engaged in a unitary business. This approach allows a state in which only the relatively unprofitable marketing operations of an oil company occur to appropriate part of the more substantial profits originating in exploration, development, and production, including those from foreign operations.

It appears that many nonproducing states are also casting about to see what else they could tax that might result in shifting of tax burdens to nonresidents. Among the ideas we have heard are a severance tax based on soil depletion to be levied on farm output and special taxes on railroads, particularly those carrying coal. This effort to find means of levying retaliatory taxes that have no other clear justification is, we believe, quite unfortunate, because it reflects not so much a healthy exercise of states' rights as the degeneration of legitimate fiscal federalism.

Effects of Fiscal Disparities

Chapter 1, by Peggy Cuciti, Harvey Galper, and Robert Lucke, and chapter 2, by Peter Mieszkowski and Eric Toder, assemble information on various forms of energy-related revenues. They show that differences in access to revenues from natural resources, which are available to a substantial degree only in a handful of states, result in large and growing disparities in the fiscal positions of various states. Montana, the state with the highest rate of severance tax, currently collects less than $200 per capita per year from natural resources. Louisiana, Oklahoma, and Texas all fall in the range of $250 to $300 per person per year. Wyoming and New Mexico have higher per-capita collections of roughly $350 per year. Finally, with its population of only about 412,000, Alaska is collecting about $8,000 per person per year from oil production. Interestingly enough, although the so-called new war between the states is often billed as a regional conflict, regional issues are not always neat and clear-cut. For example, the South produces much of the nation's oil, gas, and coal. But chapter 1 shows that these resources are very unevenly distributed, even within the South.

Figures on actual tax collections are only one way of looking at fiscal disparities. Another approach pursued in chapter 1 is to calculate how taxable capacity would vary across states if all used a representative tax system. Under this approach tax capacity is measured by applying a uniform tax structure to the revenue bases of all states. (The structure consists of all taxes typically used by state and local government, and the rates applied are national averages.) The calculations presented in chapter 1 show that the per-capita fiscal capacity of most of the major energy-producing states is well above the national average and that the primary difference between the taxable capacity of these states and that of the rest of the nation can be explained primarily by differences in the capacity to tax energy resources. For example, whereas energy-tax capacity was just over $50 per capita for the nation as a whole in 1980, it was $4,701 in Alaska, $904 in Wyoming, and $233 in Texas.

States can make a variety of uses of the extraordinary revenues they receive from natural resources. They can reduce or eliminate various non-resource taxes or they can provide higher levels of public services than found elsewhere, either to households or firms. These approaches are likely to make the resource-rich states relatively more attractive than consuming states. Economists have recently worried about the potential misallocation of scarce economic resources that could result from resource-rich states using taxes collected on natural resources to develop industries for which they have no natural comparative advantage. Among early contributors on this subject were Anthony Scott (1978), M.L. McMillan and R.H. Norrie (1980), and Charles E. McLure (forthcoming).

One of the basic objectives of chapter 2 is to quantify the possible economic inefficiency that will result, from a national perspective, if too much capital and labor migrate into energy-rich states in response to the fiscal advantages existing in those states. The analysis suffers from imprecise information on the distribution of the fiscal advantages between capital and labor and on the supply elasticities of these factors to different regions, but the tentative conclusion is that the inefficiency associated with differences in fiscal advantages of $200-300 per capita per year, at less than 10 percent of tax revenues and royalties from energy production, is not very large. Mieszkowski and Toder also argue that the potential for waste is probably much larger when per-capita tax revenues are overly abundant, as in Alaska or Alberta, since they may be squandered on public projects that have no real prospect of being economical.

Considerations such as those just enumerated can easily lead one to believe that the founders of the nation should have reserved most revenues from natural resources for the federal government. Whether this means that federal limits should be placed on state taxes on natural resources at this late date is less clear. Any such sentiments must, however, be qualified by recognition that to some extent state taxes on natural resources only compensate for various kinds of environmental damage associated with exploitation of these resources. That is, one can hardly begrudge producing states the funds they need to reclaim land that has been strip-mined, to eliminate or disguise damage done by mine tailings where possible, and so forth.

Similarly, access to a certain amount of resource revenues might be required to finance increased public expenditures on services to the resource industry and to assist states in overcoming the initial hurdles encountered in providing adequate levels of investment in public infrastructure in the boom towns often associated with development and exploitation of natural resources. Certainly, if federal limits are to be put on resource taxes, account should be taken of those costs in setting the limitations.[2] But it seems fairly clear that present levels of resource taxes cannot generally be explained by benefits provided to, or costs associated with, resource activities.

Legal and Constitutional Constraints on State Taxation

During the last several years courts in Canada and the United States have handed down significant decisions involving state (provincial) taxation of natural resources. In chapter 6 John Whyte reviews the Canadian decisions and recent constitutional developments in Canada that bear on mineral taxation.

In Canada, as in the United States, provincial taxes are subject to constitutional challenge if they substantially interfere with interprovincial and international trade. In a 1977 decision of the Supreme Court of Canada in the *CIGOL* case,[3] a windfall-profits tax imposed by Saskatchewan in 1973 was ruled invalid because it was found to be a form of indirect taxation (not allowed the provinces under the Canadian constitution) and because it was thought to interfere with the international and interprovincial trade and so represented an encroachment on a federal head of power. As the result of this decision, provincial taxes directed at oil and gas revenue will be under a constitutional cloud.

Even so, under the modified British North America Act just adopted, the provinces continue to have wide powers to tax natural resources. The act explicitly provides that the provinces may tax nonrenewable natural resources and production therefrom. The provinces also enjoy wide powers to collect royalties and to control development of natural resources. Whyte's chapter reviews the limits of the provinces' proprietary powers and related issues of the responsibility of state firms (crown corporations) to pay federal taxes.

The U.S. Supreme Court recently handed down two important decisions involving state taxation of natural resources. In chapter 4 Walter Hellerstein reviews these two cases and their implications for related issues of state taxation of energy. In *Maryland et al.* v. *Louisiana*[4] the Court struck down Louisiana's first-use tax on natural gas produced offshore on the Outer Continental Shelf and shipped into the state. The Louisiana statute was declared unconstitutional largely because it granted exemptions to Louisiana users of the offshore gas and tax credits to producers of gas who operated both in Louisiana and offshore, thereby discriminating against interstate commerce and encouraging natural-gas producers to invest in exploration in Louisiana.

In contrast with the Louisiana decision, in *Commonwealth Edison et al. v. Montana*,[5] the Supreme Court upheld the 30-percent severance tax Montana imposes on coal producers. Montana coal producers and out-of-state utility companies argued, in part, that the tax interfered with interstate commerce because it was largely borne by out-of-state consumers and was not fairly related to the services provided by the state. In reaching its decision the Supreme Court evaluated the Montana tax under the four-part test of *Complete Auto Transit v. Brady*.[6] Under that test a tax is not in violation of the commerce clause if it is applied to an activity with a substantial nexus with the state; is fair apportioned; does not discriminate against interstate commerce; and is fairly related to the services provided by the state. Nexus and apportionment were never at issue, and the Court found no evidence of discrimination, since the tax is applied equally to coal used locally and that shipped out of state. In the key part of its decision, thought by the minority to emasculate the fourth prong, the Court refused to determine whether the level of the tax was fairly related to the level of benefits provided and ruled that as long as the measure of the tax (the tax is proportional) is reasonably related to the taxpayer's contact with the state it met the constitutional test under the fourth prong.

The Court's decision not to consider either the extent of tax exporting or the relation between benefits received and taxes paid appears to have been based, at least in part, on institutional considerations; the Court is simply not equipped to deal with the economic and political considerations that would determine the acceptable rate of tax that a state could impose. It noted that if limitations are to be imposed on state taxation, beyond those in the Constitution, they must be imposed by congressional legislation. Hellerstein's basic conclusion is that the "legal constraints on the state taxation of natural resources in the American federal system are not substantial."

Charles McLure's chapter (chapter 5) on tax exporting was stimulated by the Court's decision on the Montana severance tax. A dissenting opinion to this decision argued that the commerce clause is violated if a class of out-of-state taxpayers is forced to pay a burden grossly out of line with the costs they impose on the state. The extent of tax exporting is thus central to this dissent. McLure's theoretical analysis concludes that the extent of tax exporting depends, inter alia, on the degree of market dominance of the taxing state or states. There is thus a fundamental factual question of whether coal-producing states set severance taxes independently or through implicit or explicit collusion. Moreover, in the Montana case the ability to export taxes is greatly enhanced by the existence of long-term contracts that provide for pass-through of increases in severance taxes. McLure's general conclusion is that analysis of tax exporting is so complicated that an attempt to base constitutionality on estimates of tax exporting is not advisable.

Legislative Limitations on State Taxation

Recent court decisions in both Canada and the United States strongly suggest that legal constraints on state taxation of natural resources are quite limited; the courts are reluctant to impose restrictions except in obvious cases of discriminatory taxation. Legislation has been introduced in the U.S. Congress to limit severance taxes to 12.5 percent. If this legislation were enacted, however, the limitation would affect only Montana and Wyoming, the only states whose tax rates presently exceed 12.5 percent. Moreover, binding limitations on one tax would probably lead to the substitution of alternative levies for the severance tax.

An alternate approach to dealing with the unequal distribution of natural-resource revenues is the adoption of tax-equalization schemes. In chapter 3 Robin Boadway and Frank Flatters describe the Canadian system of fiscal federalism and sharpen and extend the general case for equalization payments on both efficiency and equity grounds.

However, because of the very unequal distribution of natural resources in Canada and the United States a general-equalization scheme financed out of general federal revenues, such as that in use in Canada, would have relatively little effect on the inequality in state revenues from natural-resource taxes. Cuciti, Galper, and Lucke calculate that in 1979 the average energy-tax capacity in the United States was roughly $50 per capita. Imagine that this has doubled to $100 by 1982 and that only a small portion of states actually collect important amounts of natural-resource taxes and royalties, say states with a total population of 20 million. The remaining states with a combined population of 200 million would receive $20 billion in equalization payments from the federal government. If the payments are financed out of general federal revenues collected roughly in proportion to population, the energy-producing state would pay only about 10 percent of the additional federal taxes required. Since, in effect, the have-not states would finance 90 percent of the transfers they would receive, the net transfer resulting from a rather substantial equalization payment would be only the remaining 10 percent ($2 billion if the $20 billion is an accurate estimate).[7]

If reduction in fiscal disparities is to be taken seriously, approaches more radical than a simple rate limitation of 12.5 percent on severance taxes or an equalization scheme of the Canadian type will have to be adopted. Among possible approaches would be (1) limiting states to a certain level of total revenues per capita from natural resources, (2) requiring that producing states share some portion of their revenues from natural resources with consuming states, and (3) extending the windfall-profits tax to revenues received by government bodies as well as to other resources. Of course, these three approaches have quite different implications for the equity and efficiency of the taxation of natural resources. But any of these schemes would represent a sharp break with constitutional tradition, not to mention political realities.

Notes

1. The remaining presentation was that of Schulze et al. (1981).
2. These points were developed more fully and estimates of environmental and infrastructure costs were presented in Schulze et al. (1981).
3. Canadian Industrial Gas and Oil Ltd. v. Government of Saskatchewan (1977) 80 D.L.R. (3d) 449 (S.C.C.).
4. Maryland et al. v. Louisiana, 101 S. Ct. 2114 (1981).
5. Commonwealth Edison et al. v. Montana, 101 S. Ct. 2946 (1981).
6. Complete Auto Transit, Inc. v. Brady, 430 U.S. 274, 1977.
7. This attribute of the Canadian equalization scheme has been noted especially by Courchene (1979), for example. Equalization of this kind can adequately deal with geographically concentrated low fiscal capacity, but not high capacity.

References

Courchene, Thomas J. *Refinancing the Canadian Federation: A Survey of the 1977 Fiscal Arrangements Act*. Montreal: C.D. Howe Research Institute, 1979.

McLure, Charles E., Jr. "Fiscal Federalism and the Taxation of Economic Rents." In *State and Local Finance in the 1980s*, edited by George Break. Madison, Wis.: University of Wisconsin Press, forthcoming.

McMillan, M.L., and Norrie, R.H. "Province Building vs. a Rentier Society," *Canadian Public Policy* 6 (February 1980):213-220.

Scott, Anthony. *Central Government Claims to Mineral Revenues*. Occasional Paper no. 8, Centre for Research on Federal Financial Relations, Canberra: Australian National University, May 1978.

_____ . ed. *Natural Resource Revenues: A Test of Federalism*. Vancouver: University of British Columbia Press, 1976.

Schulze, William D.; Brookshire, David S.; d'Arge, Ralph C.; and Cummings, Ronald G. "Local Taxation for Boom-town and Environmental Effects Resulting from Natural Resource Extraction." Paper presented at the 1981 TRED Conference, Cambridge, Mass., September 10-12.

Smith, Roger S., ed. *The Alberta Heritage Savings Trust Fund: An Overview of the Issues*, a special supplement to *Canadian Public Policy* 6 (February 1980).

1 State Energy Revenues

Peggy Cuciti, Harvey Galper, and Robert Lucke

Over the eight-year period preceding the Reagan administration (1973-1981), energy was the preeminent issue on the national political agenda. The supply of energy is so pivotal to the functioning of modern society that it is not surprising that the cutback by the Organization of Petroleum Exporting Countries (OPEC) in oil supplies and the subsequent setting of vastly higher oil prices provoked a lengthy debate over the formulation of a national energy policy. The initial policy consisted of a combination of price controls and exhortations for energy independence. As the contradiction implicit in such a schizophrenic policy became manifest, a consensus emerged that all energy resources must be priced at replacement cost to encourage conservation; to increase domestic production of natural gas, oil, and coal; and to lessen dependence on imported oil. Hence, in 1978 the Congress passed the Natural Gas Policy Act calling for the gradual deregulation of natural-gas prices. And in 1979, President Carter put forward a schedule (later accelerated by President Reagan) for a decontrol of oil prices over a two-year period.[1]

Energy has moved from solely a national issue to a regional and intergovernmental issue largely because domestic energy resources are concentrated in relatively few states. Energy-price changes and federal energy policy decisions, therefore, have impacts that are differentiated geographically and are potential sources of regional conflict.[2] First producing states and then consuming states felt that their interests were ill served by national policies. And, given the new high market values assigned to energy resources, the stakes can be large indeed.

The producing states were the first to organize and express dissatisfaction with the development of national energy policy. In 1974, the Ford Administration put forward a proposal for energy independence calling for rapid development of synthetic fuels and coal resources. Governors of the western states, where much of this development was likely to occur, organized to prevent the region from becoming "an energy colony for the rest of the nation" and to ensure that "growth, change and activity will take place on our terms."[3] Their fear was that the federal government would preempt states' rights in the areas of site selection, environmental law, and water

This chapter is a preliminary presentation of some findings from a broader research project now underway at the Advisory Commission on Intergovernmental Relations. This chapter has not been reviewed by the commission and does not necessarily represent its views.

allocation and would force development detrimental to their environment and way of life.

Although issues of control over energy development are still very much alive, the decision to allow domestic prices to rise to world-market levels has pushed the concerns of energy-consuming regions to the fore. Representatives of consuming regions fear that higher energy prices will have adverse effects on their economies, since these effects are not offset, as is the case in producing regions, by growth resulting from investment in exploration and development of energy resources. The transfer of capital from consuming to producing states is believed to be exacerbated by the ability of the producing states to extract a portion of energy-resource rents through production taxes and royalties.[4]

The intergovernmental conflict stemming from energy-price changes and energy development takes two forms. First, there is a regional conflict, pitting producing states against consuming states. Rising energy prices could be the source of a permanent and serious regional economic imbalance. States rich in natural resources are likely to prosper, and consuming states may be forced to cope with an ever-declining economic base. The potential for regional conflict is heightened to the extent that the difference in economic fortunes translates into disparities in tax capacity between energy-rich and energy-poor states. Second, there is a potential conflict among levels of government. The federal government has the power to preempt state policies if they clearly run counter to the national interest. Energy-poor states have sought to enlist this federal power to offset alleged fiscal imbalances. Furthermore, the federal government can hardly avoid becoming a party to any energy-based conflict inasmuch as a large proportion of future production will occur on federally owned lands.

The Advisory Commission on Intergovernmental Relations (ACIR) decided to launch a study of the intergovernmental implications of state energy taxes and royalties in September 1980. It did so after hosting a conference on the future of federalism, when a number of experts predicted that differences in access to energy and energy revenues would be the basis for a new competition among regions and that such competition, if unchecked, could place a serious strain on the federal system.[5] The commission was especially interested in monitoring this new development, since it had just completed a major study of regional growth. This study concluded that differences in regional-growth patterns were largely benign because they were leading to a convergence in economic conditions and that, therefore, the federal government need play no additional role in regulating interstate competition to influence the location of people, capital, and jobs.[6] Thus, the commission wanted to know whether expected developments and future trends in energy production and consumption and differential access to energy-related revenues would alter its previous findings.

This chapter is the result of research directed to answering these questions. As such, it has several objectives. In the first section we review the political history of the conflicts among regions and levels of government caused by the energy crisis and resulting federal policy. Based on this review we then identify intergovernmental concerns that arise from uneven access by states to energy revenues. The second section describes several ways that states derive revenues from energy production. The third section discusses the use of the representative-tax system (RTS) for measuring state tax capacity and presents data on energy capacity as one component of total tax capacity. In the fourth section we analyze these data to assess whether energy-revenue gains may be expected to result in serious fiscal disparities and inefficient resource allocation.

Emergence of State Energy Revenues as an
Intergovernmental Issue

Producer-state tax and royalty gains first became a national issue in 1979 during the debate over oil-price decontrol and the windfall-profit tax. It was expected that price decontrol would result in large windfall gains to producers and owners of resources but that a substantial portion of these gains would in effect be recouped for the benefit of all consumers through a federal tax. In the course of debate, however, it became apparent that states where production takes place would also realize large windfall gains from decontrol in the form of increased taxes and royalties, and these gains would not be taxable by the federal government. The Department of the Treasury estimated these gains could be as great as $128 billion over a ten-year period.[7] Fearing the regional impact that could result from a transfer of such magnitude, Senator John Danforth of Missouri sought, unsuccessfully, to make the royalty portion of the state gain—that is, the amounts received by states in their capacity as owners of resources—subject to the windfall-profit tax. Danforth contended that the windfall gains would enable a few states to "conduct what amounts to economic warfare on the rest of the country. . . . They will begin doing what the OPEC countries are doing, building up their economic base at the expense of the rest of the country."[8] He elaborated on the point in the course of Senate-floor debate:

> They will package economic incentives—and they will go on a raiding party throughout the country attracting business, industry, industrial plants, job opportunities, jobs taken from the rest of the country into the state of Texas, into the state of Louisiana, into the state of California. It seems to me that is just as obvious as the nose on my face that when this kind of increased revenue goes to just a handful of states, it presents a very severe economic peril for the rest of the country.[9]

Danforth was unsuccessful in his effort to amend the tax law, in part because he was taking on Senator Russell Long—a representative of an oil-rich state and a man who usually gets his own way on tax matters. In addition, however, he lost because his amendment was seen as being contrary to traditional federal-state relationships and raising possible constitutional issues. Senator Theodore Stevens's response in floor debate reflects this view: "The Senator from Missouri has proposed a very discriminatory amendment which is, in my opinion, steering us on a new course of federalism. It is one in which the federal government will start taxing the property of the individual states. If it can tax our oil royalties, why can it not tax Missouri's court buildings? Why can it not tax every single property that states own? It is a states rights' issue."[10]

Congress also focused on state energy taxes in the context of debate over the renewal of the general-revenue-sharing grant program. Congressman Andrew MaGuire argued that a large portion of energy taxes are exported outside the boundaries of producer states and that these taxes should not be counted in the calculation of state tax effort for purposes of distributing general-revenue-sharing funds.[11] Without such an adjustment to the formula, energy-producing states might increase their share of federal-aid dollars at the same time as their fiscal capacity was increasing and their own residents' tax burdens were decreasing. The MaGuire amendment was defeated both in committee and on the House floor. Those who opposed it argued that it was impossible to determine who paid severance taxes and that it was unfair to single out energy-producing states and severance taxes when other states are capable of exporting portions of their tax burden through various other tax instruments (for example, sales taxes in tourist states such as Nevada, business taxes on cars produced in Michigan).

Tax statutes enacted in a couple of western states prompted the next congressional consideration of state severance taxes. This time the focus was on coal, and the major concern was the possible impact that high severance-tax rates could have on the price and production of an energy resource that many policymakers considered the United States's ace-in-the-hole. In 1975, the state of Montana, which contains approximately one quarter of all U.S. coal reserves and half of reserves low in sulfur content, upped its severance tax on surface mined coal from 34 cents per ton to 30 percent of the value calculated after deducting various production taxes (an effective rate of roughly 21 percent or $2.05 per ton at 1979 prices). Wyoming, another state with huge coal reserves, followed suit with substantial tax hikes in 1975 and 1977, to a statutory rate of 10.5 percent (roughly $1.02 per ton).

After relatively lengthy hearings, the House Interstate and Commerce Committee approved a bill limiting state severance taxes (on any coal destined for shipment in interstate commerce for use in any powerplant or major fuel-burning installation) to 12.5 percent of value.[12] It did so after concluding that high coal-severance-tax rates frustrated national energy policy because they posed an unnecessary burden on the production of coal when federal policy was to encourage, and indeed in some instances even mandate, its use.[13] The burden was adjudged unnecessary in that the amounts collected by the western states were considered to be far in excess of that needed to deal with direct or indirect costs attributable to production. Furthermore, the committee said "a state tax unfairly skewed to elicit revenues from out-of-state residents who are denied a voting voice in determining such tax may polarize the nation and promote fractiousness and regional divisiveness."[14]

Opposition to the bill within committee took two forms. Some members asserted that the taxes had little or no impact on the amount of coal produced or on prices to the consumer of electricity.[15] It was also argued that the committee was engaged not in drafting energy policy but rather in altering the balance of power between the states and the federal government. The severance-tax limit was said to create:

> a precedent for federal intervention into the most basic of the states activities. Under the Constitution, certain fundamental rights have been reserved to the states. One of these rights is the power of the state to tax within its borders. In limiting this power to tax, this legislation seriously calls into question the fundamental relationship between the federal and state governments under our Constitution . . . nothing less than the independence and sovereignty of the states would be forfeited.[16]

The bill limiting coal severance taxes to 12.5 percent was reported out of the House Interstate and Commerce Committee during the 96th Congress but never went to the House floor for a vote. It was caught in the backlog of business that preceded the presidential election in 1980.

Opposition to high energy taxes took yet another turn during 1979 and 1980. Two lawsuits challenging state energy taxes were decided by the Supreme Court in its 1981 term. The legal issues are briefly summarized here; they are discussed at length by Walter Hellerstein in chapter 4.

The electric-utility companies that had long-term contracts to purchase Montana coal initiated a law suit charging that the state's tax was unconstitutional on the grounds that it violated the supremacy and commerce clauses of the Constitution.[17] Under the supremacy-clause challenge, the state's tax was said to discourage production and use of coal when it was clear that federal policy was to encourage its use to decrease the nation's dependence on imported oil. The arguments under the commerce clause were multiple. The tax was said to discriminate against interstate commerce because the burden of the tax would fall largely on out-of-state consumers. Court intervention was appropriate because the interests of these consumers were not represented within the state legislature. However, the most important line of attack under the commerce clause was the contention that any tax directed at interstate commerce must bear some "fair relation" to the costs imposed on the taxing jurisdiction by the activity taxed. The Montana tax, imposed at a statutory rate of 30 percent, was said to collect much more than was required to meet any costs associated with coal mining.

The suit failed in the state courts and was appealed to the U.S. Supreme Court. In July 1981, the High Court rejected the contentions of the utility companies. It could not see a supremacy-clause issue resulting from any substantial conflict between federal energy law and the Montana tax statute. The Court also rejected the commerce-clause arguments noting that the tax was not discriminatory, since it was imposed on all coal produced, regardless of whether it was consumed in state or out of state. The Court further did not accept an interpretation of the fair-relation principle that required a balancing between taxes imposed on interstate business and benefits provided by the taxing jurisdiction. It said tax rates appropriately involve political rather than legal judgments and invited Congress to act, if, in its view, the Montana tax was contrary to the federal interest.

The Second Supreme Court decision involving state energy taxes concerned a suit filed by the states of Maryland, Illinois, Indiana, Massachusetts, Michigan, New York, Rhode Island, and Wisconsin against the state of Louisiana, contending that the Louisiana first-use tax on natural gas was unconstitutional.[18] Since the conflict involved two states, the Supreme Court accepted the case under its original jurisdiction.

The Louisiana tax effectively fell only on natural gas that was produced on the federal Outer Continental Shelf (OCS) but processed, transported, or otherwise used within the state. Louisiana claimed the tax was designed to eliminate any advantage that offshore gas might have over gas produced in Louisiana and subject to the state's severance tax. But the state provided a series of exemptions and credits to relieve instate users of OCS natural gas from any burden and to encourage offshore producers to expand their operations in the state. Furthermore, the state enacted a regulatory provision overriding certain provisions in existing contracts among producers, processors, and pipeline companies apportioning costs among the various parties. The purpose of the provision was to ensure that the burden of the first-use tax was either borne by the pipeline companies or passed forward to consumers of natural gas.

The Supreme Court ruled in favor of Maryland and other consuming states that had entered the suit, finding the Louisiana tax statute unconstitutional on both supremacy and commerce-clause grounds. The law was said to conflict with a comprehensive federal scheme regulating the production and marketing of natural gas in interstate commerce. Various provisions were found to discriminate against interstate commerce by giving an advantage to either in-state consumers or producers vis-à-vis their out-of-state counterparts.

A review of the arguments presented before the Court and in the Congress suggests that there are several concerns underlying the emergence of state energy revenues as an intergovernmental issue. These concerns may be summarized as follows:

1. Energy revenues might result in unacceptably large fiscal disparities among states in their ability to finance public services. Changes in the production and price of energy affect state finances in a variety of ways. The impacts may be of some concern if energy capacity is distributed unevenly and if the states that benefit from rising prices and production are also well situated with respect to other taxable resources. Although fiscal equalization is only of secondary importance in the U.S. federal system, a finding of major new disparities in fiscal capacity could lead to a rethinking of the need for equalizing policies.

2. The fiscal advantage accruing to producer states might be so large as to result in a distortion in the allocation of economic resources among states and regions. Such an effect might be expected if, for example, energy capacity allows a state to significantly improve its public services and/or offer tax relief to its residents and businesses. This assumes of course that location choices can be affected by fiscal variables.

3. Energy capacity may allow a state to export a disproportionate share of its tax burden to nonresidents. The distribution of tax burdens that results when some states export their tax burden may be considered unfair and may result in retaliatory actions by other states attempting to protect their own citizens' interests. Furthermore, tax exporting weakens the link within a state between public-sector benefits and burdens, thereby potentially reducing political accountability and possibly contributing to an excessive expansion of the state and local public sectors in some states.

4. Energy is so important to the functioning of the economy that national security requires a lessening of dependence on foreign-energy supplies. State tax practices might be obstructing the achievement of this goal by discouraging investment in domestic energy production or by encouraging inefficient production patterns.

5. The combination of OPEC-cartel power and federal policy allowing domestic prices to rise to world-market levels has resulted in large economic rents or windfall gains accruing to domestic energy producers and the governments that can tax them. It may be argued that the current allocation of rents is unfair in that too small a share is going to the federal government, which represents all the consumers who must bear the burden of higher prices.

Although each of these concerns raises intergovernmental issues, in this chapter we are limiting our focus to the contribution of energy revenues to state fiscal capacity and particularly to possible fiscal disparities among states. Such disparities may be a matter for concern for reasons of equity or because they affect the ability of states to compete on equal terms for other types of economic activity. Some of the other intergovernmental concerns are addressed in other chapters in this book.[19]

Energy Production as a Source of State Revenues

A description follows of the major sources of revenue derived by states from energy production: severance taxes, property taxes, corporate-income taxes, and mineral-lease receipts. Although these descriptions focus primarily on general patterns and trends using aggregate data at the national level, states vary considerably in the extent to which they make use of these revenue sources. Greater detail on specific state practices and revenue collections is included in chapter 2.[20]

Severance Taxes

The major focus of public debate thus far has been on the severance-tax collections of energy-rich states. Severance taxes are special levies on the production of natural resources. The actual taxes levied by the states may bear a variety of names (production taxes, license taxes, conservation taxes, and so on), but all are triggered by the activity of extracting a resource from the ground. Although all sorts of natural resources may be subject to severance taxes, fuel-resources account for the overwhelming share of severance-tax collections. Approximately 84 percent of severance-tax collections in 1980 were attributable to oil and gas production and an additional 8 percent to coal production.[21]

    Severance taxes take two basic forms: specific and *ad valorem*. The base for a specific severance tax is measured by the amount of production; a set fee is collected for each unit (barrel of oil, thousand cubic feet of gas, ton of coal, and so on) produced. The base for an *ad-valorem* tax is the value of the resource produced. States vary in their definition of value, some allowing various costs associated with extraction or processing to be deducted. The *ad-valorem* tax is more common.

    As shown in table 1-1, OPEC's actions to limit supply, coupled with federal policy allowing domestic prices to rise to world-market levels, have greatly increased the value of the severance-tax base. Onshore production of oil and gas has actually declined over the course of the decade, but the value of the two fuels has more than tripled in real terms (228 percent increase for oil; 260 percent for gas). The first big rise occurred between 1973 and 1975 after the Arab oil embargo. A second big increase in value occurred after 1978 as a result of another OPEC price hike following the Iranian revolution and of federal decisions to decontrol oil prices and gradually deregulate the market for natural gas.

    The picture with respect to coal is somewhat different. Here both production and value rose over the decade. The increase in value shown in table 1-1 for the early part of the decade is attributable primarily to price changes.

Table 1-1
Amount and Value of Onshore Oil, Gas, and Coal Production, 1970-1980

Year	Oil			Gas			Coal		
	Production (millions of barrels)	Value in Current Dollars[a]	Value in Constant Dollars[b]	Production (trillions of cubic feet)	Value in Current Dollars[c]	Value in Constant Dollars[b]	Production (millions of short tons)	Value in Current Dollars[d]	Value in Constant Dollars[b]
1970	2942	9355	10238	19.50	3335	3647	613	3837	4199
1971	2839	9625	10023	19.71	3587	3745	561	3966	4129
1972	2840	9627	9627	19.49	3625	3625	602	4611	4611
1973	2771	10780	10198	19.61	4236	4000	599	5109	4834
1974	2659	18268	15741	18.09	5499	4794	610	9608	8363
1975	2559	19630	15433	16.65	7409	5894	655	12596	10035
1976	2507	20531	15353	16.35	9483	7178	685	13310	10076
1977	2580	22112	15610	16.29	12869	9204	697	13814	9876
1978	2763	24871	16359	15.58	14100	9395	670	14593	9728
1979	2732	34533	21201	16.08	18942	11642	781	18354	11278
1980	2760	59591	33591	15.45	23036	13163	835	21710	12241

Source: Energy Information Administration, *1980 Annual Report to Congress*, vol. 2, Data, DOE/EIA-0173(80)/2 (Washington, D.C., 1980), tables 22,38,44,50,53,63; and U.S. Department of the Interior, Geological Survey, *Outer Continental Shelf Statistics, Calendar Year 1980*, (Washington, D.C., June 1981).

Note: Offshore production has been eliminated from the totals because most of it (that deriving from the Outer Continental Shelf) is not subject to state taxation.

[a]Value calculated by multiplying average daily production by 365 by average domestic price; figures are millions of dollars.

[b]Constant dollars based on GNP deflator, where 1972 = 100.

[c]Value calculated by multiplying production by average wellhead price.

[d]Value calculated by multiplying production by average price of bituminous coal and lignite. The average price of anthracite is significantly higher, but since anthracite accounts for a very small part of total production, its role is ignored.

The average FOB mine price per ton (in 1972 dollars) jumped from $8.07 in 1973 to $15.32 in 1975 in response to changes in the price of oil. Since that time, however, the national-average mine price has actually declined in real terms as less expensive western coal has claimed a greater share of the market. The rise in the value of production between 1975 and 1980 stemmed entirely from increases in production. Over the decade as a whole, the value in constant dollars of coal production has almost tripled.

As the value of the base has increased, so too have state severance-tax collections. Table 1-2 shows the amounts collected over the decade in both current and constant dollars. States collected $6.4 billion in fiscal 1981, 124 percent more than they had collected in fiscal 1979 and 830 percent more than in fiscal 1970. In real terms, the growth of severance taxes over the decade 1970-1980 was 216 percent, somewhat less than growth in the value of the energy-resource base (226 percent). Despite the large increase in state severance-tax collections in fiscal 1981, they still account for only a small portion (4.3 percent) of the total tax collections of state governments. For individual states, however, severance taxes make up a substantially greater proportion of total taxes. In 1981, seven states—Alaska, Louisiana, Montana, New Mexico, Oklahoma, Texas, and Wyoming—received 20 percent or more of their total tax collections from severance taxes.

Although severance taxes are highly visible as special levies imposed uniquely on the energy industry, they constitute only one of several sources of state revenue directly affected by changing energy prices and production levels.

Table 1-2
Severance-Tax Collections, Fiscal Years 1970-1981

Fiscal Year	Severance-Tax Collections		Percentage of Total State Taxes
	Current Dollars (millions)	Constant Dollars (millions)[a]	
1970	685.9	750.0	1.4
1971	733.0	763.5	1.4
1972	758.0	758.0	1.3
1973	850.4	804.2	1.3
1974	1254.2	1092.1	1.7
1975	1741.1	1386.6	2.2
1976	2028.7	1535.6	2.3
1977	2168.1	1550.5	2.1
1978	2492.9	1661.4	2.2
1979	2850.5	1751.2	2.3
1980	4207.8	2372.5	3.1
1981[b]	6379.2	3295.4	4.3

Source: U.S. Bureau of the Census, *State Government Tax Collections* (Washington, D.C.; U.S. Government Printing Office, various years).

[a]Calculated using GNP deflator where 1972 = 100.

[b]Preliminary figures.

Property Taxes

Like all owners of property, the energy industry is liable for property taxes. These taxes are imposed primarily by local governments, although some state governments use the tax as well. Since the value of energy property bears some relation to the price of output and the level of production, property-tax payments by the industry have almost certainly increased during the last ten years. Unfortunately data on property-tax payments by industry are unavailable.

States vary in how they define their base for property-tax purposes. Land and buildings are always valued and taxed, but states differ in their treatment of equipment, inventory, and especially energy reserves in the ground. In principle, a property tax ought to be imposed on the value of all reserves, regardless of the level of production. Reserves should be appraised based on the future net-income stream (appropriately discounted) that can be generated from development of the resource.[22] Appraisal requires knowledge of the characteristics of the reserve in the ground, the likely costs associated with extraction, and, of course, future prices. Needless to say, appraisal of market values is very difficult.

Indeed, the difficulties associated with the appraisal of energy resources has lead a number of states to move away from standard property taxation of mineral resources. Some retain a local property tax in name but substitute a measure of the total value of the resource produced during the taxable year for an appraisal of true market value. In these instances, the property tax is much like a severance tax, except that, as a local tax, the rate varies by location within the state. Other states exempt altogether the value of the energy rsource from the local property-tax base and rely solely on a state severance tax. It is not known whether the cumulative liability from these severance or severance/property-tax hybrids is in any way comparable to the burden that would have been borne had a uniform property tax been levied on the market value of mineral rights over time.

Unfortunately, as already indicated, there are too few data to allow the assessment of trends over time in the value of the energy-property-tax base or in the amounts collected in taxes. However, balance-sheet data compiled by the Federal Trade ,Commission (FTC) show that for corporations engaged in all mining and in the manufacture of petroleum and coal products, the real gross book value of land and mineral rights increased by 49 percent between the third quarters of 1974 and 1980.[23]

Corporate-Income Taxes

The energy industry is subject to a third major set of taxes at the state level—corporate-income and franchise taxes. Rising energy prices have increased profits, and therefore, presumably the industry's tax liability to states. Once again, data collected by the FTC provide some indication of growth in this part of the states' tax base. Between 1975 and 1980, net income before federal taxes and after adjusting for inflation increased by 48 percent for the mining industry and by 86 percent for manufacturers of petroleum and coal products.[24]

Since many of the companies that produce energy resources are vertically integrated and pursue some aspect of their operations in a large number of states, access to the energy-related corporate-income-tax base is not limited to states where production occurs. Many states use a formula to determine their share of the taxable income of multistate businesses.[25] The factors commonly used to apportion income are payroll, property, and sales by destination. The use of these factors ensures that consuming states get a share of energy-related corporate-income-tax revenue, whether production occurs within their boundaries or elsewhere.

Indeed, some consumer states have sought to capture a greater share of the profits accruing to the energy industry. There has been a flurry of state legislative activity directed toward imposing gross-receipts taxes on sales of petroleum products and/or amending corporate-income-tax statutes to increase tax collections from major integrated oil companies. Proposed changes to increase the state income-tax base include the use of unitary accounting on a worldwide basis, elimination of deductions for the federal windfall-profit tax, and even adoption of state excess-profits taxes. The Citizen/Labor Energy Coalition has been formed with organizations active in at least eight states to push for these changes in state tax laws. New York, Pennsylvania, and Connecticut have adopted gross-receipts taxes on oil-company sales, although Connecticut's tax, which incorporated an anti-pass-through provision, was later invalidated by the courts. New York has also legislated use of worldwide combined-income reporting for oil companies, and Minnesota has decided that federal windfall-profit taxes are not deductible for state tax purposes. Other proposals to impose special taxes on oil companies have been considered and are pending in several other states.[26]

Mineral-Lease Receipts

To the extent that energy production occurs on publicly owned lands, taxes do not account for all the gains in state revenues attributable to increases in the price or volume of domestically produced energy. State governments receive all or part of the lease payments made by producers for the right to explore or develop resources on state and federal lands.

Producers pay bonuses, rents, and royalties to public owners of resources in much the same way they make payments to private owners who prefer to lease rather than sell their mineral rights. Lessees of public lands are subject to all the ordinary state and federal taxes, although in some states the amount paid in royalties to federal, state, or Indian-tribe governments is excluded from the severance-tax base.

State receipts from mineral leases have grown from approximately $0.5 billion in 1972 to $3.3 billion in fiscal 1980.[27] Most of these receipts (80 percent) derive from activities on state-owned lands; the remainder results from the federal government's sharing of mineral-lease receipts with the states. Although they account for a relatively small proportion of the total, royalties from production on federal land have increased at a faster pace than state royalties.

Little information is readily available concerning energy production or reserves on state-owned lands or state policies regarding leasing. (Chapter 2 provides some information on lease terms in Texas and Louisiana.) We know somewhat more about the determinants of state receipts from energy development on federal lands. The level of receipts received by states from federal mineral leases depends on the provisions of those leases, the amount of land under lease, the level of production, and federal policy governing the allocation of its receipts.[28] Table 1-3 summarizes the provisions of federal law that determine the terms of federal leases and the distributions to states. The law varies depending on the resource and the status of land involved. Most onshore production of oil, gas, and coal under federal lease occurs on public-domain lands. Under the Mineral Leasing Act of 1920 as amended, half of all mineral-lease receipts from production on such lands are shared with the states.

Other Direct Taxes and Indirect Effects

A broader range of taxes are clearly associated with energy-extraction activity. For example, an analysis of energy taxes could consider sales taxes paid by energy-producing firms on items purchased for use in their operations, state taxes for unemployment insurance or worker's compensation, income taxes on the wages and salaries earned by the labor force engaged in energy extraction and on the dividend and royalty income received by stockholders and owners of resources. Some of these taxes are quite small, but taken together they would undoubtedly have added significantly to the total revenues attributable to energy production. We chose to restrict this analysis of the links between energy taxation and fiscal disparities among states to the major taxes and royalties for which the business entity itself is legally liable, because these payments have been the primary focus of public debate.

A more inclusive view, incorporating all taxes paid on capital and labor income derived from extraction activities, could also be justified as could an

350940 ~ LIBRARY
MURRAY STATE UNIVERSITY

Table 1-3
Major Provisions of Federal Law Governing Leasing of Federal Lands for Energy-Resource Development

Land Category	Resource	Type of Lease	Bonus Bid	Royalty	Distribution of Royalties and Bonus Bids to States
Outer Continental Shelf	Oil and gas	Competitive	Yes	Minimum of 12.5 percent; usually 16.67 percent	None
Public-domain lands[a]	Oil and gas In known geological structure[b]	Competitive	Yes	Minimum of 12.5 percent	States except Alaska get 50 percent of both royalty and bonus-bid payments; 40 percent goes to reclamation fund and 10 percent to general fund. For Alaska, 75.6 percent to state and 16 percent to Alaska native fund. No restrictions on use but priority to be given to energy-impacted areas.
	Other	Noncompetitive	No	Maximum of 12.5 percent	
	Coal[c]	Competitive	Yes	Underground 8 percent Surface-mined 12.5 percent	
Acquired lands[d]	Oil and gas In known geological structure	Competitive	Yes	Minimum of 12.5 percent	Distribution of royalties and bonus bids depends on category of land. For example, of receipts generated on national-forest lands, 25 percent goes to states to be spent on roads and schools in affected counties.
	Other	Noncompetitive	No	Maximum of 12.5 percent	
	Coal[c]	Competitive	Yes	Underground 8 percent Surface mined 12.5 percent	

Source: Compiled by authors from information reported in U.S. Office of Technology Assessment, *Management of Fuel and Non-Fuel Minerals in Federal Land* (Washington, D.C.: U.S. Government Printing Office, April 1979).

[a]Land that has been retained in federal ownership since its original acquisition by treaty, cession, or purchase as part of the general territory of the United States

[b]Areas where the character and extent of resource are known or can be estimated with a reasonable degree of confidence

[c]Before 1976, coal known to be available in commercial quantities was leased on a competitive basis with minimum royalty of 5 cents per ton, but other coal was let on a noncompetitive basis

[d]Land obtained from a state or a private owner through purchase, gift, or condemnation for particular federal purposes

alternative analysis extending beyond the extraction industry. For example, taxes imposed when energy is transported, converted to electricity, refined, or consumed could be included along with the revenues that may be generated indirectly by the reallocation of resources among industries and regions caused by changing energy prices.[29] To analyze all these effects would require a complete model of interregional and interindustry flows and the revenues associated with each state pattern of economic activity—analysis clearly beyond the scope of this chapter.

The Representative-Tax System

To analyze the impact of energy revenues on the fiscal condition of states, we will make use of the representative-tax system (RTS), a concept developed by the ACIR to compare the revenue-raising ability of the fifty states and the District of Columbia.[30] Under the RTS concept, potential revenue-raising ability or tax capacity is measured by applying a uniform taxing structure to all states. That structure consists of all taxes typically used by state and local governments. The rates applied are national averages calculated by dividing national collections from a given tax by a measure of the value of the tax base (or its proxy) nationwide. Hence, the *tax capacity* of a state and its local governments is the amount of revenue that would be raised if that state applied national-average tax rates to the particular tax bases available within the state. When the amounts calculated for each state are expressed in per-capita terms and as a ratio to the national average, an index of tax capacity can be developed. This index indicates the relationship of each state's per-capita tax capacity to the national per-capita average.

The RTS essentially provides a way to add together the various tax bases commonly used by state and local governments. By applying national-average tax rates, each base is, in effect, accorded a weight in the measure of capacity that corresponds to its contribution to the overall tax collections of state and local governments. Table 1-4 shows the types of tax included, the national-average rate applied to each base, and the relative importance of each base to the overall calculation of tax capacity.

Although the measure of tax capacity produced by the RTS builds on the taxing practices of states, the estimate for each state is independent of that state's specific decisions regarding base definition or rate. Any variation among states in tax capacity is attributable not to differences in state tax laws but rather to the distribution of uniformly defined taxable bases.

The RTS has been used by a variety of researchers over the last twenty years to measure and analyze differences in fiscal capacity among states and localities. It is not used in the United States for distributing federal grants, but in Canada a variation of the RTS is used to measure fiscal capacity and forms the basis for a comprehensive grants-equalization scheme (see chapter 3).[31]

Table 1-4
Information underlying the Representative-Tax System (RTS) for State and Local Governments, 1980

Tax	State and Local Tax Collections ($ millions)	Percent of Total	Tax Base ($ millions)	Description	RTS Tax Rate
General sales or gross receipts	51,175.5	18.8	791,261.6	Retail sales and receipts of selected service industries	6.5 percent
Selected sales	26,517.5	9.8			
Motor fuel	9,821.6	3.6	115,968.0	Fuel consumption in gallons	$.08/gallon
Distilled spirits	1,632.7	0.6	449.9	Consumption of distilled spirits in gallons	$3.63/gallon
Beer	826.9	0.3	117.8	Consumption of beer in barrels	$4.65/barrel
Wine	182.3	0.1	471.8	Consumption of wine in gallons	$.39/gallon
Tobacco	3,874.9	1.4	29,184.5	Cigarette consumption in packages	$.13/package
Insurance	3,127.9	1.2	199,158.0	Insurance permiums for life, health, property and liability insurance	1.57 percent
Public utilities	6,017.4	2.2	200,862.0	Revenues from electric, gas, and telephone companies	3.00 percent
Parimutuels	731.5	0.3	13,802.1	Parimutuel turnover from horse and dog racing	5.23 percent
Amusements	303.2	0.1	28,279.0	Receipts of amusement and entertainment business	1.07 percent
License taxes	7,702.2	2.8			
Automobiles	3,194.4	1.2	120.9	Private-automobile registrations	$26.42/registration
Trucks	2,129.6	0.8	32.2	Private-truck registrations	$66.14/registration
Motor vehicle operators	390.9	0.1	145.3	Motor-vehicle-operators licenses	$2.69/license
Corporations	1,389.1	0.5	2.71	Number of corporations	$512.58/corporation
Alcoholic beverage	180.7	0.1	0.271	Licenses for the sale of distilled spirits	$666.79/license
Hunting and fishing	417.5	0.2	62.2	Number of hunting and fishing licenses	$6.71/lic.
Individual income	41,371.8	15.2	247,386.3	Federal income-tax liability	16.72 percent
Corporate income	13,481.8	5.0	214,634.0	Corporate income	6.29 percent
Property	68,329.8	25.1			
Residential	37,384.6	13.8	2,955,168.0	Market value of residential property	1.27 percent

Commercial-industrial	21,998.9	8.1	Net book value of inventories, property, plant, and equipment of corporations	1.41 percent
Farm	4,062.0	1.5	Market value of farm real estate	0.61 percent
Public utilities	4,884.4	1.8	Net book value of fixed assets for electric, gas, and telephone companies	1.22 percent
Estate and gift	2,045.0	0.8	Federal estate and gift-tax receipts	31.54 percent
Severance	5,035.9	1.9		
Oil and gas	4,233.8	1.6	Value of oil and gas production	4.98 percent
Coal	463.7	0.2	Value of coal production	2.14 percent
Nonfuel minerals	202.9	0.1	Value of nonfuel mineral production	0.78 percent
Timber and other	135.5	a	b	100 percent[b]
Documentory and stock transfer	1,003.2	0.4	b	100 percent[b]
Other taxes	6,800.9	2.5	Disposable personal income	0.38 percent
User charges	44,373.0	16.3	Disposable personal income	2.47 percent
Rents and royalties	3,621.6	1.3	b	100 percent[b]
Payments under Mineral Leasing Act	268.0	0.1	b	100 percent[b]
Total	271,726.1	100.0		

Source: Advisory Commission on Intergovernmental Relations, *Tax Capacity of the 50 States, Supplement: 1980 Estimates*, p.6, and ACIR staff computations (Washington, D.C.: ACIR, June 1982).

[a]Less that 0.1 percent.

[b]For these sources, each state's actual collections were used as the base. Yields from these sources were added directly to the yield of the RTS.

The RTS is useful for analyzing potential fiscal disparities arising from differential endowments of natural resources because it allows the researcher to identify the contribution of particular revenue sources to the overall tax capacity of states. In the development of the RTS, analysts have concentrated almost exclusively on taxes that are commonly used by state and local governments, thereby excluding such components of capacity as user charges and fees, miscellaneous taxes, and rent and royalty income from publicly owned property. Since the conventional measure of tax capacity excludes one of the more significant sources of energy-related revenues—mineral-lease receipts—we have expanded the standard measure of fiscal capacity to include royalty payments to state or local governments from energy production on state or federal lands. Royalties were included simply by adding the amounts received per capita in fiscal 1980 to the tax capacity calculated by the RTS. This assumes that the ability of a state to raise royalty revenue is equal to the actual revenues it receives. If the general approach used in constructing the RTS had been followed, a typical royalty rate would have been established based on the value of production on public lands. However, the necessary data are not readily available.

In addition to accounting for energy royalties, we have also included user charges and miscellaneous taxes in our measure of fiscal capacity. In 1980, state and local governments raised $7.9 billion, or about 3.5 percent of all state and local taxes, through a variety of miscellaneous levies. In developing the more comprehensive measure of capacity, disposable personal income was used as the tax base for most ($6.8 billion) of these taxes. In this way, the ability to raise these various taxes was assumed to be proportionate to the disposable personal income of a state's residents. The remainder of the miscellaneous taxes ($1.1 billion) tap relatively unique tax bases, such as timber taxes or stock-transfer taxes, and were handled by adding their revenue directly to yield of the RTS; that is, collections from these special levies served as the proxy for distribution of the actual base. Finally, user charges and fees were incorporated into the RTS by using disposable personal income as the relevant base. This category includes a wide range of revenue producers, such as university tuition, highway tolls, parking facilities, airports, and public hospitals; it does not, however, include revenue from public utilities or state-run liquor stores. Although the underlying assumption—that capacity to pay user charges is directly related to disposable income—is imperfect because charges are imposed on both individuals and businesses, the present data do not allow such distinctions. In 1980, user charges and fees accounted for $44 billion in state and local revenue.

Table 1-5 displays our preliminary estimates for 1980 of the standard measure of tax capacity and the expanded measure including royalties. The differences are significant in only a few states—Alaska, Nevada, New Mexico, and Lousiana. The range of the expanded measure of tax capacity extends from $817 per capita and an index of 68.3 in the case of Mississippi to $6,161 per capita and an index of 515.1 in the case of Alaska.[32] Minnesota has a tax capacity of $1,201 which, as indicated by its index value of 100.4, is nearly equal to the national average of $1,196. (We shall refer to this expanded measure as tax capacity without further identification, although it should be understood that the measure differs from the standard measure because of the inclusion of miscellaneous taxes, user charges, and rents and royalties.)

The measure of energy-tax capacity is based on the four revenue sources described in the second section: (1) severance taxes on oil, gas, and coal production, (2) mineral-lease receipts of states from production on state or federally owned land, (3) property taxes on the energy industry, and (4) corporate-income taxes from the energy industry. The energy industry for this purpose includes oil, gas, and coal extraction.[33]

Data on the size of the severance-tax base and mineral-lease receipts are readily available and reasonably accurate. The measures of the energy-property and corporate-income tax bases are less reliable. The value of the energy-industry-property-tax base was assumed to equal the net book value of assets including inventories, depreciable assets, depletable assets and land as reported to the Internal Revenue Service. Because of the unavailability of energy-property data by state, the national totals are allocated to states according to each state's share of the industry's total payroll. This allocation procedure implicitly assumes that each industry can be characterized by a Cobb-Douglas production function and that the gross return to capital within each industry does not vary across states. In such circumstances, the share of each industry's capital stock employed within any state would equal the share of the industry's payroll within that state. Each state's total energy-related-property-tax base was then multiplied by the national-average tax rate derived for all commercial and industrial property to yield a measure of property-tax capacity. This measurement method includes offsetting errors of unknown magnitude. The basic measure and allocation method probably understate the property value of energy-rich states, since book values have not increased nearly as much as energy prices. (In contrast, for manufacturing as a whole, book values have increased faster than the general-price index.) On the other hand, the application of the composite business-property-tax rate to the energy-related base probably results in an overstatement of capacity in these same states, since in some states energy resources are not included in the property-tax base and severance taxes are substituted. On balance, we think we have understated the value of energy-property-tax capacity. The sensitivity of the results to underestimates of this measure will be determined later in the chapter.

Our measure of the energy-related-corporate-income-tax base starts with the income reported to the IRS by energy companies. We allocate

Table 1-5
Tax Capacity: Standard and Expanded Measures of the Representative-Tax System, 1980

State	Standard Tax Capacity			Expanded Tax Capacity		
	Total ($ thousands)	Per Capita (dollars)	Index	Total ($ thousands)	Per Capita (dollars)	Index
Alabama	2,799,780	718.08	75.7	3,507,489	899.59	75.2
Alaska	990,293	2,463.42	259.7	2,476,721	6,161.00	515.1
Arizona	2,291,663	841.29	88.7	2,885,299	1,059.21	88.6
Arkansas	1,717,155	749.52	79.0	2,124,731	927.43	77.5
California	26,331,802	1,109.69	117.0	32,776,753	1,381.30	115.5
Colorado	3,094,400	1,068.51	112.6	3,837,547	1,325.12	110.8
Connecticut	3,297,188	1,058.49	111.6	4,169,340	1,338.47	111.9
Delaware	631,239	1,057.35	111.4	783,739	1,312.80	109.8
Washington, D.C.	672,793	1,051.24	110.8	862,492	1,347.64	112.7
Florida	9,355,327	949.01	100.0	11,710,262	1,187.89	99.3
Georgia	4,262,375	778.09	82.0	5,306,490	968.69	81.0
Hawaii	978,257	1,010.60	106.5	1,211,965	1,252.03	104.7
Idaho	786,111	830.11	87.5	979,953	1,034.80	86.5
Illinois	11,687,956	1,021.05	107.6	14,640,633	1,278.99	106.9
Indiana	4,814,798	874.94	92.2	5,993,649	1,089.16	91.1
Iowa	2,913,978	997.94	105.2	3,554,509	1,217.30	101.8
Kansas	2,445,803	1,032.42	108.8	3,017,078	1,273.57	106.5
Kentucky	2,888,891	787.16	83.0	3,570,728	972.95	81.3
Louisiana	4,368,436	1,036.40	109.2	5,812,660	1,379.04	115.3
Maine	856,451	759.27	80.0	1,076,193	954.07	79.8
Maryland	3,977,646	941.01	99.2	5,013,634	1,186.10	99.2
Massachusetts	5,248,268	912.58	96.2	6,627,252	1,152.37	96.3
Michigan	8,537,076	919.94	97.0	10,722,101	1,155.40	96.6
Minnesota	3,961,646	969.33	102.2	4,907,898	1,200.86	100.4
Mississippi	1,662,290	657.81	69.3	2,063,629	816.63	68.3
Missouri	4,376,434	887.89	93.6	5,439,841	1,103.64	92.3
Montana	841,538	1,066.59	112.4	1,039,227	1,317.14	110.1
Nebraska	1,445,462	918.34	96.8	1,794,287	1,139.95	95.3

Nevada	1,173,647	1,465.23	154.4	1,386,380	1,730.81	144.7
New Hampshire	845,046	915.54	96.5	1,065,462	1,154.35	96.5
New Jersey	7,365,925	996.88	105.1	9,287,963	1,257.00	105.1
New Mexico	1,324,114	1,016.20	107.1	1,943,546	1,491.59	124.7
New York	15,057,553	855.25	90.1	19,712,309	1,119.64	93.6
North Carolina	4,441,553	754.34	79.5	5,564,873	945.12	79.0
North Dakota	672,138	1,027.74	108.3	880,401	1,346.18	112.5
Ohio	9,940,257	918.44	96.8	12,410,869	1,146.71	95.9
Oklahoma	3,360,458	1,107.97	116.8	4,060,279	1,338.70	111.9
Oregon	2,582,257	978.50	103.1	3,220,693	1,220.42	102.0
Pennsylvania	10,451,293	878.63	92.6	13,196,513	1,109.42	92.8
Rhode Island	755,072	794.81	83.8	982,279	1,033.98	86.4
South Carolina	2,232,948	713.86	75.2	2,807,553	897.56	75.0
South Dakota	592,945	855.62	90.2	727,617	1,049.95	87.8
Tennessee	3,448,535	749.36	79.0	4,337,405	942.50	78.8
Texas	16,723,511	1,172.51	123.6	20,539,648	1,440.07	120.4
Utah	1,195,045	815.73	86.0	1,486,911	1,014.96	84.9
Vermont	411,164	801.49	84.5	512,230	998.50	83.5
Virginia	4,818,051	899.06	94.8	6,043,550	1,127.74	94.3
Washington	4,041,326	976.17	102.9	5,142,458	1,242.14	103.8
West Virginia	1,736,662	888.77	93.7	2,107,683	1,078.65	90.2
Wisconsin	4,238,961	898.66	94.7	5,268,529	1,116.92	93.4
Wyoming	880,512	1,861.55	196.2	1,134,857	2,399.28	200.6
Totals	215,524,056	948.73	100.0	271,726,131	1,196.13	100.0

Source: Advisory Commission on Intergovernmental Relations, *Tax Capacity of the 50 States, Supplement: 1980 Estimates*, pp. 15, 19, and ACIR staff computations (Washington, D.C.: ACIR, June 1982).

this income to states by a method intended to replicate the three-factor formula, generally used by state administrators, which equally weights payroll, property, and sales by destination. Payroll data are readily available. The measure of property is the same as described previously. The sales factor is a combination of retail sales and intermediate sales, with the latter estimated through use of an input-output table.[34]

Table 1-6 presents information on these four elements of energy capacity in per-capita terms for each state. In the aggregate, energy capacity represents roughly 4.4 percent of total tax capacity or about $11.7 billion in 1980. Of this total capacity, severance taxes account for $4.7 billion or 40 percent, royalties for $3.3 billion or 28 percent, corporate taxes on the energy-production industry for $1.4 billion or 12 percent, and property taxes for $2.2 billion or 19 percent.[35]

Although the RTS provides the best available measure of state tax capacity including energy-related capacity, there are several limitations associated with this approach.

First, the data needed to measure the size of the various state tax bases within the RTS are not always complete, timely, or accurate, and proxies (such as book values rather than market values of commercial and industrial property) sometimes have to be used.

Second, the RTS fails to take account of the interrelated nature of the various taxes. The capacity to tax any given base within a state may be affected by the size of another base. For example, the ability to levy property taxes may depend in part on the income level of residents. In the energy area, a state's severance-tax capacity may depend on the profitability of firms engaged in energy production.[36] Our calculation of capacity using the RTS, which assumes each state can tax its own bases at the national-average rates, ignores these interrelationships.

A third weakness of the RTS is that it cannot take account of a government's policies, which may influence the size of its base. Two states with equal-quality coal reserves may have differing levels of production if one, in pursuit of environmental goals or life-style considerations, erects regulatory roadblocks thereby limiting development. In one sense these states could be viewed as having equal capacities, since, absent regulation, their production levels would be the same. Under the RTS, however, severance-tax capacity is measured by production value and thus reflects not just the inherent ability of states to produce energy but also their choices regarding desirable levels of production.[37]

Two additional points should be made clarifying the scope of our analysis. This chapter does not provide a fully comprehensive analysis of the fiscal effects of changing energy prices, because we have used a somewhat restricted definition of energy-tax capacity. We look at energy-tax capacity as deriving only from the income, property, and severance taxes and royalties paid by the energy-extraction industry. We do not include in energy-tax capacity taxes paid by employees or stockholders nor taxes generated when production activity spurs additional economic development. Also, we do not consider energy-tax capacity resulting from the ability to tax energy downstream (for example, taxes on refining, pipelines, or retail sales). All these other tax bases, however, are included in total capacity and, therefore, in nonenergy-tax capacity. The result of this categorization is that changing energy prices may have effects on the fiscal condition of states over and beyond those identified in this analysis.

Finally, it should be noted that we measure fiscal disparities based on a consideration of tax capacity independent of any assessment of public-service needs and requirements. We are assuming implicitly that public-service requirements are roughly comparable across states after controlling for population. This assumption is a debatable one in any study of fiscal disparities. Some may argue, however, that it poses special problems when energy revenues are the focus of analysis. Some types of energy production could have such deleterious effects on the environment or require such abnormally high per-capita public-sector expenditures that the increment to tax capacity that production provides may result in no net fiscal advantage whatsoever.[38] Whether energy production in fact imposes higher costs than other activities is an open empirical question.

Energy Taxes and Fiscal Disparities

There are two distinct reasons for focusing on fiscal disparities in analyzing the intergovernmental implications of energy taxation. The first reflects concern with the equity of the state-local fiscal structure. Fiscal or tax disparities are undesirable from this perspective because they may permit citizens to enjoy vastly different access to public services depending on where they live. This means that an individual living in a state rich in revenue bases has access to either more public services at any given tax price or a lower tax price for the same public services (and, therefore, more private goods and services).

Differential access to state and local services may be tolerated within fairly wide limits under our federal system, but at some point government action may be taken to correct extreme imbalances. For example, during the 1970s, major school-finance-reform efforts were undertaken to reduce inequities in access to resources.[39] Fiscal disparities are a source of concern because they not only result in differences in current public or private goods consumption but also may lead to differences in future income streams and consumption as well. This occurs because services such as health and education contribute to human-capital formation and hence, to future earning capabilities.

Table 1-6
Components of Energy-Tax Capacity, 1980
(dollars per capita)

State	Severance Taxes	Royalties	Subtotal	Corporate Income Taxes	Property Taxes	Total
Alabama	14.19	0.00	14.19	2.94	6.07	23.20
Alaska	1167.49	3404.68	4572.17	42.74	86.49	4701.40
Arizona	1.18	0.63	1.81	1.14	0.83	3.78
Arkansas	11.38	0.07	11.45	3.61	4.97	20.03
California	18.58	13.32	31.90	4.82	5.05	41.78
Colorado	17.94	10.80	28.75	13.78	27.98	70.50
Connecticut	0.00	0.00	0.00	1.35	0.94	2.29
Delaware	0.00	0.00	0.00	4.19	0.40	4.60
Washington, D.C.	0.00	0.00	0.00	2.01	0.56	2.58
Florida	4.44	0.00	4.44	0.81	0.31	5.56
Georgia	0.00	0.00	0.00	0.90	0.10	0.99
Hawaii	0.00	0.00	0.00	1.38	0.09	1.48
Idaho	0.00	2.81	2.81	0.75	0.38	3.94
Illinois	6.45	0.00	6.45	4.22	4.26	14.94
Indiana	4.15	0.00	4.15	2.84	2.48	9.47
Iowa	0.09	0.00	0.09	0.73	0.21	1.03
Kansas	55.38	0.37	55.75	12.65	19.63	88.03
Kentucky	28.76	0.00	28.76	8.20	21.35	58.31
Louisiana	99.42	129.61	229.03	35.79	63.77	328.58
Maine	0.00	0.00	0.00	0.63	0.11	0.74
Maryland	0.52	0.00	0.52	0.94	0.38	1.84
Massachusetts	0.00	0.00	0.00	0.90	0.01	0.90
Michigan	6.07	1.46	7.53	1.84	1.48	10.86
Minnesota	0.00	0.00	0.00	1.31	0.28	1.59
Mississippi	19.19	0.01	19.20	6.69	11.30	37.19
Missouri	0.43	3.60	4.04	1.34	0.56	5.94
Montana	55.06	35.41	90.47	12.33	21.77	124.58
Nebraska	6.09	0.07	6.15	1.57	2.05	9.77

Nevada	0.00	8.66	8.66	2.37	3.01	14.04
New Hampshire	0.00	0.00	0.00	0.62	0.13	0.75
New Jersey	0.00	0.00	0.00	3.29	0.10	3.39
New Mexico	150.43	195.54	345.97	17.80	34.47	398.24
New York	0.17	0.00	0.17	2.50	0.76	3.43
North Carolina	0.00	0.00	0.00	0.69	0.05	0.74
North Dakota	53.61	3.54	57.14	15.88	31.03	104.06
Ohio	5.50	0.00	5.50	4.17	5.07	14.74
Oklahoma	115.44	10.42	125.87	38.78	73.38	238.02
Oregon	0.00	0.07	0.07	0.97	0.25	1.29
Pennsylvania	6.98	0.00	6.98	4.77	5.88	17.62
Rhode Island	0.00	0.00	0.00	0.51	0.13	0.63
South Carolina	0.00	0.00	0.00	0.77	0.01	0.78
South Dakota	1.83	0.95	2.78	0.78	0.52	4.08
Tennessee	1.67	0.00	1.67	0.96	1.64	4.26
Texas	109.29	36.89	146.19	31.72	55.35	233.25
Utah	25.01	10.20	35.21	7.24	13.71	56.17
Vermont	0.00	0.00	0.00	0.48	0.00	0.48
Virginia	6.73	0.00	6.73	1.94	5.18	13.86
Washington	0.34	0.01	0.35	1.38	0.44	2.16
West Virginia	65.40	0.00	65.40	16.12	48.43	129.95
Wisconsin	0.00	0.00	0.00	0.74	0.06	0.80
Wyoming	413.41	281.56	694.97	69.12	140.53	904.61
Totals	20.68	14.52	35.20	6.37	9.88	51.45

Source: Advisory Commission on Intergovernmental Relations, *Tax Capacity of the 50 States, Supplement: 1980 Estimates*, pp. 45, 46, and ACIR staff computations (Washington, D.C.: ACIR, June 1982).

The second reason for concern with fiscal disparities is economic efficiency. If economic resources locate themselves geographically in response to relative prices, then tax prices as well as the prices of private goods or factor inputs should have a resource-allocation effect.[40] If differences in tax prices reflect not just real differences in the cost of providing public services but also differential access to captive tax bases that serve to lower the tax prices borne by mobile resources, then the geographic allocations of resources responding to these differences in tax prices will be inefficient. In this section, we will be concerned with fiscal disparities from both of these perspectives.

Equity Considerations

The effects of energy revenues on fiscal disparities can be shown in several ways. We may take as the starting point the RTS figures presented in table 1-5. For 1980, the index of the expanded RTS has a standard deviation of 22.2 when states are weighted for population. In dollar terms, this is a per-capita standard deviation of $266 compared to the national-average fiscal capacity in 1980 of $1,196 per capita. In contrast, if all energy revenues were distributed according to population among all states, the resultant index of tax capacity would have a standard deviation of 11.1. In per-capita terms, the standard deviation would be $132. Thus, although energy capacity in the aggregate represents only 4.3 percent of total capacity, a uniform per-capita distribution of this capacity would reduce overall fiscal disparities by 50.2 percent. The contribution of energy to fiscal disparities is clearly disproportionate to the relative importance of such revenues in the aggregate fiscal structure of the states.

The reason for this result, of course, is that the revenue capacity from energy sources is much more unevenly distributed among states than is the revenue capacity from nonenergy sources. Table 1-7 shows the coefficients of variation for total energy capacity as well as its four components (severence taxes, royalties, energy-industry property taxes, and energy corporate-income taxes) and also for selected nonenergy taxes (personal-income taxes, nonenergy corporate taxes, nonenergy property taxes, and sales taxes). Income, property, and sales taxes are the major revenue producers in the state and local fiscal structures. Among the sources of energy revenue, royalties are by far the most unevenly distributed, followed by severance taxes (coefficients of variation are 10.008 and 2.960 respectively). The energy corporate-income and property-tax bases are less unevenly distributed, but, as table 1-7 shows, the coefficient of variation for each source of energy capacity is higher by factors of 8 to 54 than those for any of the major nonenergy tax bases.

Table 1-7
Coefficients of Variation for Sources of Energy-Tax and Nonenergy-Tax Capacity

Item	Coefficient of Variation
Total energy capacity	4.168
Severance taxes	2.960
Energy property taxes	1.922
Energy corporate-income taxes	1.555
Royalties	10.008
Total nonenergy capacity	.116
Personal-income taxes	.168
Nonenergy corporate-income taxes	.128
Nonenergy property taxes	.185
Sales taxes	.146
Total fiscal capacity	.222

We noted earlier that since our measure of energy-industry-property-tax capacity is based on the book value of land and mineral rights, the contribution of energy tax capacity to fiscal disparities is likely to be understated. To determine the sensitivity of our results to possible measurement error, we arbitrarily adjusted the value of energy property and tax capacity—first by doubling and then tripling the recorded book value of land and mineral rights—and reexamined the distribution of fiscal capacity among states. Under these two new scenarios, the reduction in fiscal disparities that could be achieved by a uniform per capita distribution of energy capacity was 51.2 percent or 51.4 percent (depending on whether energy-property-tax capacity was doubled or tripled as compared to 50 percent in the base case). The standard deviation of the tax capacity indices is 22.8 when energy-property-tax capacity is doubled and is 23.4 when it is tripled. Recall that the standard deviation of the original measure of capacity is 22.2, and is 11.1 when all energy capacity is evenly distributed. Although the remainder of the analysis relies on only the base case, the results presented here should not be sensitive to the possible understatement of energy-property-tax capacity.

Table 1-8 shows total capacity, nonenergy capacity, and energy capacity for each of the fifty states and the District of Columbia in both per-capita and index-number terms. In addition, capacity resulting solely from severance taxes and energy royalties has been isolated. At the top of the table are thirteen high-energy-capacity states (states with energy capacity per capita above the national average) and at the bottom are all other states.

Table 1-8
Total Tax Capacity, Nonenergy-Tax Capacity, and Energy-Tax Capacity, 1980

	Total Tax Capacity		Nonenergy Tax Capacity		Royalty and Severance Tax Capacity		Total Energy Tax Capacity	
	Dollars per Capita	*Index*	*Dollars per Capita*	*Index*	*Dollars per Capita*	*Index*	*Dollars per Capita*	*Index*
Energy-rich states								
Alaska	6161.00	515.1	1459.60	127.5	4572.17	12989.1	4701.40	9137.8
Colorado	1325.12	110.8	1254.62	109.6	28.75	81.7	70.50	137.0
Kansas	1273.57	106.5	1185.53	103.6	55.75	158.4	88.03	171.1
Kentucky	972.95	81.3	914.64	79.9	28.76	81.7	58.31	113.3
Louisiana	1379.04	115.3	1050.46	91.8	229.03	650.6	328.58	638.6
Montana	1317.14	110.1	1192.57	104.2	90.47	257.0	124.58	242.1
New Mexico	1491.59	124.7	1093.36	95.5	345.97	982.9	398.24	774.0
North Dakota	1346.18	112.5	1242.12	108.5	57.14	162.3	104.06	202.2
Oklahoma	1338.70	111.9	1100.68	96.2	125.87	357.6	238.02	462.6
Texas	1440.07	120.4	1206.81	105.4	146.19	415.3	233.25	453.4
Utah	1014.96	84.9	958.79	83.8	35.21	100.0	56.17	109.2
West Virginia	1078.65	90.2	948.70	82.9	65.40	185.8	129.95	252.6
Wyoming	2399.28	200.6	1494.67	130.6	694.97	1974.3	904.61	1758.2
Subtotal	1384.71	115.8	1133.96	99.1	177.63	504.6	250.75	487.4
Other states								
Alabama	899.59	75.2	876.39	76.6	14.19	40.3	23.20	45.1
Arizona	1059.21	88.6	1055.44	92.2	1.81	5.1	3.78	7.3
Arkansas	927.43	77.5	907.39	79.3	11.45	32.5	20.03	38.9
California	1381.30	115.5	1339.51	117.0	31.90	90.6	41.78	81.2
Connecticut	1338.47	111.9	1336.18	116.7	0.00	0.0	2.29	4.5
Delaware	1312.80	109.8	1308.20	114.3	0.00	0.0	4.60	8.9
Washington, D.C.	1347.64	112.7	1345.07	117.5	0.00	0.0	2.58	5.0
Florida	1187.89	99.3	1182.33	103.3	4.44	12.6	5.56	10.8
Georgia	968.69	81.0	967.70	84.5	0.00	0.0	0.99	1.9
Hawaii	1252.03	104.7	1250.55	109.2	0.00	0.0	1.48	2.9
Idaho	1034.80	86.5	1030.86	90.1	2.81	8.0	3.94	7.7

Illinois	1278.99	106.9	1264.06	110.4	6.45	18.3	14.94	29.0
Indiana	1089.16	91.1	1079.69	94.3	4.15	11.8	9.47	18.4
Iowa	1217.30	101.8	1216.27	106.3	0.09	0.2	1.03	2.0
Maine	954.07	79.8	953.34	83.3	0.00	0.0	0.74	1.4
Maryland	1186.10	99.2	1184.25	103.5	0.52	1.5	1.84	3.6
Massachusetts	1152.37	96.3	1151.46	100.6	0.00	0.0	0.90	1.8
Michigan	1155.40	99.6	1144.54	100.0	7.53	21.4	10.86	21.1
Minnesota	1200.86	100.4	1199.27	104.8	0.00	0.0	1.59	3.1
Mississippi	816.63	68.3	779.44	68.1	19.20	54.6	37.19	72.3
Missouri	1103.64	92.3	1097.70	95.9	4.04	11.5	5.94	11.5
Nebraska	1139.95	95.3	1130.19	98.7	6.15	17.5	9.77	19.0
Nevada	1730.81	144.7	1716.77	150.0	8.66	24.6	14.04	27.3
New Hampshire	1154.35	96.5	1153.60	100.8	0.00	0.0	0.75	1.5
New Jersey	1257.00	105.1	1253.61	109.5	0.00	0.0	3.39	6.6
New York	1119.64	93.6	1116.21	97.5	0.17	0.5	3.43	6.7
North Carolina	945.12	79.0	944.38	82.5	0.00	0.0	0.74	1.4
Ohio	1146.71	95.9	1131.97	98.9	5.50	15.6	14.74	28.6
Oregon	1220.42	102.0	1219.13	106.5	0.07	0.2	1.29	2.5
Pennsylvania	1109.42	92.8	1091.79	95.4	6.98	19.8	17.62	34.3
Rhode Island	1033.98	86.4	1033.35	90.3	0.00	0.0	0.63	1.2
South Carolina	897.56	75.0	896.77	78.3	0.00	0.0	0.78	1.5
South Dakota	1049.95	87.8	1045.87	91.4	2.78	7.9	4.08	7.9
Tennessee	942.50	78.8	938.25	82.0	1.67	4.7	4.26	8.3
Vermont	998.50	83.5	998.02	87.2	0.00	0.0	0.48	0.9
Virginia	1127.74	94.3	1113.88	97.3	6.73	19.1	13.86	26.9
Washington	1242.14	103.8	1239.98	108.3	0.35	1.0	2.16	4.2
Wisconsin	1116.92	93.4	1116.13	97.5	0.00	0.0	0.80	1.5
Subtotal	1158.86	96.9	1146.80	100.2	7.05	20.0	12.06	23.4
Total	1196.13	100.0	1144.68	100.0	35.20	100.0	51.45	100.0

Source: Advisory Commission on Intergovernmental Relations: Staff Computations.

The average tax capacity of the energy-rich states is about 19.5 percent above the average for all other states—an index of 115.8 compared to 96.9. This difference is entirely because of the energy capacity of these states. As a group their nonenergy capacity (99.1) is virtually identical to that of other states (100.2).

There is significant variation, however, within the group of energy-rich states. Alaska, for example, is an extreme case. In per-capita terms, its energy capacity (an astounding $4,701 per person) exceeds the total capacity of any other energy or nonenergy state. Wyoming's energy capacity is also very high—$905 per capita or 76 percent of the average total capacity of nonenergy-producing states. Both Alaska and Wyoming have high capacity from nonenergy sources to complement their energy capacity, so their overall capacity measures are also the highest among states.

Other energy-rich states are not so fortunate. Kentucky, Utah, and West Virginia have below-average total capacity despite high levels of energy capacity. The nonenergy capacities of these states are among the lowest in the nation, averaging 15 percent below the national average. Louisiana, New Mexico, and Oklahoma also have nonenergy capacities below the national average; their energy tax bases, however, are so large that on the index of total fiscal capacity these states score 11 to 25 percent above the national average.

Per-capita income is often used as a generalized measure of a state's ability to raise revenues.[41] The population-weighted correlation between per-capita income and nonenergy capacity across states is .89 indicating that per-capita income may be a fairly good proxy for the ability of states to raise revenues from nonenergy sources. However, the correlation between per-capita income and energy capacity is only .08. Thus, per-capita income very poorly reflects the revenue capability of energy-rich states.

In summary, the distribution of fiscal capacity among states is substantially more unequal than it would otherwise be because of the differential accessibility to energy revenues among states. Of the ten highest-capacity states, seven are in our group of energy-rich states. The fiscal disparities resulting from uneven access to energy revenues are moderated, however, by the fact that several energy-rich states have other tax bases that are relatively small.

Efficiency Considerations

We now turn to a consideration of the issue of economic efficiency raised by fiscal disparities among the states. As a general proposition, a state that is able to impose a large share of its total tax burden on a captive tax base may be able to reduce significantly the tax burdens on more mobile resources and, as a consequence, induce the relocation of individuals and businesses. The extent to which capital and labor move in response to differences in state tax attractiveness is still an unsettled issue.[42] Nonetheless, if movements of capital and labor are induced by tax-price variations that do not result from real economies in the provision of public services, a geographic misallocation of resources could occur.

In general, the potential reduction in the tax price borne by residents of a state as a result of energy taxation is given by the ratio of energy tax capacity to nonenergy tax capacity. Thus, if a state having an energy tax capacity equal to 10 percent of its nonenergy capacity were denied access to its energy tax base, taxes on nonenergy sources would have to be increased by 10 percent to maintain the same level of public services. As shown in table 1-8 above, energy tax capacity in 1980 was 22.1 percent of nonenergy capacity for the thirteen energy-rich states and only 1.1 percent of nonenergy capacity for the other states. This implies that if the energy-rich states were unable to tap energy tax bases, they would have had to increase tax rates on nonenergy tax bases by 22.1 percent, on average, to raise their 1980 level of revenues. Other states, in constrast, would only have had to increase their nonenergy tax rates by 1.1 percent.

This same result can be expressed in terms of the *tax effort* of each state, a companion concept to that of tax capacity. A state's tax effort is given by the ratio of its actual tax, user charge, and rent and royalty collections to its fiscal capacity. This is essentially an aggregate effective tax rate for each state expressed as an index number relative to the national average of 100. Table 1-9 shows total per-capita tax and royalty collections in each state and our measure of total effort.[43]

On average, energy-rich states have an effort index of 83.5, 20 percent below that of all other states taken as a whole (for which the average index is 103.9). Even this lower level of effort by the energy states may be overstated, however, for it results in part from the apparently high level of effort made by the state of Alaska (131.1). In Alaska's case the effort reflects an extraordinarily high rate of energy taxation, more than compensating for the very high energy tax bases located in that state. The more general finding is that the energy-wealthy states are able to reduce overall tax rates relative to other less-fortunate states.

The third column of table 1-9 shows the effort that would be required by each state to maintain total tax collections without resorting to use of energy-related bases—it is the required tax rate on nonenergy sources to maintain total revenues at current levels. If no use could be made of energy taxes and royalties, energy-rich states would still be making smaller tax efforts than other states (102.0 compared to 105.0), but the percentage difference would be narrowed from 20 percent to 3 percent. This occurs because, as shown in the fourth column, effective tax rates on nonenergy-related bases

Table 1-9
Actual Tax Effort and Effort Required to Maintain Revenues without Energy Capacity

	Per-Capita Collections (dollars)	Actual-Tax Effort Index	Required-Tax-Effort Index	Change in Tax Effort (percent)
Energy-rich states				
Alaska	8,078.81	131.1	553.5	322.1
Colorado	1,244.22	93.9	99.2	5.6
Kansas	1,129.00	88.6	95.2	7.4
Kentucky	884.20	90.9	96.7	6.4
Louisiana	1,158.28	84.0	110.3	31.3
Montana	1,191.33	90.4	99.9	10.4
New Mexico	1,344.90	90.2	123.0	36.4
North Dakota	1,282.63	95.3	103.3	8.4
Oklahoma	1,055.00	78.8	95.8	21.6
Texas	1,024.51	71.1	84.9	19.3
Utah	1,043.41	102.8	108.8	5.9
West Virginia	960.41	89.0	101.2	13.7
Wyoming	1,986.00	82.8	132.9	60.5
Subtotal	1,156.19	83.5	102.0	22.1
Other States				
Alabama	907.18	100.8	103.5	2.6
Arizona	1,180.52	111.5	111.9	0.4
Arkansas	816.78	88.1	90.0	2.2
California	1,396.41	101.1	104.2	3.1
Connecticut	1,189.31	88.9	89.0	0.2
Delaware	1,340.37	102.1	102.5	0.4
Washington, D.C.	1,613.75	119.7	120.0	0.2
Florida	952.72	80.2	80.6	0.5
Georgia	1,018.98	105.2	105.3	0.1
Hawaii	1,477.35	118.0	118.1	0.1
Idaho	954.03	92.2	92.5	0.4
Illinois	1,234.56	96.5	97.7	1.2
Indiana	948.33	87.1	87.8	0.9
Iowa	1,203.73	98.9	99.0	0.1
Maine	980.30	102.7	102.8	0.1
Maryland	1,304.26	110.0	110.1	0.2
Massachusetts	1,387.91	120.4	120.5	0.1
Michigan	1,326.14	114.8	115.9	0.9
Minnesota	1,366.82	113.8	114.0	0.1
Mississippi	868.98	106.4	111.5	4.8
Missouri	917.20	83.1	83.6	0.5
Nebraska	1,217.92	106.8	107.8	0.9
Nevada	1,247.04	72.0	72.6	0.8
New Hampshire	908.28	78.7	78.7	0.1
New Jersey	1,312.11	104.4	104.7	0.3
New York	1,689.50	150.9	151.4	0.3
North Carolina	915.49	96.9	96.9	0.1
Ohio	997.82	87.0	88.1	1.3
Oregon	1,221.10	100.1	100.2	0.1
Pennsylvania	1,114.98	100.5	102.1	1.6
Rhode Island	1,166.75	112.8	112.9	0.1
South Carolina	896.71	99.9	100.0	0.1
South Dakota	990.29	94.3	94.7	0.4
Tennessee	848.20	90.0	90.4	0.5
Vermont	1,060.62	106.2	106.3	0.0
Virginia	1,043.93	92.6	93.7	1.2
Washington	1,215.55	97.9	98.0	0.2
Wisconsin	1,305.98	116.9	117.0	0.1
Subtotal	1,204.02	103.9	105.0	1.1
Totals	1,196.13	100.0	104.5	4.5

Source: Advisory Commission on Intergovernmental Relations: Staff Computations.

would have to increase by 22.1 percent for the energy-producing states but only by 1.1 percent in other states. Thus, to the extent that the availability of taxable energy sources has enabled energy-rich states to reduce taxes levied on nonenergy sources (both business and individuals), the possibility exists of a greater fiscal attractiveness of energy-rich states.

Whereas in table 1-9 we addressed the issue of how high state tax efforts would have to rise to maintain their current level of spending if they had to make do without their energy tax bases, in table 1-10 we take a different approach and control for spending differences across states. This was done by computing the level of tax effort that states would have to apply to their nonenergy tax bases, given their current energy receipts, to raise the national-per-capita-average amount of revenue. In this table, *energy* strictly refers to severance and royalty collections or capacity; energy-related property and corporate income have been retained as part of the nonenergy category.[44]

The first two columns of table 1-10 present each state's current overall tax collections per capita and tax effort. The third column is a measure of each state's current nonenergy tax effort; this is the ratio of a state's actual nonenergy tax collections to its nonenergy base. The fifth column contains a standardized measure of state nonenergy tax effort. This index can be interpreted as the average rate that would have to be applied to a state's nonenergy bases, given revenues already collected from severance taxes and royalties, to finance the national-average level of spending. For example, Colorado's index of 90.9 indicates that by applying tax rates that are 90.9 percent of the national average to its nonenergy tax bases, and adding its 1980 collections from severance taxes and royalties, the state would be able to raise the average per-capita amount of revenue.

The disparity between the energy and nonenergy states indicated by this standardized measure of effort is dramatic. The energy-rich states, with an index of 82.7, would have to put forth only 80 percent as much effort as the nonenergy states (82.7 ÷ 103.6) to raise the same per-capita amount of revenue. Thus, the energy-rich states, on average, can provide the same level of spending as the other states at a tax rate on nonenergy sources of 20 percent less. This difference is, however, less than the differential in nonenergy tax efforts that currently exists (24 percent) because, on average, the energy-rich states have tax collections that are below the national norm. In fact, most of the energy states—Kansas, Kentucky, Oklahoma, Louisiana, Montana, Texas, Utah, and West Virginia—would have to increase their nonenergy tax rates to provide the average level of revenue. Even after these hypothetical increases, however, only Kentucky, Utah, and West Virginia would have nonenergy tax efforts in excess of the national average. The 20-percent-lower tax effort on nonenergy sources of the energy-rich states is a measure of the relative fiscal attractiveness of these states to potential businesses or residents.

Although the 20-percent discount represents the average of the energy states, there is extreme variation among the states within that group. Alaska

Table 1-10
Nonenergy-Tax-Effort Index, Standardized for Average Revenue, 1980

	Collections Per Capita (dollars)	Tax-Effort Index	Nonenergy-Tax-Effort Index	Percentage Difference	Standardized Nonenergy-Tax-Effort Index	Percentage Difference
Energy-rich states						
Alaska	8,078.81	131.1	102.7	−21.7	−330.5	−421.7
Colorado	1,244.22	93.9	94.6	0.8	90.9	−3.9
Kansas	1,129.00	88.6	92.6	4.5	98.2	6.0
Kentucky	884.20	90.9	88.5	−2.6	121.6	37.3
Louisiana	1,158.28	84.0	78.9	−6.1	82.2	4.2
Montana	1,191.33	90.4	84.8	−6.2	85.2	0.5
New Mexico	1,344.90	90.2	87.1	−3.4	74.1	−14.9
North Dakota	1,282.63	95.3	94.0	−1.3	87.3	−7.1
Oklahoma	1,055.00	78.8	74.3	−5.8	85.9	15.7
Texas	1,024.51	71.1	68.1	−4.3	81.4	19.5
Utah	1,043.41	102.8	105.0	2.1	120.6	14.8
West Virginia	960.41	89.0	87.1	−2.2	110.4	26.7
Wyoming	1,986.00	82.8	87.2	5.3	40.8	−53.2
Subtotal	1,156.19	83.5	79.4	−4.9	82.7	4.2
Other states						
Alabama	907.18	100.8	101.6	0.7	134.2	32.1
Arizona	1,180.52	111.5	111.6	0.1	113.1	1.3
Arkansas	816.78	88.1	88.4	0.4	129.8	46.9
California	1,396.41	101.1	102.5	1.4	87.6	−14.5
Connecticut	1,189.31	88.9	88.9	0.0	89.4	0.6
Delaware	1,340.37	102.1	102.1	0.0	91.1	−10.8
Washington, D.C.	1,613.75	119.7	119.7	0.0	88.8	−25.9
Florida	952.72	80.2	80.0	−0.2	100.6	25.7
Georgia	1,018.98	105.2	105.2	0.0	123.5	17.4
Hawaii	1,477.35	118.0	118.0	0.0	95.5	−19.0
Idaho	954.03	92.2	92.2	0.0	115.6	25.5
Illinois	1,234.56	96.5	97.0	0.5	94.0	−3.1
Indiana	948.33	87.1	87.4	0.4	110.2	26.1

Iowa	1,203.73	98.9	98.9	0.0	98.3	-0.6
Maine	980.30	102.7	102.7	0.0	125.4	22.0
Maryland	1,304.26	110.0	110.0	0.0	100.9	-8.3
Massachusetts	1,387.91	120.4	120.4	0.0	103.8	-13.8
Michigan	1,326.14	114.8	115.0	0.2	103.7	-9.8
Minnesota	1,366.82	113.8	113.8	0.0	99.6	-12.5
Mississippi	868.98	106.4	106.5	0.1	147.5	38.5
Missouri	917.20	83.1	83.1	0.0	108.5	30.5
Nebraska	1,217.92	106.8	107.2	0.4	105.3	-1.8
Nevada	1,247.04	72.0	71.9	-0.2	69.0	-4.1
New Hampshire	908.28	78.7	78.7	0.0	103.6	31.7
New Jersey	1,312.11	104.4	104.4	0.0	95.2	-8.8
New York	1,689.50	150.9	150.9	0.0	106.8	-29.2
North Carolina	915.49	96.9	96.9	0.0	126.6	30.7
Ohio	997.82	87.0	87.4	0.4	104.8	19.9
Oregon	1,221.10	100.1	100.1	0.0	98.0	-2.0
Pennsylvania	1,114.98	100.5	101.1	0.6	108.5	7.3
Rhode Island	1,166.75	112.8	112.8	0.0	115.7	2.5
South Carolina	896.71	99.9	99.9	0.0	133.3	33.4
South Dakota	990.29	94.3	94.4	0.1	114.1	20.8
Tennessee	848.20	90.0	90.1	0.1	127.1	41.0
Vermont	1,060.62	106.2	106.2	0.0	119.8	12.8
Virginia	1,043.93	92.6	93.1	0.6	106.7	14.6
Washington	1,215.55	97.9	97.9	0.0	96.3	-1.6
Wisconsin	1,305.98	116.9	116.9	0.0	107.1	-8.4
Subtotal	1,204.02	103.9	104.3	0.4	103.6	-0.7
Totals	1,196.13	100.0	100.0	0.0	100.0	0.0

Source: Advisory Commission on Intergovernmental Relations: Staff Computations.

is the only state with a negative tax effort, reflecting that it collects so much revenue from severance taxes and royalties that it could refund nearly $4,000 per capita and still maintain the national-average level of spending. Indeed, if Alaska is excluded from the group of energy states, the group's nonenergy tax rate would increase from 82.7 to 88.6 to maintain an average spending level, and the advantage of the energy-rich states as a whole would decline by nearly a third, from 20 percent to .14 percent. One criticism that has been leveled against the use of the tax-effort measure is that it abstracts from differences in public-service burdens and costs. However, it is unlikely that such differences would alter the assessment that Alaska currently enjoys an enormous revenue advantage over other states.

A related criticism may be also directed at overall state variations in tax capacity as an indicator of the extent to which resources may be misallocated as a result of tax differentials. These overall comparisons imply that the competition for capital and labor pits each state against every other state. In fact, this may not be the case. Various regions may have their own comparative advantages—proximity to markets, supplies of raw materials, skilled labor, physical and cultural amenities—with tax considerations of decidedly second-order importance. Within each region, however, tax factors may be more likely to influence locational decisions.

Based on this reasoning, we have developed an alternative measure of differences in tax capacity, a measure of each state's position relative to neighboring states. That is, instead of comparing each state with the national average (and therefore with every other state), our alternative tax-capacity measure is an index calculated for each state by dividing its capacity by the population-weighted average capacity of bordering states. Table 1-11 shows the relevant data for all states. Alaska and Hawaii have been omitted from this analysis since they have no immediate neighbors. Also, in some instances noncontiguous states are included in regional groupings, (for example, Massachusetts and Maine are considered to be neighbors).

This calculation can substantially change the index numbers for individual states. Low-capacity states in low-capacity regions, such as South Carolina and Alabama, have their capacity measures increased; on the other hand, some high-capacity states such as Texas and California have their relative capacities decline because their neighbors are also relatively well off.

If a lot of the variation in tax capacity is attributable to regional differences, then tax capacity is less likely to influence location decisions and result in resource misallocations. By comparing the dispersion for each of the two measures of capacity, we can determine whether disparities are primarily an interregional phenomenon. Table 1-12 shows the means and standard deviations, both population weighted, and the coefficients of variation of the initial and the new neighboring-tax-capacity calculations. A comparison of the two coefficients of variation—.139 in the initial case and .120 for the new capacity index—indicates that the clustering of high- and low-tax-capacity states reduces dispersion in tax capacity by 13.7 percent. This reduction in variation is 81 percent of that achieved by a uniform distribution of energy tax capacity.[45] Furthermore, the average value for the energy-rich states under the new measure of capacity (105.7) is much closer to that average for all other states (102.4). Therefore, if one accepts the assumption that the neighboring-state analysis more accurately reflects tax competition than did the nationwide analysis, adverse efficiency effects of unequally distributed energy capacity may be too small to worry about.[46]

These results should come as no surprise, since energy resources are found in specific areas of the country. Energy-rich states are often competing against states with similar fiscal advantages. However, states such as Arkansas, Arizona, and Idaho, which have few energy resources under production but which border on states that do, may face the worst tax competition as a result of energy-related fiscal disparities. Interestingly, one energy-rich state—Utah—nevertheless is seriously disadvantaged in the intraregional competition. In contrast, Wyoming with its very large fiscal capacity retains its advantage whether the reference group is the nation or its region.

Trends in Fiscal Disparities

Attention thus far has been focused on the effects of energy revenues on fiscal disparities for the year 1980, but it is also important to be aware of trends in fiscal disparities. Can 1980 be considered a typical year for examining the future role of energy taxes? When past studies of the RTS are examined to determine fiscal disparities, the conclusion emerges that, although fiscal disparities appear to have narrowed through the early 1970s, they have widened in more recent years. The data are shown in table 1-13. In particular, the population-weighted measure of the standard deviation for the RTS index first decreased from 15.3 in 1967 to 10.5 in 1975 but since then has increased to 13.7 in 1979 and to 22.2 in 1980. Thus, disparities in fiscal capacity have grown by 45 percent since 1967 and by 109 percent since 1975. This rapid rise in disparities, however, is largely a reflection of Alaska's expanding affluence. Excluding Alaska, the standard deviation declined from 15.3 in 1967 to 10.1 in 1975; since then it has risen to 13.8 in 1980. Therefore, if Alaska is omitted from the analysis, disparities are still found to have grown in recent years, but they remain lower than they were in 1967.

Although it has been impossible to determine the precise contribution of energy taxes to fiscal capacity in 1967 and 1975, it is likely that energy tax capacity has played a role in widening fiscal disparities. This conclusion is

Table 1-11
Tax Capacity of States, Based on Regional Groupings

State/ Tax Capacity	Neighboring States/ Tax Capacity						Capacity Indexed on a Regional Basis
Alabama (AL) 75.2	FL 99.3	GA 81.0	TN 78.8	MS 68.3			86.3
Arizona (AZ) 88.6	CA 115.5	NV 144.7	UT 84.9	CO 110.8	NM 124.7	MO 92.3	77.2
Arkansas (AR) 77.5	MS 68.3	TN 78.8	LA 115.3	TX 120.4	OK 111.9		73.7
California (CA) 115.5	OR 102.0	NV 144.7	AZ 88.6				113.6
Colorado (CO) 110.8	NM 124.8	UT 84.9	KS 106.5	WY 200.6	NE 95.3	AZ 88.6	107.1
Connecticut (CT) 111.9	NJ 105.1	NY 93.6	MA 96.3	RI 86.4			115.9
Delaware (DE) 109.8	MD 99.2	PA 92.8	NJ 105.1				112.2
District of Columbia (DC) 112.7	MD 99.2	VA 94.3					116.8
Florida (FL) 99.3	GA 81.0	AL 75.2					126.4
Georgia (GA) 81.0	FL 99.3	AL 75.2	SC 75.0				90.7
Idaho (ID) 86.5	OR 102.0	NV 144.7	UT 84.9	WY 200.6	MT 110.1	WA 103.8	79.5
Illinois (IL) 106.9	IN 91.1	KY 81.3	MO 92.3	IA 101.8	WI 93.4		116.7
Indiana (IN) 91.1	IL 106.9	MI 96.6	OH 95.9	KY 81.3			92.8

State									Value
Iowa (IA) 101.8	NE 95.3	MO 92.3	SD 87.8	MN 100.4	IL 106.9				101.9
Kansas (KS) 106.5	OK 111.9	CO 110.8	NE 95.3	MO 92.3					104.6
Kentucky (KY) 81.3	TN 78.8	VA 94.3	IL 106.9	IN 91.1	OH 95.9	WV 90.2			85.2
Louisiana (LA) 115.3	MS 68.3	TX 120.4	AR 77.5						106.4
Maine (ME) 79.8	NH 96.5	VT 83.5	MA 96.3	RI 86.4					84.5
Maryland (MD) 99.2	VA 94.3	DC 112.7	DE 109.8	PA 92.8	WV 90.2				105.5
Massachusetts (MA) 96.3	NY 93.6	CT 111.9	VT 83.5	NH 96.5	RI 86.4	ME 79.8			101.5
Michigan (MI) 96.6	IN 91.1	OH 95.9	WI 93.4						102.7
Minnesota (MN) 100.4	ND 112.5	SD 87.8	IA 101.8	WI 93.4					103.4
Mississippi (MS) 68.3	LA 115.3	AL 75.2	AR 77.5	TN 78.8					77.7
Missouri (MO) 92.3	AR 77.5	KS 106.5	IA 101.8	IL 106.9	TN 78.8	NE 95.3	OK 111.9	KY 81.3	94.9
Montana (MT) 110.1	ID 86.5	WY 200.6	ND 112.5	SD 87.8					97.9
Nebraska (NB) 95.3	KS 106.5	SD 87.8	IA 101.8	CO 110.8	WY 200.6	MO 92.3			91.9
Nevada (NV) 144.7	CA 115.5	UT 84.9	OR 102.0	ID 86.5	AZ 88.6				131.9
New Hampshire (NH) 96.5	VT 83.5	ME 79.8	MA 96.3	RI 86.4					104.7

Table 1-11 *(continued)*

State/ Tax Capacity	Neighboring States/ Tax Capacity							Capacity Indexed on a Regional Basis
New Jersey (NJ) 105.1	PA 92.8	DE 109.8	CT 111.9	NY 93.6				110.3
New Mexico (NM) 124.7	AZ 88.6	CO 110.8	UT 84.9	TX 120.4				110.8
New York (NY) 93.6	VT 83.5	PA 92.8	MA 96.3	NJ 105.1	CT 111.9			95.0
North Carolina (NC) 79.0	SC 75.0	VA 94.3	TN 78.8					93.8
North Dakota (ND) 112.5	MT 110.1	MN 100.4	SD 87.8					112.3
Ohio (OH) 95.9	IN 91.1	PA 92.8	WV 90.2	MI 96.6	KY 81.3			104.1
Oklahoma (OK) 111.9	KS 106.5	AR 77.5	TX 120.4	MO 92.3				102.6
Oregon (OR) 102.0	WA 103.8	ID 86.5	CA 115.5	NV 144.7				89.7
Pennsylvania (PA) 92.8	NY 93.6	NJ 105.1	MD 99.2	OH 95.9	WV 90.2	DE 109.8		95.8
Rhode Island (RI) 86.4	MA 96.3	CT 111.9	VT 83.5	NH 96.5	ME 79.8			82.8
South Carolina (SC) 75.0	NC 79.0	GA 81.0						93.8
South Dakota (SD) 87.8	ND 112.5	NE 95.3	WY 200.6	MN 100.4	IA 101.8	MT 110.1		87.8
Tennessee (TN) 78.8	NC 79.0	KY 81.3	AR 77.5	AL 75.2	MS 68.3	MO 92.3	VA 94.3	95.1
Texas (TX) 120.4	OK 111.9	NM 124.7	AR 77.5	LA 115.3				112.0

Utah (UT) 84.9	AZ 88.6	CO 110.8	NV 144.7	WY 200.6	ID 86.5	NM 124.7	76.3
Vermont (VT) 83.5	NY 93.6	NH 96.5	ME 79.8	MA 96.3	RI 86.4		89.3
Virginia (VA) 94.3	NC 79.0	MD 99.2	DC 112.7	WV 90.2	KY 81.3	TN 78.8	110.3
Washington (WA) 103.8	OR 102.0	ID 86.5					106.0
West Virginia (WV) 90.2	OH 95.9	PA 92.8	KY 81.3	VA 94.3	MD 99.2		96.4
Wisconsin (WI) 93.4	MN 100.4	IL 106.9	IA 101.8	MI 96.6			91.6
Wyoming (WY) 200.6	MT 110.1	ID 86.5	SD 87.8	CO 110.8	UT 84.9	NE 95.3	203.7

Note: The regionally based index is the ratio of a state's capacity to the population-weighted average of its neighbors' capacity (multiplied by 100).

Table 1-12
Two Measures of Tax Capacity

Measure	Mean	Standard Deviation	Coefficient of of Variation
Original tax capacity[a]	99.24	13.78	.139
Neighboring tax capacity[a]	102.87	12.38	.120
Energy-rich states	105.68	nr[b]	nr
Other states	102.42	nr	nr

Source: Advisory Commission of Intergovernmental Relations: Staff Computations.
[a]Statistics were calculated excluding Alaska and Hawaii.
[b]nr = not reported

based on the increased relative importance of energy taxes in overall state-revenue systems combined with the uneven distribution of energy tax capacity. It is also consistent with the pattern of changes in state indexes of tax capacity since 1967. The difference in average fiscal capacity between the thirteen states identified as energy rich in 1980 and other states has substantially increased between 1967 and 1980. In 1967, the energy-rich states had an average fiscal capacity slightly lower than other states, 97.1 compared to 100.5. By 1975, when the effects of the Arab oil embargo on energy prices had begun, the energy-rich states pulled slightly ahead of the other states. Coincident with the second big energy-price rise in 1979, the gap in fiscal capacity between the energy-rich and other states increased to 11 points in 1979, and to 19 points in 1980. Thus, it seems likely that energy revenues have contributed to increasing disparities in tax capacity since the mid-1970s.

It is more difficult to determine the future role of energy taxes in influencing fiscal disparities. In the short run, energy capacity will almost certainly increase its contribution to fiscal disparities. The long-range picture, however, is more clouded.

Energy taxes will definitely account for a larger share of state revenues through fiscal-year 1981 and possibly through 1982. The fiscal 1980 data, on which our analysis is based, do not reflect the full effect of the federal decontrol of the price of oil, or the continued rapid rise in natural-gas prices. Oil was priced at about $33.00 per barrel in mid-1981, roughly triple the price underlying fiscal-1979 tax collections. Natural-gas prices have also risen substantially from an average wellhead price of $0.91 per thousand cubic feet in 1978 to $1.74 during the first half of 1981. As one would expect from these price changes, severance-tax collections, as reflected in preliminary census data, have increased by more than 120 percent between fiscal years 1979 and 1981. No other source of revenue has increased at such an

Table 1-13

Expanded-Tax-Capacity Estimates for 1967, 1975, 1979, and 1980

State	1980	1979	1975	1967
New England	97	96	100	98
Connecticut	112	109	111	109
Maine	80	80	84	'79
Massachusetts	96	95	99	97
New Hampshire	97	95	100	101
Rhode Island	86	87	89	89
Vermont	83	84	93	85
Mideast	96	96	102	103
Delaware	110	107	123	120
District of Columbia	113	110	117	115
Maryland	99	99	101	98
New Jersey	105	104	110	104
New York	94	93	101	113
Pennsylvania	93	93	99	86
Great Lakes	98	103	103	102
Illinois	107	111	112	109
Indiana	91	97	97	98
Michigan	97·	104	100	105
Ohio	96	100	101	97
Wisconsin	93	98	97	96
Plains	99	102	100	101
Iowa	102	106	104	103
Kansas[a]	106	108	107	106
Minnesota	100	103	97	100
Missouri	92	96	95	93
Nebraska	95	99	105	118
North Dakota[a]	113	108	101	113
South Dakota	88	93	93	95
Southeast	87	87	88	82
Alabama	75	76	77	72
Arkansas	78	77	78	74
Florida	99	100	102	103
Georgia	81	81	85	80
Kentucky[a]	81	84	84	78
Louisiana[a]	115	105	99	101
Mississippi	68	70	69	66
North Carolina	79	81	84	76
South Carolina	75	76	77	65
Tennessee	79	81	83	81
Virginia	94	93	94	85
West Virginia[a]	90	90	87	72
Southwest	115	110	104	98
Arizona	89	91	92	101
New Mexico[a]	125	114	101	108
Oklahoma[a]	112	106	96	102
Texas[a]	120	114	109	96
Rocky Mountain	108	106	102	105
Colorado[a]	111	109	106	107
Idaho	87	90	89	91
Montana[a]	110	110	103	106
Utah[a]	85	86	86	90
Wyoming[a]	201	178	158	160

Table 1-13 *(continued)*

State	1980	1979	1975	1967
Far West	118	115	110	124
California	115	115	110	125
Nevada	145	145	138	169
Oregon	102	106	99	111
Washington	104	105	100	123
Alaska[a]	515	247	172	136
Hawaii	105	102	110	104
Mean Capacity				
All states	100	100	100	100
Energy-rich states	116	109	102	97
Other states	97	98	100	101
Standard Deviation[b]				
All states:	22.2	13.7	10.6	15.3
Excluding Alaska	13.8	12.2	10.1	15.3

Source: Advisory Commission on Intergovernmental Relations, *Tax Capacity of the 50 States, Supplement: 1980 Estimates,* p. 13, and ACIR staff computations (Washington, D.C.: ACIR, June 1982).

[a]Energy-rich state.

[b]Population weighted.

explosive rate. Therefore, when the data become available to calculate fiscal capacity in fiscal-year 1981, we anticipate a continuation of the trend toward increasing fiscal disparities, largely because of energy tax capacity.

Beyond 1981, the situation is less certain. Indeed, there are forces that now seem to be working in opposite directions. On the one hand, continued real increases in energy prices, which were the basis of most energy forecasts just a year ago, now appear less likely, given relatively high supplies of oil. Indeed, declines in price have already occurred. Similarly, the share of corporate profits attributable to the energy-extraction industry may well have peaked in 1980. Finally, if recent trends continue, energy-producing states will continue to experience higher-than-average population growth owing to both greater employment opportunities generally and, to some degree, to the greater fiscal attractiveness of these states. Although the latter outcome may, as noted, give rise to inefficiencies in resource allocation, the net result, in any event, would be a reduction in the per-capita fiscal advantages of the energy-rich states. These factors suggest that fiscal disparities resulting from energy tax capacity will stabilize over the longer term.

On the other hand, there are countervailing forces. Future decontrol of natural-gas prices should give rise to significant increases in energy capacity from that source, much as occurred in 1974-1975 and 1979-1980 from the rise in domestic oil prices. The result could be an increasing ability of gas-producing states to raise both severance taxes and corporate-income taxes from gas production. Second, a larger share of onshore production is expected to come from public lands; hence states will receive greater royalty income in addition to energy taxes. Third, the market for energy is still vulnerable to supply disruptions, which could cause a sharp increase in prices similar to that experienced in past years. The longer-run outlook, therefore, is a mixed one, although on balance some increase in the relative tax capacity of energy-producing states still seems to be in the cards.

Concluding Comments

Differential access to energy tax bases is clearly a significant source of disparities in tax capacity among the states. Whether the equalizing effects that would result from distributing energy revenues uniformly with population—a reduction of the standard deviation of tax capacity from about $266 per capita (or $165 excluding Alaska) to about $132—are sufficiently large to warrant taking federal action, or indeed whether federal action is even feasible, are questions that cannot be easily answered. Much depends on whether disparities in tax capacity will continue to grow, generating increasing pressure for government action, or whether such disparities will diminish over time, as occurred through the mid-1970s.

Notes

1. Oil prices were first controlled under President Nixon's wage-price freeze of August 1971. The system of controls was extended by the Emergency Petroleum Allocation Act of 1973 and the Energy Policy and Conservation Act of 1975. Controls were mandatory through May 1979. Between June 1979 and October 1981 the president was given discretionary authority to control oil prices. President Carter decided to exercise this authority by phasing out price controls over the two-year period.

2. Richard Corrigan, "Economic War over Oil also Looms at the State Level," *National Journal*, 22 December 1979, pp. 2137-2138; Richard Corrigan and Rochelle L. Stanfield, "Rising Energy Prices—What's Good for Some States Is Bad for Others," *National Journal*, 22 March 1980, pp. 468-474; James Coates, "A New Civil War Looms over State Taxes on Natural Resources," *Washington Post*, 19 August 1981, p. A7; Jerry Hagstrom, "The Severance Tax Is the Big Gun in the Energy War between The States," *National Journal*, 29 August 1981, pp. 1544-1548.

3. The organization formed was the Western Governors Regional Energy Policy Organization, the forerunner of the Western Governors Policy Office (WESTPO). The statements are by Governor Apodaca of New Mexico and Governor Herschler of Wyoming, as quoted in, Lynton R. Hayes, *Energy, Economic Growth, and Regionalism in the West* (Albuquerque, N.M.: University of New Mexico Press, 1980), pp. 3-4.

4. See J. Appleton and J. Kingsley, *Western Energy Production: Related Taxes, Subsidies, and the Impact upon the Northeastern Region*, Governor's Office of Policy and Planning, State of New Jersey, January 1980; Tom Cochran and J.R. Prestidge, *The United American Emirates: State Revenues from Non-Renewable Energy Resources* (Washington, D.C.: Northeast-Midwest Institute, June 1981); Task Force on Energy and Natural Resources, *Energy and the Economy* (prepared for the Midwest Governors Conference, 19 August 1981).

5. Advisory Commission on Intergovernmental Relations, *Conference on the Future of Federalism: Report and Papers* (M-126) (Washington, D.C.: U.S. Government Printing Office, July 1981).

6. Advisory Commission on Intergovernmental Relations, *Regional Growth: Historic Perspective* (A-74) (Washington, D.C.: U.S. Government Printing Office, 1980), and *Regional Growth: Interstate Tax Competition* (A-76) (Washington, D.C.: U.S. Government Printing Office, 1981).

7. The Department of Treasury estimated that oil-producing states would collect $94.5 billion in corporate-income, severance, and property taxes and $33.1 billion in royalty income through 1990 as a direct result of the decision to decontrol the price of oil. See Corrigan, "Economic War over Oil," p. 2138.

8. Ibid.

9. U.S., Congress, Senate, *Congressional Record*, 96th Congress, 1st Session, 1979, p. S.18292.

10. Ibid., p. S.18297.

11. U.S., Congress, House, *Congressional Record*, 96th Congress, 2nd Session, 1980, pp. H.10601-H.10607. Also, for an estimate of the impact of severance taxes on the general-revenue-sharing program, see U.S. Department of the Treasury, Office of State and Local Finance, *The Outlook for Severance Tax Collections and the Interstate Allocation of Revenue Sharing* (Washington, D.C., 5 November 1981).

12. U.S., Congress, House, Committee on Interstate and Foreign Commerce, *Limitation on Coal Severance Taxes*, Report 96-1527, part 1 to accompany H.R. 6625, 4 December 1980 (hereinafter cited as Report 96-1527).

13. The Powerplant and Industrial Fuel Use Act of 1978 limits the use of oil and gas by electric utilities and other major fuel-burning installations. The provision of law affecting existing electric-utility plants has since been repealed.

14. Report 96-1527.

15. Dissenting view of representative Tim Wirth, Report 96-1527, pp. 20-23.

16. Minority views submitted by representatives James Corlins, Tim Lee Carter, Carlos J. Moorhead, and Dave Stockman, Report 96-1527, p. 19.

17. Commonwealth Edison v. State of Montana, 101 S. Ct. 2946 (1981).

18. Maryland et al. v. Louisiana, 101 S. Ct. 2114 (1981).

19. See chapters 2 and 5.

20. Other sources of information on state tax practices include: Karl Starch, *Taxation, Mining and the Severance Tax*, Information Circular 8788 (Washington, D.C.: U.S. Department of the Interior, Bureau of Mines, 1979). Thomas Stinson, *State Taxation of Mineral Deposits and Production*, Rural Development Research Report no. 2 (Washington, D.C.: U.S. Department of Agriculture, 1978); Donna Sammons, *Coal Industry Taxes: State-by-State Guide* (New York: McGraw-Hill, 1981); and Committee on Energy Taxation, Assembly of Behavioral and Social Sciences, National Research Council, *Energy Taxation: An Analysis of Selected Taxes*, Energy Policy Study, vol. 14 (Washington, D.C.: U.S. Department of Energy, September 1980).

21. These figures are ACIR estimates based primarily on census data using the Bureau's definition of severance taxes.

22. Traditional appraisal techniques in other applications—appraisals based on replacement value or market sales of like property—are not generally feasible in this case. For further information on energy property-tax-appraisal methods, see Abraham Goldman, "The Appraisal of Oil and Gas Properties: Systems and Procedures" (Conference on Assessment Administration, Chicago, International Association of Assessing Officers, 1975), pp. 142-165; Robert McGeorge, "Approaches to State Taxation of The Mining Industry," *Natural Resources Journal* 10 (January 1970):156-170.

23. U.S. Federal Trade Commission, *Quarterly Financial Report for Manufacturing, Mining and Trade Corporations* (Washington, D.C.: U.S. Government Printing Office. First quarter 1975 report, June 1975, tables C-2 and K-2; data for the third quarter 1980 are from first quarter 1981 report, June 1981, tables C-2 and K-2. The balance sheet items have been deflated by the corresponding quarterly GNP deflators).

24. Ibid (Data for 1975 are profits before income tax and extraordinary items taken from U.S. Federal Trade Commission, op. cit. first quarter 1976 report, June 1976, table C-1 and K-1; data for 1980 are from first quarter 1981 report, June 1981, tables C-1 and K-1. The income items have been deflated by the corresponding annual GNP deflators).

25. For general information on state corporate-income taxes as applied to multistate firms see: Oliver Oldman and Ferdinand P. Schoettle, *State and Local Taxes and Finance: Text, Problems and Cases* (Mineola, N.Y.: Foundation Press, 1974), pp. 550-660; and Jerome R. Hellerstein and Walter Hellerstein, *State and Local Taxation: Cases and Materials* (St. Paul, Minn.: West, 1978), pp. 397-547.

26. Conversations with Citizen/Labor Energy Coalition. For reviews of current developments in state taxation, see *Multistate Tax Commission Review*, published quarterly by the Multistate Tax Commission, Boulder, Colorado; and *State Tax Report*, published monthly by the Committee on State Taxation, Council of State Chambers of Commerce, Washington, D.C.

27. ACIR estimates based on Bureau of the Census, *State Government Finances*; U.S. Department of Treasury, *Federal Aid to States*; and contacts with state revenue officials.

28. The most important statutes governing lease terms and receipts allocation are the Mineral Leasing Act of 1920, as amended, 30 USC 191 and 286, and the Mineral Leasing Act for Acquired Lands of 1947, 30 USC 355.

29. These shifts have been analyzed in Irving Hoch, "The Role of Energy in the Regional Distribution of Economic Activity" (paper prepared for Conference on Balanced National Growth and Regional Change, University of Texas, 24 September 1977); William Miernyk, "The Differential Effects of Rising Energy Prices on Regional Income and Employment" (paper prepared for the RFF—Brookings Conference on the Differential Impact of High and Rising Energy Costs, Washington, D.C., 9-10 October 1980); David J. Bjornstad, *Changes in Economic Capacity at the Federal Region Level due to NEP-1 Energy Price Changes* (Oakridge, Tenn.: Oakridge National Laboratory, April 1980).

30. See ACIR, *Measures of State and Local Fiscal Capacity and Tax Effort*, M-16 (Washington, D.C.: U.S. Government Printing Office, October 1962) and ACIR, *Measuring the Fiscal Capacity and Effort of State and Local Areas*, M-58 (Washington, D.C.: U.S. Government Printing Office, March 1971). For further work on this subject, see Kent D. Halstead, *Tax Wealth in 50 States* and *Tax Wealth in 50 States, 1977 Supplement* (Washington, D.C.: National Institute of Education, 1978, 1979); and Robert Reischauer, "Rich Governments—Poor Governments," staff paper (Washington, D.C.: Brookings Institution, 1974). The most recent data on the RTS are available in the ACIR report entitled *Tax Capacity of the Fifty States: Methodology and Estimates*, M-134 (Washington, D.C.: U.S. Government Printing Office, March 1982). The 1980 data used in this chapter will be available from the ACIR in a forthcoming report.

31. Advisory Commission on Intergovernmental Relations, *Studies in Comparative Federalism: Canada*, M-127 (Washington, D.C.: U.S. Government Printing Office, July 1981), pp. 42-47.

32. Alaska's extraordinary capacity for 1980 is partly due to exceptionally high bonus payments for the sale of oil-extraction leases on state property in that year. If these payments had been excluded, Alaska's tax capacity would be $5,027 per capita and its index would be 420.

33. The data underlying our estimates of the business-property tax and corporate-income tax bases came from the Internal Revenue Service, *Statistics of Income* (SOI) and the Bureau of Economic Analysis, respectively. Since many oil- and coal-extraction firms are integrated businesses, there is some difficulty in relying on the industrial classifications used by these sources. A number of major oil-production companies appear not in the extraction classification but rather as petroleum refiners. Coal-production companies are sometimes owned by steel or utility companies, and their incomes are included in those other classifications. To the extent possible, the data have been adjusted to reflect these patterns of industrial organization; the assets and income associated with extraction but reported in other categories were estimated and combined with the SOI extraction totals for this analysis.

34. A detailed description of the methodology underlying the RTS is included in ACIR, *Tax Capacity*.

35. In table 1-6, Alaska's special corporate-income and property taxes on oil corporations and West Virginia's gross-receipts tax on coal and oil companies are included in severance taxes, rather than in corporate or property taxes, since they are much closer in nature to a tax on production. As a result, the amount shown for severance taxes in table 1-6 exceeds the amount shown in table 1-2, which is based strictly on the census definition of a severance tax.

36. See Gerald Boyle in "Taxation of Uranium and Steam Coal in the Western States," NonRenewable Resource Taxation in the Western States: A Conference on Tax Policy, January 31-February 1, 1977, Lincoln Institute monograph #77-2. Boyle argues that tax rates should be set to "maximize economic benefits to the state" and that these can be determined by measuring the competitive advantage that a state enjoys in a production industry.

37. Although the RTS will treat states with potential production differently depending on their *actual* production, over time the RTS will tend to account for the full amount of a state's potential production as it is realized. Thus, to the extent that capacity is reduced in one period due to low production, it will rise when higher production occurs.

38. An assessment of the relationship between severance taxes and costs imposed by energy development was provided in William Schulze, David Brookshire, Ralph D'Arge, and Ron Cummings, "Taxation, Boomtowns and Environmental Effects" (paper read at 1981 TRED Conference, Cambridge, Mass., September 10-12).

39. See Robert D. Reischauer and Robert W. Hartman, with the assistance of Dan J. Sullivan, *Reforming School Finance* (Washington, D.C.: The Brookings Institution, 1973) and Allen Odden and John Augenblick, *School Finance Reform in the States: 1981* (Denver, Colo.: Education Commission of the States, 1981).

40. See Charles E. McLure, Jr., "Fiscal Federalism and the Taxation of Economic Rents," in *State and Local Finance in the 80s*, ed. George F. Break (Madison, Wis.: University of Wisconsin Press, forthcoming), and chapter 2 of this book.

41. For a discussion of the comparison between the RTS and per-capita personal income as a measure of tax capacity see ACIR, *Tax Capacity*.

42. See Advisory Commission on Intergovernmental Relations, *Interstate Tax Competition*, A-76 (Washington, D.C.: U.S. Government Printing Office, 1981), pp. 32-34; Roger Vaughn, *State Taxation and Economic Development* (Washington, D.C.: Council of State Planning Agencies, 1979), pp. 77-79. Also see the discussion in chapter 2 of this book.

43. Unlike tax capacity, tax effort encompasses both the relative scale of the state-local sector in a particular state and the state's capacity to raise revenues. A high tax-effort index, for example, could reflect a below-average capacity and a public sector of average size (in per-capita terms) or a higher-than-average capacity and an even larger public sector. This characteristic of the tax-effort index has no bearing on the calculations in the text relating to changes in tax effort resulting from eliminating access to energy tax bases. However, the comparisons of tax effort across states implicitly assume that states are doing equally well in meeting the needs of their residents. Depending on the particular comparison, this assumption may not be correct.

44. We have not been able to develop a comprehensive measure of energy tax effort that includes corporate-income and property taxes on oil, gas, and coal-extraction industries, as well as severance taxes and royalties, because data are not available on tax collections specifically for those industry classifications.

45. We reported earlier that a uniform distribution of energy tax capacity would reduce the overall dispersion of tax capacity by 50 percent. This calculation, however, is inclusive of Alaska and Hawaii. When those two states are omitted to compare the results with the neighboring-state analysis, a uniform distribution of energy tax capacity reduces dispersion by 17 percent (from .139 to .115). The reduction in dispersion of 13.7 percent achieved in the neighboring anlaysis equals 81 percent of this 17-percent figure.

46. The inefficiencies resulting from geographical movements of capital and labor may be small for another reason as well. To the extent that more resources flow to energy-rich states, a larger share of the total state-local public sector will be financed with taxes on rents associated with energy production, which may be less distorting than other revenue sources. This efficiency in finance could mitigate the inefficiencies from resource migration.

Comments

Roy Bahl

Peggy Cuciti, Harvey Galper, and Robert Lucke have added much to what is known about the intergovernmental dimension of state energy taxation. Using the RTS approach, they have provided a first careful set of estimates of the influence of the uneven distribution of energy resources on interstate variations in taxable capacity. Their result is important: there is a growing gap in taxable capacity between the energy-rich and other states. The purpose of this comment is not to quibble with this general finding, for it is essentially correct. Rather, the purpose here is to point out an inherent problem with the measurement of taxable capacity using the RTS approach and to raise a question about the efficiency implications of the results.

Measurement Problems

A correct measure of taxable capacity will permit interstate comparison of the resource base available for taxation. In theory, measured taxable capacity in state i should be independent of actual fiscal decisions taken in state i or in any other state. Cuciti, Galper, and Lucke see this as a virtue of the RTS approach: "Any variation among states in tax capacity is attributable not to differences in state tax laws but rather to the distribution of uniformly defined taxable bases." This, unfortunately, is not quite the case, since the RTS estimates of taxable capacity are sensitive to the fiscal choices made. One can demonstrate, for example, that New York State's estimated taxable capacity is sensitive to Texas's choice to raise $701 per capita in taxes in 1979 as well as to Texas's choice as to how to raise this amount.

Taxable capacity of state i ($\hat{T}_i$) is defined under the RTS as

$$\hat{T}_i = \sum_j \bar{r}_j B_{ji}$$

where $\bar{r}_j$ = the average tax rate employed in the fifty states for the jth tax and B_{ji} = the base of the jth tax in state i. Quite clearly, $\bar{r}_y$ is influenced by tax laws and fiscal choices in all states. For example, New York's choice to cut income taxes lowers the average national rate and therefore affects the estimated taxable capacity ($\hat{T}_i$) of every state. By the same token, Texas's choice to tax natural resources rather than individual income dampens the estimated taxable capacity of energy-poor states such as New York because it results in a lower average income-tax rate (New York's income-taxable

61

base is strong) and a higher average energy tax rate (New York has little capacity to tax natural resources).

This problem can lead to a number of misleading inferences. For example, these rate effects could produce estimates of future declines in taxable capacity in industrialized but energy-poor states, even if per-capita income, consumption, and property values were increasing. It would only be necessary for the national-average rates on traditional bases to fall and for energy tax rates to increase.

Related to the measure of taxable capacity ($\hat{T}_i$) is tax effort (E_i), a measure of how intensively a state actually uses its capacity, defined as $E_i = T_i / \hat{T}_i$ where T_i equals the actual taxes collected. Again, the fiscal-choices issue raises problems. A limitation movement such as Proposition 13 in California could lower $\hat{T}_i$ in other property-tax-dependent states and increase tax effort in state i, even though state i had not increased the rate at which it was taxing its existing bases.

Efficiency Effects

Cuciti, Galper, and Lucke offer the proposition that a state that can impose a large share of its total tax burden on a captive tax base may be able to reduce the tax burden on more mobile resources, thereby attracting capital and labor. This happens because residents of the energy-rich state face a lower tax price if energy taxes are chosen as the means of finance. Although the point is essentially correct, the second-round effects raise a number of interesting questions for research. Two are especially important: the possibility that public-expenditure effects will offset some of the tax price advantage, and the possibility that federal-grant effects will reinforce this tax-price advantage. In neither case is the result unambiguous.

Although a greater energy tax base offers a greater potential tax-price reduction, there may be offsetting public-expenditure effects. As the relative price of public goods falls in energy-rich states, and as inmigration of capital and labor is induced, the quantity of public goods demanded will increase. If the supply curve is perfectly elastic in both growing and declining states, the story ends here and the tax-price disparity induced by taxing the natural-resource rent remains. The energy states end up taxing mobile factors at a lower rate to provide the same quantity of public output. On the other hand, there is a body of research that suggests that the unit cost of government goods rises with increased output in that sector, in part because of increases in the scope and quality of services required.[1] In this case an increase in population and income will cause a shift in demand and will increase expenditures and drive the tax price back up if the traditional, non-energy channels of finance are used. If the supply curve were downward sloping, as in the pure-public-good case, the tax-price advantage of energy-rich states would be reinforced by inmigration.

The interregional migration of capital and labor may also induce a change in the rate of flow of intergovernmental transfers to energy-rich and other states. Under a per-capita-income-equalizing federal-grant system, the relative level of grants to such states would fall and the reduction in public output would depend on which grants were reduced and on the income and price elasticity of demand for public goods. The current federal-grant system, however, is not equalizing, and one would expect that states gaining relative shares of population and income would also gain an increased share of federal grants. If grants are primarily substitutive, the tax-price advantage of energy-rich states will be further reinforced. Certainly the potential for an important federal-grant effect is present. Indeed, energy taxes account for only about 4 percent of total taxable capacity, far less than the federal-grant share of taxable capacity.

Implications

These caveats do not detract from the basic findings of the Cuciti, Galper, and Lucke chapter. The taxable capacity of energy-rich states is high and growing, and an important fiscal advantage is being created. But we need to know much more. Do these advantages induce significant migration of labor and capital? Do inmigrants and increased economic activity in the growing region lead to public-sector expansions that will eventually erase the fiscal advantage of energy-rich states? Does the federal-grant system reinforce or offset the comparative fiscal advantage of energy-rich states?

Note

1. See Roy Bahl, Jesse Burkhead, and Bernard Jump, Jr., eds., *Public Employment and State and Local Government Finances* (Cambridge, Mass.: Ballinger, 1980).

2 Taxation of Energy Resources

Peter Mieszkowski
and *Eric Toder*

The dramatic increases in the price of fossil fuels that have occurred since 1973 have greatly complicated intergovernmental relations and economic policy generally in both Canada and the United States. In both countries, to varying degrees, the huge wealth transfers from energy consumers to energy producers resulting from the increase in the world price of oil have influenced pricing regulations, allocation policies, and the taxation of energy resources at all levels of government.

In the United States, price controls on crude oil dating from the Nixon administration's general wage and price controls were maintained for many years after price controls generally had ended. The decision to phase out crude-oil-price controls in 1979 was accompanied by passage of a windfall-profit tax on crude-oil producers. This tax is assessed on the difference between the sales price of crude oil and a legislated base price. Both the tax rate and the base price vary among defined production tiers, and independent producers are allowed special reduced tax rates. For tier-1 oil (old oil), the tax rate is 70 percent while for tier-3 oil (new oil and certain categories of high-cost oil) the tax imposed is 30 percent.[1]

States and localities have also sought to capture some of the increased revenues from rising energy prices. Revenues from severance taxes and royalties on state-owned land have increased, and producing states have raised rates on existing taxes and imposed new ones:

Alaska imposed a severance tax whose effective rate is 11.5 percent of the value of production, exclusive of the tax. In 1978, it introduced a special corporate tax on oil and gas production that imposes separate accounting for the profits earned on oil production in Alaska. Separate accounting was also introduced for the taxation of profits earned from the Alaska pipeline. Alaska also collects a special property tax on the property of oil companies.

The authors would like to acknowledge the many helpful comments by Charles McLure on an earlier draft of this chapter. We also are grateful to Albert Church and Harvey Galper for useful comments, to Cabell Chinnis and Cynthia Wallace for supplying data on domestic oil production and windfall-profit taxes, and to Donna Harrell, Geri Huggins, and Vera Wallis for typing the manuscript. The views expressed in this chapter are those of the authors alone and do not represent the official position of the Department of the Treasury.

Louisiana imposed a first-use tax on the production of natural gas on federally controlled offshore property shipped through the state. Recently, this law was declared to be unconstitutional by the U.S. Supreme Court, and Louisiana was ordered to refund $500 million that it has collected since 1979.

Montana has imposed a 30-percent severance tax exclusive of the value of the tax on the production of surface coal. The constitutionality of this highly controversial tax was recently upheld by the U.S. Supreme Court. Wyoming taxes coal production at an effective rate of 17 percent by combining a 10.5-percent severance tax with a local property tax, which is equivalent to a tax of 6.5 percent on the value of coal output.

There remains considerable scope for increases in severance taxes in major producing states. The severance tax on oil in Texas is 4.6 percent, well below the rates in Alaska and Louisiana. The severance tax on natural gas in Louisiana is a per-unit tax and has declined as a fraction of the value of natural gas as prices have increased. There are indications that Louisiana is planning to increase this tax significantly in November 1981, possibly to 15 percent of value.

Oil-consuming states have also attempted to capture some of the increased revenue from oil production. Both New York and Connecticut enacted taxes on the gross revenues of oil companies and attempted, unsuccessfully, to exploit provisions in then-existing price regulations to prevent the full pass-through of these taxes to within state consumers. The provisions of the Connecticut tax that forbade passing through the cost of the tax to instate consumers were overruled by a federal court in July 1980. In addition, New Jersey has contemplated the imposition of a refinery tax. Other states and localities have considered similar initiatives.

The impetus for these taxes on energy producers by consuming states stems less perhaps from rational economic calculation than from a general resentment about the burden imposed on them, and the benefits to energy companies and energy-producing states, from rising energy prices. In part, this resentment results from a perception that increases in taxes on energy production by energy-producing states are exacerbating interregional inequities caused by the rise in energy prices.

Decontrol of natural gas, scheduled to occur in 1985, will provide an additional fiscal windfall for producer states, especially Texas and Louisiana. It is expected that decontrol will more than double the price of natural gas. This potential fiscal windfall to producing states, by increasing resentment in other regions, could increase political opposition to decontrol. This would place a further strain on intergovernmental relations and could perpetuate the serious inefficiencies that result from regulations that keep the price paid by consumers for most natural gas significantly below its replacement cost.

This chapter will review some of the equity and efficiency issues relating to the effort of different levels of government to capture the economic rents from energy production. The following section details the major taxes imposed by states, localities, and the federal government on domestic energy production. For completeness, we also discuss royalties captured on federal and state-owned lands. An important theme of this section is that focusing on state severance taxes alone provides a very incomplete picture of the fiscal transfers and that local property taxes and royalty earnings are often close substitutes for severance taxes. For this reason, federally legislated limits on state severance taxes may not be sufficient to accomplish the objectives of their sponsors.

The third section of the chapter presents rough estimates of the distribution of the additional oil revenues from decontrol and higher oil prices in the two major oil-producing states, Texas and Alaska. We show that most of the increased revenue from higher oil prices was captured by governments, not private producers. However, the state government took a much larger share of the increased revenue in Alaska than it did in Texas, and the private producers captured a smaller share. The federal government's share of the increased oil revenue is somewhat larger in Texas than in Alaska because the higher state revenues collected in Alaska are exempt from the federal crude-oil windfall-profit tax.

The final section discusses the economic inefficiencies that may result from the various ways that different levels of government capture revenues from energy production. These potential inefficiencies include adjustments to taxes and royalties that cause too little domestic energy production, prevent energy from being produced in the lowest-cost locality or region, cause too much migration to energy-producing states, and may cause too many resources to be allocated to the public sector in some states. We will discuss what types of policies are likely to be connected with what inefficiencies and provide a rough assessment of the magnitude of the welfare loss from excessive migration to energy-producing states.

Sources of State and Federal Revenue from Energy Production

This section provides an overview of the various ways in which the states and the federal government capture a portion of the revenues from energy production. It should be noted that there are also important subsidies to private energy producers, particularly in provisions of the federal income tax that significantly reduce the effective tax rate on income from oil and gas production.

Federal Windfall-Profit Tax

The major federal tax targeted specifically at energy revenues is the Crude Oil Windfall Profit tax, enacted in March 1980. This tax is not actually a net-profits tax; it is imposed on the gross value of production above a base price adjusted for inflation. However, the tax for any producer is limited to 90 percent of net income from crude-oil production.

The windfall-profit tax is calculated by applying the tax rate to the difference between the selling price of oil and the base price. Oil owned by governmental interests and by certain qualified charitable interests is exempt from the tax. Therefore, state royalties are not subject to the tax. In addition, state severance taxes up to 15 percent of the value of crude oil are deductible in calculating the net windfall profit. However, taxes levied on the value of reserves, on the net proceeds from production (that is, a state corporate-income tax), or on the physical volume of production are not deductible. Moreover, taxes imposed by local governments are not deductible. Table 2-1 summarizes the provisions of the windfall-profit tax as of June 1981.

In the Economic Recovery Tax Act of 1981, Congress reduced the windfall-profit tax in several ways. First, the tax rate on tier-3 oil is to be reduced from 30 percent to 15 percent in 1986 in a series of steps. Second, stripper oil produced by independent producers was made exempt from tax. Third, the $1,000 royalty-owner credit, enacted at the end of 1980, was increased to $2,500 in 1981. Under this provision, owners of royalty rights to crude oil will receive an annual tax credit for the first $2,500 of windfall-profit tax withheld on their share of oil revenues. For 1982 through 1984, 2 barrels per day of royalty-owner oil is exempt from tax; after 1985 this tax exemption is increased to 3 barrels per day. At a price of $34/barrel, the 3-barrel-per-day exemption is equivalent to exempting from windfall-profit tax the first $37,000 of annual royalty income from oil property.

Although the windfall-profit tax diminishes to some degree private incentives for oil production, provisions of the federal corporate-income tax favor oil production relative to other uses of private capital. Oil producers are allowed to expense rather than to capitalize intangible drilling costs. In addition, in 1980, independent oil producers were allowed to deduct 22 percent of gross revenues from crude-oil production as percentage depletion.[2]

Estimation of the net incentive to oil production, relative to other uses of capital, provided by the entire federal tax system is beyond the scope of this chapter. However, we note that the windfall-profit tax and the corporate- and personal-income taxes combined do capture a significant share of any windfall that might result from an unanticipated increase in energy prices. That is, although the *ex-ante* tax treatment of a planned oil venture might be light because a large share of initial investment costs are tax deductible, the federal government shares in the profits as well as the

Table 2-1
Base Prices, Inflation Adjustments, and Rates of Tax Applicable to Windfall Profits

	Base Prices	Inflation Adjustment	Major-Producer Rate (percent)	Independent Producer Rate[a] (percent)
Tier 1: Oil not in Tiers 2 and 3. Mostly old oil classified as lower-tier or upper-tier oil under pre-June 1979 U.S. Department of Energy price-control regulations	May 1979 upper-tier price less 21 cents (An average of $12.81)	Increase in GNP deflator since June 1979	70	50
Tier 2: Stripper-well oil and National Petroleum Reserve oil	$15.20 (adjusted for grade, quality, and location)	Increase in GNP deflator since June 1979	60	30
Tier 3: Newly discovered oil, heavy oil, and incremental tertiary oil[b]	$16.55 (adjusted for grade, quality, and location)	Increase in GNP deflator since June 1979 plus 2 percent a year, compounded quarterly	30	30

[a]Independent producers are crude-oil producers without significant interests in refining or retailing. According to 1980 Department of Energy estimates, independent producers accounted for 12 percent of tier-1 production and 44 percent of tier-2 production (mostly stripper wells).

[b]Newly discovered oil is oil from an onshore property that was not in production in 1978 or from a lease entered into since 1979 on the Outer Continental Shelf. Heavy oil is defined as oil from a property with a weighted average gravity of 16 degrees or less API for the taxable period. Incremental tertiary oil is oil from a property where the producer uses a tertiary recovery method such as steam injection, polymer-augmented water flooding, alkaline flooding, and other approved methods. A stripper-well property is a property whose average daily production is less than 10 barrels per day.

costs. If earnings from an oil property are higher than anticipated, the federal government, through the corporate- and personal-income taxes and the windfall-profit tax, captures a large share of these additional revenues. Thus, the federal government has captured a large share of the revenues of oil companies from decontrol and the post-1979 increases in the world price of oil.

State Severance Taxes

Severance taxes are production taxes imposed either on the value or on the physical volume of resources extracted from the mine or wellhead. Generally, for purposes of comparison, one examines the relative effective *ad-valorem* rates imposed by different states on a resource. For some resources, the same *ad-valorem* rate among states would imply vastly different tax rates per unit of physical output. For example, the minemouth price of coal mined in Montana is about one third the price of coal mined in the East. If the external costs from mining are viewed as related to the number of units extracted rather than the total cost of extraction, then a somewhat higher *ad-valorem* rate in Montana than in the East may be attributable to social costs of mining.

The effective tax rate on mineral extraction in any state depends on the interaction between property taxes and severance taxes. Some states exempt the value of the mineral in the ground from local property taxes if a severance tax has been paid. In other states, property taxes have exactly the same incidence as a severance tax, because the property assessments are based on the annual value of minerals extracted. Even in the states with no explicit severance tax, there may still be substantial taxes on the extraction of mineral wealth, depending on the methods of determining property values used by local tax assessors. For example, Albert Church (1978) shows that taxes on the value of coal output may be substantial even in the absence of a state severance tax. This suggests that a closer look at the tax systems of states without severance taxes is warranted.

Notwithstanding these qualifications, it is worth noting the significant differences among states both in *ad-valorem* severance-tax rates (expressed as a percentage of output exclusive of tax) and in the amount by which rates have changed in recent years. In general, states with expanding mineral production have been the most aggressive in recent rate increases. Alaska increased its nominal severance-tax rate on oil to 12.25 percent just before the rapid expansion of production in 1978. Wyoming has progressively increased its severance taxes in recent years, as coal production has expanded. Montana, another state with rapidly expanding coal production, has the nation's highest severance-tax rate of 30 percent of the value of coal mined. Kentucky and New Mexico have also increased rates in recent years.

Louisiana, a mature oil and gas producer, has the highest rate on oil—12.5 percent—but Texas, another mature producer, has a low rate of 4.6 percent, which has remained unchanged since 1951. Louisiana's gas tax of 7¢/thousand cubic feet currently about 3.5 percent of value, is likely to be increased significantly in the near future; the Texas tax on natural gas is 7.5 percent of value, unchanged since 1969.

Table 2-2 summarizes severance-tax rates for oil, gas, and coal in the major producing states. Table 2-3 shows the yield from all severance taxes collected by the major energy-producing states.

The very large increases in revenue between fiscal 1979 and fiscal 1981 for the oil-producing states largely reflect the effects of oil-price decontrol.

Table 2-2
Severance-Tax Rates in Key Fossil-Fuel-Producing States

	Oil	Gas	Coal
Alaska	12.25[a]	10	
Texas	4.6	7.5	
Louisiana	12.5	$.07/thousand cubic feet	
New Mexico[b]	6.3	2.55 plus $.26/ thousand cubic feet	
Oklahoma	7.0	7.0	
Montana	2.9		30.0
Wyoming	6.0		10.5
Kentucky			4.5
California	0.0	0.0	

Note: All numbers except those for gas taxes in Louisiana and Mexico are in percent. Rates are expressed as a percentage of the value of output, exclusive of tax.

[a]This is a nominal rate. It is adjusted by a complicated limit factor (not described here), which lowers the effective tax rate to about 11.5 percent.

[b]New Mexico has a number of taxes on mineral production. The rates reported in the table are for the oil and gas severance tax and a privilege tax (emergency school tax). Two taxes, the oil and gas *ad-valorem*-production tax and the equipment-production tax, are discussed in the section on property taxes.

For example, the average price of Alaskan crude oil rose from approximately $8.50 per barrel in May 1979 to slightly over $20 per barrel in December 1980 and to about $22 per barrel following full decontrol after January 1981.

Tables 2-4 and 2-5 present more detailed data on severance-tax collections in Texas and Louisiana. The Texas data show that increased collec-

Table 2-3
Severance-Tax Collections for Selected States
(millions of dollars)

	1978	1979	1980	1981	Tax revenues Per Capita 1981 (dollars)
U.S.A.	2,494	1,979	4,167	6,379	28
Alaska	107	174	506	1,170	2,920
Kentucky	128	154	177	194	52
Louisiana	477	511	526	815	194
Montana	45	54	95	99	124
New Mexico	146	159	214	322	248
Oklahoma	230	281	436	501	200
Texas	960	1,026	1,525	2,198	154
Wyoming	66	87	106	138	276

Source: U.S. Bureau of the Census, *State Government Tax Collections* Washington, D.C., Series GS 79.

Table 2-4
Severance-Tax Collections in Texas

Fiscal Year	Total Severance Tax (millions of dollars)	Oil Production (million barrels)	Severance Tax, Oil (millions of dollars)	Average Price, Oil (dollars/barrel)
1981	2,220	925	1,330	31.00
1980	1,518	936	784	18.70
1979	1,019	990	465	10.70
1978	953	1,054	435	9.00
1977	900		426	
1976	796		429	

	Gas Production (billion cubic feet)	Severance Tax, Gas (millions of dollars)	Average Price, Gas (dollars/thousand cubic feet)
1981	7,000	890	1.80
1980	7,073	734	1.38
1979	6,933	554	1.10
1978	7,050	518	.97
1977		474	
1976		367	

Source: U.S. Bureau of Census, *State Government Tax Collections* Series GS-76-81-no. 1, and unpublished data, Texas Revenue Department, Austin, Tx.

tions are entirely due to increases in oil and gas prices between 1976 and 1981; during that period, oil production declined slightly and gas production remained approximately level.

Property Taxes

The tax treatment of mineral property by local governments varies widely among states. For analytical purposes, it is useful to distinguish between three general types of state practice: (1) states where there is no tax on reserves or land under production; (2) states where the gross value of current production is used to determine the assessment of mineral property; and states where an attempt is made to assess mineral reserves in terms of their market value.

Alaska, Louisiana, and Oklahoma do not tax reserves or land under production. Alaska's statewide property tax on mineral reserves expired in 1978. In addition, Oklahoma exempts from tax much of the personal property (equipment) used in mining.

Wyoming, Montana, and New Mexico use the gross value of current production to determine the assessment of mineral property. Thus, the tax base for the property tax in these three states for mining property is essentially the same as the tax base for a severance tax.

Table 2-5
Severance-Tax Collections in Louisiana
(millions of dollars)

Fiscal Year	Total Severance Tax	Oil	Gas
1981	815	639	161
1980	525	335	174
1979	512	260	202
1978	477	270	210
1977	495	276	226
1976	558	282	251

Source: U.S. Bureau of Census, *State Government Tax Collections* Series GS-76-81, no. 1, and unpublished data, Louisiana Revenue Department, Baton Rouge, La.

Somewhat different practices exist in these three states. In Wyoming, land is taxed according to value until development is complete. Once mining begins, the land is exempt and production is taxed. The assessment is 100 percent of the value of gross output, to which local tax rates are applied. Improvements in personal property at the surface remain taxable, but reserves in oil, gas, and coal are effectively subject to a local severance tax.

In Montana, assessment is determined on the basis of gross proceeds. Surface-mining property is assessed at 100 percent of the value of annual gross output, and the tax base is 45 percent of assessed value.

New Mexico has local production taxes and production-equipment taxes. Under the local production tax, assessed value, which is the tax base, is one third of taxable value. Taxable value is defined to be 150 percent of the value of annual gross product, less royalties. Under the production-equipment levy, the tax base is 27 percent of the value of production. In effect, these two taxes are local severance or gross-receipts taxes. Oil and gas properties in New Mexico are exempt from other local property taxes if they are subject to the *ad-valorem* production tax and the production-equipment tax.

Texas and California are the only two producing states that attempt to assess mineral and energy reserves in terms of their market value. Under state law, assessment practices are supposed to estimate the market value of a property. In the case of oil, when a well begins production, the level of recoverable reserves is established based on petroleum-engineering studies. Initial reserves, combined with historical information on similar properties, including data on the pattern of production decline, are used to establish estimates of annual output in future years. Local assessors have informed us that net proceeds for all years are then estimated by subtracting extraction costs, severance taxes, and the windfall-profit tax from estimated gross revenues. The stream of net proceeds is discounted to obtain an estimate of the present value of the property. (In Texas, the current discount rate is 14 percent.)

According to state law, assessment in any year should reflect current estimates of the value of output. Properties are to be reassessed every year as estimates of output, costs, and prices are changed. Annual reassessments should also take account of any new information on the level of reserves. We have no information on the extent to which local assessment practices in Texas and California are consistent with the formulas in state law.

The form and level of the property tax affects both revenue and production incentives. Where assessment is based on the gross value of output, property taxes will discourage production and delay exploitation of known reserves. Property taxes imposed on the expected value of net proceeds—as the taxes in California and Texas theoretically are designed to do—should encourage production, once the level of reserves has been established. The form of property tax will also influence the extent to which states and localities share in the benefits from unanticipated price increases. For a given price increase, revenues will be most responsive in those states taxing on the basis of gross proceeds and least in those states exempting mineral reserves.

Both the economic equivalence of severance taxes and property taxes based on gross value and the fact that some states grant property-tax exemptions tied to severance taxes suggest that the burden of severance taxes in any state cannot be properly evaluated without taking into account property-tax practices in the state.

To date, there have been few efforts to compile comparative data on effective property-tax rates on mineral reserves. Church (1978) reports effective property-tax rates on gross revenues in coal production for sixteen states. His calculations do not make any distinction between improvements and reserves. Church finds a very high variance in tax rates among states, with Montana the highest at 7 percent of the value of output. Arthur Anderson and Company (1978) estimates the property taxes in Wyoming to be 6.5 percent of gross value. Combining this gross value-based property tax with the 10.5-percent severance tax implies an effective severance-tax rate of 17 percent for Wyoming coal.

Information provided to us by tax assessors in the Houston area suggests an effective tax rate of 2 percent of the value of oil reserves. Oil-company representatives believe this rate is representative of the rate for all of Texas. Arthur Anderson and Company reports property taxes to be 2.5 percent of gross value for Texas oil. Assuming the same effective rate for natural gas, we estimate that local property taxes on oil and gas properties in Texas yield an annual revenue of $775 million, about 30 percent of severance-tax collections. This is probably a high estimate because it assumes that localities reassess values immediately when prices increase.

Based on the fragmentary information available, it appears that local property taxes on energy resources are either small or zero in all states except Texas, Montana, and Wyoming. Some states such as Arizona receive substantial property-tax revenues from copper reserves.

State Corporate Taxes

Many states impose taxes on net corporate income patterned in varying degree after the federal corporate-income tax. These taxes will capture some share of increased revenue accruing to energy producers from rising energy prices.

However, estimation of incremental tax revenues on a state-by-state basis is quite complex. A precise calculation of effective tax rates on the income from natural-resource properties would require information on how companies apportion their net income among states. Generally, corporations engaged in interstate commerce pay corporate tax to most states. Net income is typically apportioned on the basis of a three-factor formula:

$$T_L = \frac{t_L P \left(\frac{S_L}{S} + \frac{W_L}{W} + \frac{K_L}{K} \right)}{3}$$

where P = total profits for entire nation
S = sales
W = wages
K = property
L = state in question

States differ considerably in the way they define various factors that go into the formula and the weight accorded to them. Calculation of T_L would require data on sales, wages, and property in each state on a firm basis or for energy industries as a whole. This information is not available and cannot easily be approximated. Therefore, we have made no attempt to estimate state revenues from corporate taxes imposed on the additional private earnings from higher energy prices.

We have, however, taken account of the special corporate tax imposed by Alaska on oil companies and pipeline companies operating in Alaska that prevailed during the period 1978-1981. Under this tax, companies were required to use separate accounting for earnings on Alaskan oil production. The tax is imposed at a rate of 9.4 percent on oil-production revenues net of royalties, severance taxes, and some designated deductions designed to reflect the cost of production. The law allows a deduction for the federal windfall-profit tax, but the federal corporate-income tax is not deductible. The estimated share of additional revenue from decontrol captured by the

Alaska tax is included in the calculations presented in the next section on the division of revenues from decontrol and higher prices.

Other oil-producing states have no or modest corporate taxes. Texas and Wyoming have no state corporate tax. Louisiana imposes an 8-percent tax with formula apportionment but allows a 38-percent depletion allowance for all oil companies. New Mexico and Oklahoma impose corporate taxes of 6 percent and 4 percent, respectively. Oklahoma allows a 22-percent depletion allowance.

Royalty Payments

Citizens of a state reap a fiscal advantage from state revenues from energy production whether they arise from taxes or from royalties on state-owned lands. However, there are different production incentives from taxes and royalty payments. In addition, the right of states to receive royalties on state-owned land is much more firmly established than the unlimited right to impose severance taxes, which has been subject to judicial and legislative challenges.

States also receive royalties from minerals and energy produced on federally owned lands within their boundaries. The minimum federal royalty rate is fixed at 12.5 percent. Of federal royalties, 50 percent are allocated to states in all states other than Alaska. Although there is currently no production on federal lands in Alaska, current legislation allocates 90 percent of royalties on federal land to Alaska.

In fiscal 1978, states received $228 million of royalties on federally owned land. Of this, two thirds were received by Wyoming and New Mexico and virtually nothing by Alaska, Texas, Louisiana, and Oklahoma. However, the potential growth in royalties from coal leased on federal lands is very large. The U.S. Department of the Interior estimates that the federal government owns 80 percent of the land in the Powder River Basin of Wyoming and Montana. This area might produce as much as 300 million tons of coal per year by the late 1980s, up from the current combined-production levels in Wyoming and Montana of 100 million tons.

It is estimated that two thirds of our remaining oil reserves and 40 percent of remaining gas reserves are found on the Outer Continental Shelf. The rights to these reserves belong to the federal government, and the revenues from these leases are not shared with the states.

Royalties earned on state-owned land are another story, particularly in Alaska. Alaska owns all the land in areas currently producing oil. From the one eighth royalty share it receives from production, it collects about $2.3 billion annually at current price and output levels. Alaska also collected $900 million in bonus payments when the land was leased.

Royalty earnings of other states are considerably lower than the income received by Alaska. Table 2-6 summarizes the avilable information on state royalty earnings from energy production.

The most complete information available to us on royalties is for Texas. About 16 percent of natural gas and 5 percent of oil in Texas is produced on state property (exclusive of university land). In general, the state sold these lands but retained the mineral rights. The average royalty rate to the state, net of the share received by the private landholder, is 10 percent. However, with rising energy prices, both royalty rates and bonus payments determined by competitive bidding have been rising. The conventional royalty rate, formerly 12.5 percent, has risen to 25 percent on leases currently being negotiated. On some unusually rich natural-gas property, the state's share is 44 percent. Moreover, total royalties have also risen because of the increases in oil and natural-gas prices.

Table 2-6
Royalties Collected by States on State and Federal Lands, by Fiscal Year
(millions of dollars)

	1979	1980	1981
Alaska	186	866	1119
Texas	266[a]	442	600
Louisiana	262	262[b]	326[c]
New Mexico	143[d]	111[e]	
Oklahoma	20	20	
Wyoming	92[f]		
Montana	20[g]	28	
California	72	293	

Sources: For 1979, U.S. Bureau of the Census, *State Government Finances* (Washington, D.C., 1979); unless otherwise indicated, figures for 1980 come from U.S. Bureau of the Census, *State Government Finances* (Washington, D.C., 1980); figure for 1981 for Alaska is from Alaska, Office of the Governor, *Budget in Brief FY 1982* (Juneau: Division of Budget and Management, 1982), p. 10; 1980 and 1981 figures for Texas are estimates from the Texas Department of Revenue; 1981 figure for Louisiana is from the Louisiana Revenue Department.
[a]Does not include $75 million in bonus payments.
[b]Does not include $281 million in bonus payments (Louisiana Revenue Department).
[c]Does not include $136 million in bonus payments (Louisiana Revenue Department).
[d]Includes $60 million from federal lands.
[e]Does not include $92 million in mineral-lease revenue other than oil and gas royalities.
[f]For 1978, includes $70 million from federal lands.
[g]For 1978, includes $8 million from federal lands.

Louisiana officials confirmed the upward trend in royalty rates. The minimum rate in Louisiana is currently one sixth, and on some properties the government's share has exceeded 60 percent. Louisiana claims to have an abundance of unexplored property in the eastern part of the state, some of it offshore. Leases are not granted for indefinite periods, thus with re-negotiation the state's share could rise significantly. In addition, Louisiana royalties will be increased by the expected increase in the state severance tax on natural gas. Under current federal price regulations the tax will be passed through to consumers, thus increasing the value of the state's royalty share.

In conclusion, state royalties comprise an important share of state revenues from energy production in some states. Royalties have risen with rising energy prices, both because total revenues have increased and because, as unleased property has become scarcer, firms have bid up the share of lessors. Royalties from resources on state lands may continue to increase. In addition, royalties received by states from federal lands will probably increase, especially in Wyoming, New Mexico, Montana, and possibly Alaska. Federal policy, as determined by the Mineral Leasing Act, will have an important impact on state revenues by affecting future state royalties on federal land.

Distribution of Economic Rents from Price Decontrol

In this section, we integrate the data on state and federal taxes described in the preceding section to compute estimates of the share of revenues from crude-oil decontrol captured by different levels of government. This distribution differs among states both because of differences in state and local taxes on the returns to energy production and because of the different treatment of different classes of oil production and oil producers under the Federal Crude Oil Windfall Profit Tax.

We present calculations for two states, Alaska and Texas, of the division of revenues from two changes—the decontrol of oil between May 1979 and January 1981 and an arbitrarily assumed $10-per-barrel increase in the price of oil in January 1981. Thus, we show how the increased revenues are distributed from a change that has occurred and from a potential change (using January 1981 data and tax rules in effect then) if a decline in foreign oil production caused a further increase in the world price of oil.

Alaska and Texas are selected because they are the two leading oil-producing states and because we have more complete information on state and local taxes in Alaska and Texas than we have for other states.

The calculations reveal some substantial differences between the two states. Under the legislation that existed between 1978 and 1981, the state government in Alaska captured approximately 24 percent of the additional oil revenues from decontrol and from a $10-per-barrel increase in the price of oil. In contrast, the state government of Texas captured only about 10-percent of these revenues. Private producers captured 24 percent of the increased revenues from decontrol in Texas, but they captured only 13 percent in Alaska. If the price of oil had risen by $10 per barrel in January 1981, private producers would have captured 21 percent of the additional revenue in Texas and only 12 percent in Alaska.

State and federal tax rates on private oil producers are higher in Alaska than in Texas. The federal tax rate on private oil production is higher in Alaska than in Texas because almost all oil in Alaska is tier-1 oil produced by majors, the oil subject to the highest rates under the Crude Oil Windfall Profit Tax. Texas has relatively more oil taxed at lower rates, both because independent producers pay lower windfall-profit taxes and because independent producers are allowed to deduct 22 percent of gross revenues from taxable income as percentage depletion. However, the percentage of the revenue increase captured by the federal government is smaller in Alaska than in Texas because the state of Alaska preempts a much higher share of taxable revenue than does Texas. All state taxes and royalties are deductible under the federal corporate-income tax, and state severance taxes and royalties are deductible from the windfall-profit tax.

Some qualifications to these calculations need to be mentioned:

1. These calculations do not estimate the share of all oil-company revenues or profits captured in the long run by different levels of governments. Specifically, they fail to account for the share of investment financed by different levels of government through tax depreciation, investment credits, expensing of certain capital costs, and other tax-accounting rules. What they do measure is the extent to which different levels of government share in so-called unanticipated revenues.

2. The calculations do not measure the net increase in federal tax revenues from oil-price increases. Domestic oil-price increases resulting from either decontrol or an increase in OPEC prices are not necessarily associated with an increase in nominal national income, if the targets of aggregate monetary and fiscal policies are unchanged. If nominal GNP were unaffected by changes in the price of energy, the total tax base for the corporate- and personal-income taxes would remain constant. Income would shift from consumers of oil products to crude-oil producers, and revenues would be reallocated within the economy. More revenue would be collected from oil companies under the corporate-income tax, but this revenue increase would be offset by reduced corporate- and personal-income-tax collections from other corporations and households experiencing a decline or slower growth in nominal income than would otherwise have occurred. Net federal revenues rise because the windfall-profit tax is applied only to oil-company revenues, but federal revenues would increase by less

than the total amount of increased collections from oil producers,[3] unless nominal GNP increases by the amount of oil-company revenues.

3. The calculations do not precisely measure increases in economic rents to the oil industry. To the extent that production has increased in response to higher prices, higher costs were probably incurred in adding marginal units of output. Thus, part of the increased revenues represents economic rent to suppliers, and part represents increases in marginal production costs. In the short run, with most production from older wells that would have produced approximately the same output without the price change, it is reasonable to argue that most of the revenue change represents increased rents.

Results for Alaska

For Alaska, it is assumed that the state collects a 12.5-percent royalty on all production in Alaska. The effective severance tax is 10 percent, and the special state corporate tax of 9.4 percent is applied to all the additional revenues generated by the price increase. The property tax on reserves is assumed to be 0.

A sample calculation for the windfall-profit tax base for tier-1 oil for major producers is as follows. The price change between May 1979 and December 1980, ΔP, is $31.65 - 8.31 = \$23.34$ per barrel. The change in state royalties is $.125\Delta P = \$2.92$ per barrel; the change in severance tax is $.10(\Delta P - \Delta \text{royalties}) = \$2.04$; and the change in state corporate tax is $.094(\Delta P - \Delta \text{royalties} - \Delta \text{severance tax} - \text{windfall-profit tax}) = \$0.59$. The change in total state revenues in dollars/barrel is $\$2.92 + \$2.04 + \$0.57 = \$5.53$, and the windfall-profit tax base is: [Price − Severance Tax Adjustment − Adjusted Base Price] $(1 - r)$ where Severance Tax Adjustment is (Price − Adjusted Base Price) × severance tax rate. r is the public royalty rate (the state's share in output). So for Alaska the tax base is $[31.65 - (31.65 - 9.38) \times 10 - 9.38] \times 875 = \$17.54$. Therefore, the windfall-profit tax for major producers for tier-1 oil (WPT) $= 0.7$ base $= \$12.28$.

We assumed that the additional federal taxes paid by major producers is 46 percent. In making this assumption, we ignore taxes on additional corporate distributions resulting from higher oil revenues and thus slightly understate the total federal share. The increase in corporate profits subject to federal tax is equal to change in price − state taxes and royalties − federal windfall-profit tax, or $\$23.34 - \$5.53 - \$12.28 = \$5.53$. Therefore, the increase in corporate-tax revenues is equal to $0.46 \times \$5.53 = \$2.54$, and the total increase in federal tax revenues is equal to $\$14.82$. To summarize, the change in price is $\$23.34$, of which state taxes and royalties

are $5.53, the increase in federal tax revenues is $14.82, and the private
share (return) is $2.99. The production numbers for December 1980 are us-
ed to calculate the absolute level of rents. Total output in barrels per day was
1,584,900. Independents produced 1.3 percent of the total and major producers 98.7 percent.

The calculations for independent producers are essentially the same except that the price change is greater, the windfall-profit tax is 50 percent,
and the additional federal income tax is assumed to be 40 percent of the
change in the net income of producers. The federal tax is a weighted average
of the marginal tax rate of corporations and individual taxpayers holding
partnership shares. In addition, independent producers are allowed to claim
22 percent of additions to gross revenues as percentage-depletion deductions in computing net income. The summary for independent producers,
tier 1, is: change in price is $20.44, of which state taxes and royalties are
$5.15, the increase in federal tax revenues is $9.82, and the private share
(return) is $5.47. There was no tier-2 or tier-3 oil in Alaska as of May 1979.

Multiplying the increase in revenue per barrel for each category of producer by total output, and combining the revenue changes for major and independent producers, the summary total for additional revenues from oil
production in Alaska resulting from decontrol between May 1979 and January 1981 is:

	Changes in Revenue (millions of dollars/year)
State	3,195 (23.7 percent)
Federal	8,536 (63.3 percent)
Private share (return)	1,749 (13.0 percent)
Total revenue	13,480

Results for Texas

Texas differs from Alaska in that less than 10 percent of the oil is produced
on state land. The overall royalty rate for the state is just over 1 percent in
contrast to 12.5 percent for Alaska. There is no corporate-income tax in
Texas and the severance tax is 4.6 percent. Texas levies property taxes on oil
reserves. The increase in property taxes resulting from price increases is difficult to compute without knowledge of actual practices. According to state
regulations, local governments are supposed to assess at 100 percent of
value and should use a 14-percent discount rate in converting projected net
earnings into a present value. The effective property-tax rate on value so
assessed is 2 percent. Assuming ten years of production left in the average
well, we estimated that the property tax would increase by about $1.50 per

barrel from the $28.00-per-barrel price increase from decontrol if state rules were followed. The implied rate of tax is much higher than the Arthur Anderson estimate of 2.5 percent of the gross annual value of production. For the purposes of our computations, we assumed an in-between effective marginal rate on gross value of 4.6 percent, a rate equal to the Texas severance tax. Further work on this issue is needed, since Texas is one of the few states with a property tax on oil reserves. A finding of a high implied tax rate on gross value would correct the impression that Texas is a low-tax state. However, an adequate estimate of the effective rate requires a thorough study of actual assessment practices.

The summary totals for Texas expressed as revenues per year (in millions of dollars) are as follows:

State revenues	2,202 (10.2 percent)
Federal revenues	14,187 (62.7 percent)
Private revenues	5,274 (27.1 percent)
Total revenues	21,663

The results for Texas and Alaska probably bracket the results we shall obtain for other states, because Alaska is a relatively high-tax state and Texas is a low-tax jurisdiction. The main differences are the higher state share in Alaska and the higher private share in Texas. Lower state and local royalties and taxes in Texas increase the private share as does a somewhat large proportion of production accounted for by independents. Table 2-7 shows the distribution of rents for Alaska and Texas from a $10-per-barrel price increase in January 1981.

Table 2-7
Distribution of Rents per Barrel for an Increase in the Price of Oil, per $10 of Increase

	Tier-1 Independent		Tier-1 Major		Tier-2 Independent	
	Alaska	Texas	Alaska	Texas	Alaska	Texas
State	2.50	1.01	2.34	1.01	2.65	1.01
Federal	4.10	5.55	6.54	7.70	3.48	4.41
Private	3.40	3.44	1.12	1.29	3.87	4.58

	Tier-2 Major		Tier-3		All Tiers Weighted Average	
	Alaska	Texas	Alaska	Texas	Alaska	Texas
State	2.41	1.01	2.65	1.01	2.35	1.01
Federal	6.08	7.19	4.64	5.38	6.50	6.85
Private	1.51	1.80	2.71	3.61	1.15	2.14

Efficiency Aspects of
Government Capture of Energy Rents

This section considers inefficiencies that result from attempts by different levels of government to capture rents from energy resources. We then discuss the potential magnitude of the welfare loss from an inefficiency first discussed by Charles McLure (forthcoming)—the misallocation of labor and capital among regions in response to fiscal disparities caused by differences in natural-resource endowments.

In general, most taxes distort the allocation of resources by driving a wedge between the price paid by the buyer for the taxed good or factor of production and the price received by the seller. These tax wedges prevent resources from flowing to their highest-value use. We can identify four types of distortions that might result from tax policies and allocations of property rights that enable governments to capture rents from energy production:

Allocation of Capital between
Energy and Other Investments

Most special taxes on energy industries, including the Crude Oil Windfall Profit Tax and state severance taxes, are imposed on gross revenues. (The windfall-profit tax attempts to impose a heavier burden on properties where the rent component of return is relatively large by taxing newly discovered oil and tertiary oil at lower rates than old oil.) Therfore, they reduce the prospective rate of return on new investments in energy, relative to other uses of capital, and provide an incentive for capital to move to less-productive uses.

Royalty payments represent an allocation of a share of the mineral to the landowner (in this case, the state) and therefore have their major impact on the value of mining rights by affecting the bonus bids for mineral properties. However, the fact that the landowner receives a return by capturing a share of the output, rather than by charging a fixed annual rental for mining rights, does discourage marginal investments in developing the property by reducing the return to an extra unit of output.

Property taxes do not discourage investment in energy properties, relative to other uses of capital, if the taxes are based on the value of property and the assessment of energy property is equal to the assessment of all other property.[4] Similarly, a corporate-income tax does not per se distort the incentive to invest in energy property, relative to other investments, if the rules for measuring taxable income are applied in a uniform manner to the return from all investments. As noted, certain provisions of the current U.S. corporate-income tax—specifically, expensing of intangible drilling costs and of exploration and development expenses for mines and percentage depletion—do provide special incentives for investment in energy and mineral-resource development.

Timing of Production from Developed Wells or Mines

Once a mine or well has been developed, taxes on output could distort the timing of production by causing relative after-tax returns for different time periods to differ from the relative returns across time periods in the absence of tax. The windfall-profit tax contains this distortion because, under current law, the tax is scheduled to be phased out beginning in 1987 and also because the tax on new oil (property developed after 1979) is being phased down gradually from 30 percent in 1981 to 15 percent in 1986. The phased reduction in the tax provides an incentive to defer production.

More generally, even severance taxes and royalty formulas that capture a constant percentage of revenue over time will distort the timing of output if the producer's discount rate is not equal to the expected rate of price change of the resource. Robert Conrad and Bryce Hool (1981) have shown that an *ad-valorem* severance tax or royalty could cause either a postponement or an advancement of production when real extraction costs are constant over time but vary positively with the level of production in any period.[5]

Corporate-income taxes and property taxes do not distort the timing of output, if based on a consistent and correct measurement of net income and market value of the property, respectively.

Local Choice between Public and Private Goods

Assignments of property rights that allow subnational fiscal units to capture rents from energy (or other natural resources) lower the average cost to residents of financing a dollar of public expenditures. However, in some cases, this will not lower the marginal cost of additional public goods because potential revenue from such rents will be far less than local public spending. At the margin, such localities will still need to impose an additional dollar of tax on their own residents for every additional dollar of public services they provide.

In the case of Alaska, where state royalties from oil production exceed the state's budget, there are likely to be incentives for excessive public expenditures because of constraints on simply distributing the surplus to citizens. In addition, it could be argued that Alaska's fiscal prosperity may result in inefficient choices among alternative public investments. However, a conclusion that Alaska's wealth would be invested inefficiently must be based on a judgment about the working of the political process. If Alaska were maximizing the welfare of its citizens, its energy royalties by themselves would provide no incentive for inefficient choices among public expenditures.

Taxes imposed on energy properties at the national level do not distort local choices between private and public goods or among types of public investments.

Locational Choice among Regions

If a state or local government has a fiscal advantage because of natural resources within its boundaries, tax rates on suppliers of labor and capital services required to finance a given level of public services will be lower than in other states or localities. An incentive will therefore be provided for immigration of labor and capital to the favored fiscal entity. This migration incentive is unrelated either to factor productivity or to desirable living characteristics of the area. The magnitude of the inefficiency created by this fiscally induced distortion of locational choice will be discussed further.

Table 2-8 summarizes the inefficiencies resulting from various ways of capturing private revenues from energy resources.

Migration Inefficiency

McLure (forthcoming) argued that the collection of mineral taxes and royalties by energy-producing states will attract labor and capital and thus lead to a misallocation of resources throughout the economy. The essence of the argument is that from the standpoint of the nation the net social marginal productivity of labor and capital should be equalized across states but that, in making locational decisions, individuals equalize utilities based on after-tax incomes (including public services as part of income). In this section, we provide some rough estimates of the magnitude of this component of the welfare loss resulting from state energy taxes and royalties.

The seven states with significant revenues from energy taxation are Texas, Alaska, Louisiana, Oklahoma, Wyoming, New Mexico, and Montana. These states had a total population of about 22 million and collected about $6.6 billion per year in special energy taxes and royalties, or about $300 per capita, in 1980. Personal income in the seven states averaged about $9,000 per capita. Thus, benefits from the taxation of energy-related resources either in the form of reduced taxes or increased public goods represented a 3.7-percent subsidy rate measured as a proportion of personal income.

Table 2-8
Inefficiencies from Government Capture of Returns to Energy Resources

	Activity Distorted			
Form of Revenue	Energy Investment	Timing of Output	Local Public Good	Migration
State severance tax	yes	yes	sometimes	yes
Property taxes[a]	no	no	sometimes	yes
National corporate-income tax[b]	no	no	no	no
State corporate-income tax[c]	no	no	sometimes	yes
Federal windfall-profit tax[d]	yes	yes	no	no
State royalties	yes	yes	sometimes	yes

[a]If based on value of property (present discounted value of net future income) and neutral among types of capital.

[b]If neutral among types of capital

[c]If neutral among types of capital

[d]Tax of the form of the current windfall-profit tax, which is actually an excise tax imposed on the value of oil above a legislated base price.

We estimate the efficiency loss from misallocation of capital and labor among regions by treating energy revenues as if they provided a special, discriminatory subsidy to movement of labor and capital into the seven-state region. We assume there is a single industry in the seven-state region, which is treated as a unit, and that the industry is characterized by a Cobb-Douglas production function. The supply of capital to the region is assumed to be perfectly elastic; the after-tax rental price of capital in these states is taken as equal to the after-tax rental price of capital in the rest of the country. The supply of labor to the region is a function of the wage rate with the subsidy from energy revenues included as part of the total wage to labor. In our calculation, we use a labor supply elasticity equal to $+1.0$[6]

The formal model is as follows. Production in the region is characterized by the equation:

$$Y = AL^aK^b \tag{2.1}$$

where Y = value of output (price level taken to be unity)
$\quad\quad\quad L$ = labor input in employed workers/year
$\quad\quad\quad K$ = capital stock (equal to 100 units)
$\quad\quad\quad a$ = labor's share of output
$\quad\quad\quad b$ = capital's share of output
$\quad\quad\quad A$ = constant

The value of A in the base case is computed using selected initial values of Y, L, a, and b. The value of Y is total personal income in the seven states in 1980, about \$198 billion. From the U.S. national-income accounts, we calculate that compensation of employees accounted for about 76 percent of national income in 1980. Therefore, we set a equal to 0.76 and b equal to 0.24. Total employment is taken to be about 45 percent of population, or 9.9 million workers. Thus, income is about \$20,000 per employed worker, of which \$15,200 is wages and the remaining income is return to suppliers of capital.

Differentiating equation 2.1 with respect to L and K and setting marginal products equal to factor prices, we obtain demand curves for labor and capital services in the region:

$$w = Aa K^b L^{(a-1)} \tag{2.2}$$

and

$$r = Ab L^a K^{(b-1)} \tag{2.3}$$

where w = unit cost of labor, and r = unit-rental price of capital services. The supply of capital is given by the equation:

$$r = r_0 - s_k \tag{2.4}$$

where r_0 = the return to suppliers of capital services (net of taxes and subsidies) and s_k = the subsidy per unit of capital services. Since the supply of capital to the region is perfectly elastic, the cost of capital services to the region is reduced by the full amount of the subsidy.

The supply of labor to the region is given by the equation:

$$L = c(w + s_L) \tag{2.5}$$

where s_L = the subsidy per worker, and c = a constant calibrated from initial values of L and w.

Finally, the total amount of subsidy to labor and capital is equal to the amount of revenue raised by energy taxes and royalties:

$$E = s_k K + s_L L \tag{2.6}$$

where E = total energy revenues (\$6.6 billion in the seven states).

We solve equations 2.2 through 2.6 simultaneously for two extreme cases. In the first case, all energy revenues are used to provide subsidies to capital ($s_L = 0$) either in the form of public services that directly enhance capital values or in reduced taxation of capital income below average levels prevailing in the rest of the country. In the second case, all energy revenues are used to provide subsidies to labor ($s_K = 0$).

With all the subsidy provided to capital, the capital stock increases in the long run by 21.8 percent. The inflow of capital, in the equilibrium solution, raises wages and the supply of labor by 4.1 percent. These factor movements increase total income in the seven states by $16 billion per year, an increase of 8.1 percent.

Following Arnold Harberger (1966), we compute the total deadweight loss of the subsidy as equal to $0.5s_k \Delta K$, where s_k = the subsidy per unit of capital ΔK is the change in the capital stock. The subsidy per unit is the total subsidy divided by the new total stock of capital, or $54.21 per unit. We calculate the welfare loss to be about $590 million per year, or slightly under 9 percent of energy revenues.

If the entire subsidy were provided to labor, the welfare-loss estimate would be smaller because of the lower assumed elasticity of labor supply. Solving the model with $s_k = 0$, total labor supply rises to 10.317 million, an increase of 4.2 percent. The capital supply also increases by 4.2 percent, and the unit cost of labor is unchanged. Income rises by 4.2 percent to $206.3 billion. The subsidy per unit of labor is equal to $639.72 or about 4.2 percent of wages before subsidy. The deadweight loss is about $133 million, only 2 percent of energy revenues.

Thus, our very rough estimates of the deadweight loss from distortion of locational decisions caused by state and local energy taxes and royalties range from 2 percent to 9 percent of the total revenue raised, depending on whether the revenue is used to provide subsidies for, or to reduce relative tax burdens on, labor or capital. These estimates are extremely sensitive to elasticity assumptions. We have used fairly high elasticities of supply to indicate the likely upper range of the welfare loss.

There is no precise way of dividing the benefits of the taxes on energy between labor and capital. The Advisory Commission on Intergovernmental Relations (1980) estimates the business share of total state and local taxes to be about 30 percent for the nation as a whole. This estimate of capital's share of the tax burden is a measure of legal liability rather than incidence and is higher in the energy-producing states because severance taxes are included in the figures as capital taxes. The estimates suggest that it is unlikely that more than 30 percent of the benefits of energy taxes (in the form of reduced taxes on capital and expenditure benefits) accrue to capital. Thus, if the elasticity of labor supply is equal to or less than 1.0, our calculations suggest that the inefficiency associated with migration is less than 4 percent of energy revenues, or no more than $265 million per year.

There are several reasons our rough analysis may overstate the efficiency loss from migration. First, in some states residents own a significant share of the energy property and consume a significant fraction of the output from that property. For example, in Texas about two thirds of the natural gas produced in the state is used by consumers and industry in the state. In assuming that all the costs of energy taxes are imposed on nonresidents of the energy-producing region, we overstate the incentive for migration of labor and capital provided by these revenues.

Second, we have ignored the existence of other, fixed factors of production, such as land. If fixed factors are important, inmigration of labor and capital will drive down marginal returns to both factors and reduce the net effect of energy revenues on factor movements. Thus, ignoring fixed factors overstates the potential efficiency losses from migration.

Finally, we have overstated efficiency losses by assuming that state tax systems are optimal in the absence of energy revenues. To the extent that energy revenues allow states to reduce taxation of labor and capital, they permit reduction in other distortions imposed by the tax system. If energy revenues arise purely from land rents, energy taxes could cause fewer economic distortions than taxes on labor and capital.[7]

Thus, our preliminary analysis suggests that the efficiency losses associated with migration of capital and labor to energy-producing states may, on balance, be relatively small. However, as noted, there is also a potential efficiency loss from the misspending of public funds in energy-rich states. In considering the efficiency costs of state and local energy revenues, we have assumed that state and local governments operate efficiently in the sense that additional revenues are used to provide public goods (or to lower taxes) that at the margin yield benefits equal to marginal costs. The size and composition of the public sector are assumed to be optimal. This assumption appears reasonable for states with energy revenues in the range of $250-$300 per capita.

Alaska presents a contrasting picture. In Alaska, the migration elasticities are likely to be smaller than in other energy-producing states, and therefore the inefficiencies arising from locational choice are likely to be lower. However, it is possible that revenues per capita from energy resources are too large to be used efficiently. The state appears constrained or unwilling to return much money directly to the taxpayers. Thus, there is potential for either overprovision of public services or uneconomic investments in capital projects.[8] Thus, even though locational distortions are smaller, it is possible that the concentration of funds in Alaska gives rise to larger efficiency losses, per dollar of revenue, than the $6 billion currently collected in the Southwest and Mountain states.

Notes

1. The 1981 Revenue Act reduces the tax rate on new oil in stages to 15 percent by 1986 and allows for a series of additional exemptions for independent producers and recipients of royalty income.

2. The percentage-depletion rate was phased down to 20 percent in 1981 and 18 percent in 1982 and, under current law, will continue to decline to 16 percent in 1983 and 15 percent in 1984 and thereafter.

3. The net increase in nominal GNP could equal the increase in oil-company revenues if the monetary authorities expanded the money supply in response to an increase in the price of imported oil so as to keep all other prices from falling. Although this type of monetary response to higher oil prices is possible, it is not the only or necessarily the most probable scenario. The main point here is that the net increase in federal revenues need not equal the increased revenue collected from oil producers, and that our figures therefore should not be interpreted as estimates of the effects of decontrol on federal revenue.

4. This assumes that property values are based on net income.

5. An *ad-valorem* tax or royalty will not capture the same present value of revenue in every time period if the expected rate of price appreciation and the firm's discount rate are not equal. If the expected growth in prices is greater than the discount rate, the present value of tax liability can be reduced by accelerating production; if the expected growth in prices is less than the discount rate, the present value of tax liability can be reduced by deferring production. Therefore, an *ad-valorem* severance tax or a fixed-percentage royalty payment is not neutral with respect to the decision of how to allocation production over time.

6. This assumed elasticity of the supply of labor to a region is slightly higher than the highest elasticity (0.8) estimated by P.M. Sommers and D.B. Suits (1973) in a study of the determinants of interstate migration. See also Samuel Bowles (1970) and R.L. Raimon (1962).

7. If energy taxes are less distortionary than taxes that would be imposed to finance public services in their absence, then there may be an efficiency gain from migration to energy-rich states because such migration enables more people to live in regions with an efficient tax system. That is, migration partially offsets the inefficiency that results because the ability to tax energy revenues is limited to particular jurisdictions. There still remains potential inefficiency in comparison to a situation in which the rights to tax energy rents were not linked to residence within particular geographic boundaries. See chapter 1 of this book.

8. Legislation has just been enacted that would spend $5 billion on local hydroelectric development. The project is expected to reduce the cost of electric power from 16 cents per kilowatt hour to 3 cents per kilowatt hour. The consumer will not be charged for the capital costs of the project. Although it is premature to conclude that this project is wasteful, it illustrates the potential for waste resulting from the abundance of state revenues in Alaska.

References

Advisory Commission on Intergovernmental Relations. *Significant Features of Fiscal Federalism, 1979-80* (Washington, D.C., October 1980).

Arthur Anderson and Company. "Prudhoe Bay Field and Trans-Alaska Pipeline System." Mimeo, January 1978.

Bowles, Samuel. "Migration as Investment: Empirical Tests of the Human Investment Approach to Geographical Mobility." *Review of Economics and Statistics* 32 (November 1970):356-362.

Church, Albert M. "Conflicting Federal, State and Local Interest: Trends in State and Local Energy Taxation—Coal and Copper—A Case in Point." *National Tax Journal* 31 (September 1978):269-284.

Conrad, Robert F. and Bryce Hool."Resource Taxation with Heterogeneous Quality and Endogenous Reserves." *Journal of Public Economics* 16 (August 1981):17-34.

Harberger, Arnold C. "Efficiency Effects of Taxes on Income from Capital." In *Effects of the Corporation Income Tax*, edited by Marian Krzyzaniak. Detroit: Wayne State University Press, 1966.

McLure, Charles E., Jr. "Fiscal Federalism and the Taxation of Economic Rents." In *State and Local Finance in the 80s*, edited by George F. Break. Madison, Wis.: University of Wisconsin Press, forthcoming.

Raimon, R.L. "Interstate Migration and Wage Theory." *Review of Economics and Statistics* 44 (November 1962):428-438.

Sommers, P.M., and D.B. Suits, "Analysis of Net Interstate Migration," *Southern Economic Journal* 39 (October 1973):193-201.

Comments

Albert M. Church

In chapter 2 Peter Mieszkowski and Eric Toder define, distinguish, and evaluate the efficiency and distribution issues that arise both theoretically and empirically from taxation of crude-oil production.

The authors quite correctly point out both the significance and difficulty of analyzing the effects of tax and royalty structures that are interrelated. Taxes other than those on output include excise, payroll, and other taxes applied to various inputs separately and the property and corporate-income taxes. The last two are more difficult to classify, particularly when they are applied to natural resources and fall on resource rents and the opportunity cost of capital. Either by legislative intent or by administrative practice, the property tax, as applied to natural resources, is most frequently in effect a tax on output. The authors take care to apply each tax to its actual tax base. To estimate the efficiency loss engendered by resource distortions and the effects on the distribution of income and wealth, one must be able to trace direct and indirect effects on prices and resource allocation. Preexisting nonneutral tax and regulatory treatment of the resource industries and the wide array of tax structures recently put in place (and those being contemplated by state legislatures) necessitate a full-fledged general-equilibrium approach. However, certain implications can be garnered from a simplified model when the more immediate impacts are of interest. This is the approach the authors have selected.

The analysis may be carried out on various orders of detail and over various time horizons. The short-run impact on private- and public-income flows may be labeled a first-order analysis. The second-order effects concern how the energy firm and industry and their consumers respond as the extent, technology, and location of investment becomes a variable. This level requires estimates of the price and resource-allocation effects and, because of interfuel competition, calls for a general-equilibrium model. Because of the complexity of these models, estimating tax shifting and incidence is uncertain. (See chapter 5.) The third order concerns the effects of resource development and the altered private- and public-income streams on other industries and induced migration of capital and labor. This requires an analysis of how natural resources *in situ* are extracted and transformed into publicly and privately owned fungible financial assets and how these are invested and ultimately used to finance consumption. These activities may in turn result in cross-subsidization of other activities and industries and may distort regional movement of industry, capital, and labor. My reading of public discussions concerning interjurisdictional energy conflicts in Canada and the United States (so-called Balkanikzation) is that the first order of analysis of the immediate effects on public- and private-income flows and the third-order analysis of the induced effects on capital flows and economic growth in the nonenergy sectors in energy-rich states are those foremost in the minds of elected officials and the public. These are also the issues focused on by the authors.

The effects of the decontrol of oil prices, the enactment of the Windfall Profits Tax, and an assumed $10-per-barrel-oil-price increase in January of 1981 are simulated for the tax and royalty structures in Texas and Alaska. The authors assume that the price of oil is established in world markets and that the rate of extraction in these states is unaffected by the simulated perturbations. Consequently the burden of taxes and royalties are borne by producers and resource owners, and the nominal tax structures are used to estimate how the windfalls are distributed. Price changes and resource reallocations caused by these events, other taxes and regulations (the depletion allowance, expensing, investment tax credits, and so on) are ignored. The authors conclude that the Texas government captures 10 percent and the Alaska government captures 24 percent of the windfalls (unanticipated increases in resource-based income) by means of taxes and royalties (approximately $250 per capita in Texas and roughly the same amount in other western oil-rich states, but $10,000 per capita in Alaska). Some of the causes of this disparity are readily apparent. A pro-oil constituency is well established in Texas, and a significant portion of oil and natural gas is processed and consumed there (roughly two thirds of natural gas is consumed in state). At present all Alaskan production occurs on state lands; virtually no oil is used in Alaska as input for further processing, and, because of the recent discovery and public ownership, no pro-oil constituency yet exists. Furthermore, the state received relatively small bonus payments at the original lease sales in light of the bonanza and may view its high severance (production) and special corporate-income taxes on oil producers as mechanisms to recoup its share as resource owner.

The authors use these income estimates to evaluate potential third-order effects of induced relocation of capital and labor. They conclude that the net migratory impact will be relatively small in the western energy-rich states because of the relatively small per-capita amounts; thus the associated net welfare losses would also be modest. They are, however, concerned that the magnitude of Alaska's oil income will cause wasteful public spending and induce a distortion in public vis-à-vis private choice. Effects on labor supply in Alaska will be minimal. However, should nonresource industries be cross-subsidized, the incremental labor demand may induce excess migration, which will dissipate Alaska's natural heritage and good fortune. Moreover, it may increase unemployment if the time lags and costs to prospective migrants of acquiring accurate information cause excess labor to migrate. This rise in unemployment as rapid resource development or large-scale construction projects begin has been observed during the construction of the Trans Alaska Pipeline and in examples in other states.

The second-order level of analysis requires further examination. The authors' position regarding energy industry and other distortions is summarized in their table 2-8. The severance- and property-tax distortions (whether assessed as a de-facto tax on output or on the present value of future net income) on the rate of extraction are consistently well documented in the literature (see Church 1981). Although these effects have not been accurately quantified, they cannot be ignored. It may be argued that the authors' assumption regarding the neutrality of the property tax (see footnote to table 2-8) is unrealistic, and there is evidence, at least in the case of coal, that states trade off the property and severance tax. The severance tax is unneutral in a regime of other taxes and increasing marginal exploration and production costs, and thus it distorts extraction rates. The property tax affects the rate of extraction, as shown by H. Stuart Burness (1976) among others. These effects and the distortions they create become potentially important, particularly as the time horizon becomes greater. The authors' final analysis of resource distortions pertains to public and private choice and effects on migration of labor and capital. Here the effects of cross-subsidization occasioned by resource-financed public expenditures on both capital and labor flows are long-term phenomena. This presents an important first step. However, other effects and other methods of distributing publicly captured resource revenues need to be looked at.

For example, the New Mexico severance-tax permanent fund has been heavily invested in local financial institutions, and there have been proposals to subsidize business loans and local savings-and-loan institutions by purchasing mortgages at below-market interest rates and allocating funds to subsidized mortgages for new construction. A concern among energy-consuming states is that low general tax rates in energy-rich states, subsidization programs, and federal-grant formulas will result in capital inflows that will stimulate economic growth, which is being perceived as being unfair.

The way in which natural-resource revenues are distributed will have important implications on both long- and short-term resource allocations, which the authors methods fail to take into account. For example, there are a number of ways in which the state may distribute its share. It can give it to its residents via grants, tax reductions, or enhanced quantity and quality of public services, it can establish a heritage fund which may pursue a number of investment policies, including investing in national- and world-capital markets to maximize returns, or it can invest locally to subsidize consumption (for example, subsidized home-mortgage loans) or industries that aid in diversifying the economy and create jobs. Clearly, direct distribution to residents will increase incomes and increase local demands for goods and

and services, as well as increase private wealth. To the extent that taxes are reduced or a higher level of public services provided, both inefficiencies may arise. But evidence from resource-based boomtowns also indicates a trade-off between wages and publicly supplied amenities. The effect is to subsidize labor costs and thereby shift benefits to capital due to lower labor costs.

To the extent that public-resource revenues reduce business taxes and otherwise subsidize capital, then capital will deepen until after tax and subsidy rates of return are everywhere equal, except of course in those enterprises directly in the public sector, and the demand for labor (job creation) will shift, resulting in increases in real wages. What all this means is that the effects of natural-resource revenues captured by the public sector affect the migration of capital and labor in diverse ways and depend on how those revenues are distributed. As a first step the authors were justified in estimating the maximum impacts on labor and capital flows without attempting to pinpoint the precise mix. Furthermore, the literature on rent seeking tells us that the size of the induced distortions will rise to 100 percent of the rents as various agents and their organizations compete for them. Thus, the overriding public-policy concern should not be differential rates of growth in economic activity, wages, and incomes but rather the preservation of man's total stock of natural and manmade wealth. Certainly these considerations go beyond the authors' intended objectives.

I will mention how others have estimated the second-order effects on discovery, development and extraction rates as well as on general economic activity. David Kresge (1980), for example, has estimated the effects of future Alaskan Outer Continental Shelf petroleum development on employment, private income, and directly and indirectly induced state revenues and expenditures necessary to supply public services. He concludes that public-sector deficits will result and that these will exceed the instate net private benefits. Robert Shelton and David Vogt (in press) analyze the effect of state taxes on the delivered price of steam coal to electric utilities as reported on Form 423 submitted to the Department of Energy for the 1976-1980 period. They conclude that an average of 6 percent of severance taxes are forward shifted and an additional 23.5 percent for shipments from western states to the east are forward shifted ($0.87 per ton for Montana and $0.23 per ton for Wyoming). Church (1981) estimates that the 1977 state tax structure increases coal prices 2 percent to 8 percent and imposes net aggregate welfare losses of $83.8 million per year for producing states and $4.25 million per year on consuming states. However, if Wyoming and Montana simultaneously impose a revenue-maximizing severance tax (maximizing the present value of revenues from 1978 through 2000 results in a 62.5 percent to 75 percent tax rate) it produces annual (in 1991) net welfare losses in producing states of $1,428 million and $12.6 million in consuming states. The tax increases electricity costs by 1 percent to 2 percent in eastern and west-northcentral states and in the Rocky Mountain states. It increases coal prices by 10 percent to 16 percent in these states, and approximately 50 percent of the northern-plains coal-production revenues produced under 1977 tax rates either shift to other western and midwestern states or are foregone. These examples illustrate that long-run energy-industry effects on incomes and resource allocation need to be evaluated, since a significant portion of the tax burdens are likely borne by resource rents, renewable capital, and labor. The exported tax share depends both on the amount forward-shifted to consumers (functions of both regional demand and supply elasticity) and the amount borne by out-of-state resource and capital owners. Of course, oil prices are determined in international markets, and therefore individual state tax and royalty policies have negligible effects on consumer prices. Furthermore each natural resource is geologically and economically unique, which renders universal statements based on highly abstract models of limited value.

Regional conflicts are certainly not new to the United States or Canada. However, the nature of these conflicts and the possible resolution may be undergoing change. During the postdepression, post-World War II period, the federal government took an active role in dealing with existing and potential regional conflict. This was accomplished in some cases by usurping power and overriding states and, more frequently, by defusing potential conflicts by providing incentives for voluntary participation by private parties and political jurisdictions. This required distributing positive benefits to all participants whose sum may often have exceeded net benefits. Water projects are classic examples. Sewerage collection and treatment facilities have been heavily underwritten by the U.S. Environmental Protection Agency and other federal programs. The costs of irrigation, recreation, and flood-control facilities of massive western water projects have been borne primarily by taxpayers in other jurisdictions, and benefits were distributed among the jurisdictions and interest groups more immediately affected by the projects. However, the philosophy of a federal Santa Claus appears to be changing, and the withdrawal of federal incentives has left a vacuum.

The authors consider the implications of energy-resource taxation for intergovernmental relations. However, they fail to consider how the situation that their simulations portray came to pass or its implications for future intergovernmental relationships. Clearly, the federal government is retreating from its former policy of redistributing income among jurisdictions via grants and direct expenditures. Furthermore, its deregulation efforts, particularly in the energy and communications sectors, have created a void that states are seeking to fill. The policy objectives of deregulation and a reduced share of government in the economy mean that the federal government is emasculating a major tool in mediating interjurisdictional and interregional disputes—namely, bribing affected parties to agree by en-suring that all receive benefits financed from economic growth and rising tax revenues. Slow productivity and economic-growth rates and massive tax reductions (including institutionalized indexing) have changed this negotiating environment. Thus, future interjurisdictional conflicts and negotiations may occur in a different context and will undoubtedly involve issues beyond the distribution of natural-resource tax revenues. The federal government has placed the responsibility for the storage of nuclear waste at the state and regional level, and toxic-waste cleanup, control, and storage may increasingly become interstate issues that will be solved regionally. Energy development and the associated population and economic growth are making ever-larger demands for water in the arid West, where inter-jurisdictional conflicts have previously been bailed out with federal projects and dollars. The interdependencies of energy, environmental quality, and water imply that bargains will be struck within a political and economic en-vironment where the federal government plays an ever-decreasing role.

References

Burness, H. Stuart. "On the Taxation of Nonreplenishable Resources." *Journal of Environmental Economics and Management* (December 1976):289-311.

Church, Albert M. *Taxation of Nonrenewable Resources*. Lexington, Mass.: Lexington Books, D.C. Heath and Company, 1981.

Kresge, David T. "Regional Impacts of Federal Energy Developments." Paper presented at the American Economics Association meeting, Denver, Colorado, September 1980.

Shelton, Robert B. and David P. Vogt. "The Incidence of Coal Severance Taxes: Political Perceptions (Realities?) and Economic Realities (Perceptions?)." *Natural Resources Journal*, forthcoming.

3

Efficiency, Equity, and the Allocation of Resource Rents

Robin Boadway and
Frank Flatters

The distribution of resource rents in the Canadian federal system has been the subject of considerable discussion in recent years. The magnitude of the rents created by the post-OPEC resource-price boom has been enormous. Consequently it is not surprising that the question of the division of the spoils has been very contentious. At issue has been the allocation between Canadians and non-Canadians, between the private and public sectors, between federal and provincial governments, and between the resource-rich and resource-poor provinces. It is the intergovernmental allocation of resource revenues, and the particular problems and issues that arise because of Canada's federal system of government, that we address in this chapter.

In this context the sharing of resource revenues must be examined along with the general system of revenue sharing in Canada. The Canadian fiscal system has long included various measures for transferring fiscal resources from so-called rich to so-called poor provinces. The most important of such current programs is the Provincial Fiscal Equalization Program of the federal government. This is a program of transfers to have-not provinces based on a measure of their deficiency in fiscal capacity (relative to the national average) across twenty-nine revenue sources. Nine of these revenue sources are natural-resource based.[1] Under the current equalization program resource revenues are treated differently from other revenue sources in several important respects. The general effect of these differences is to reduce the amount of equalization that occurs in respect to resource revenues. Even so, according to early estimates for the 1981-1982 fiscal year, resource revenues will account for 30 percent of the equalization entitlements of recipient provinces. It is clear that the general problem of revenue sharing and the particular issues related to resource revenues cannot be considered separately.

Revenue sharing is an issue that is common to most federal states. Serious theoretical discussions of the economic rationale for interregional transfers began with the work of James Buchanan (1950). A useful compendium of some of the ensuing discussions can be found in B.S. Grewal, G. Brennan and R.L. Mathews (1980). The controversies have centered on the question of whether there are efficiency and/or equity arguments for

99

interregional-equalizing transfers and whether there is any conflict between these two primary policy goals.

A review of the main features of Canada's current equalization program and its evolution follows. The fundamental questions of the equity and efficiency arguments for an equalization program and the appropriate treatment of resource revenues in this context are then discussed, followed by an evaluation of the current system of equalization payments.

The Existing Equalization Scheme and Its Evolution

Although unconditional transfers from the federal government to the provinces have been with us since confederation, equalization payments as we know them are a post-World War II phenomenon. The use of equalization-type payments as a tool for interprovincial redistribution was first advocated in the momentous Rowell-Sirois Royal Commission on Dominion-Provincial Relations (1940). Although their proposals in this regard were not adopted until some two decades later, the role of the Rowell-Sirois Report cannot be overestimated. Not only has the equalization scheme gradually evolved into one very much akin to that they had suggested but also, as important for our purposes, the rationale offered by Rowell-Sirois for a transfer scheme of such type and magnitude is still widely accepted in policy circles.

It is worth reminding ourselves of the context in which the Rowell-Sirois Report was written. The period was the late 1930s when the consequences of the Great Depression were very much evident. Economic activity was still at a relatively low level, especially in the drought-stricken prairie provinces. Provincial treasuries, laden with the heavy cost of relief payments, were seriously depleted. The tax system was in some disarray. Provincial and federal governments occupied similar tax fields but used vastly differing tax bases and rates, thereby causing inevitable inefficiencies and inequities. The economic study of public finance was in its infancy, and economic data, especially on the provincial economies, were virtually nonexistent. Given the circumstances in which the Rowell-Sirois Report was conceived, it is quite remarkable (and a tribute to the insight of its members) that the proposals regarding fiscal federalism remain intact today with such an apparently wide degree of support.

At the risk of oversimplification, the Rowell-Sirois Report's proposals regarding federal-provincial fiscal arrangements consisted of two interdependent parts, which were jointly aimed at improving the financial position of the provinces. First, the provinces should renounce the use of personal-income taxes, corporate taxes, and succession duties. The commission viewed this as indispensable to the efficient operation of the economy. At the same time, the federal government should refrain from competing with the provinces for the revenue sources left to the latter. In this way it was hoped to eliminate the inefficiencies and inequities arising from overlapping tax jurisdictions.

The second part of the recommendations can be viewed, at least in part, as a compensation to the provinces for their loss of revenue-raising power. The federal government was advised to institute a scheme of annual federal-provincial transfers, called "national adjustment grants," to be allotted to provinces according to their shortfall between provincial expenditures required to provide the "normal Canadian standard of services" and the tax revenues that would be obtained from "taxation of normal severity." In fact, to select an enduring quote, the commissioners stipulated "the amount, if any, which each individual province should receive from the Dominion annually to enable it to provide normal Canadian services with no more than normal Canadian taxation." In other words, provinces below the national-average ability to provide normal services with normal tax rates were to be brought up to the national average with national-adjustment grants. These grants, in conjunction with the acceptance by the federal government of the net debt accumulated by the provinces as a result of the Depression, were intended to secure the financial position of the provinces. As will be discussed further, the objective of equalization grants varies little from that of the proposed national-adjustment grants, despite the facts that provinces are no longer in any financial difficulty and that they occupy the same lucrative personal- and corporate tax fields as the federal government.

The exigencies of wartime finance precluded action on the Report.[2] By the end of the war circumstances had changed considerably. For example, the provinces had temporarily given up their power to levy personal and corporate taxes in the joint interest of the war effort. In the early postwar period the federal government continued to be the sole occupant of these tax fields and compensated the provinces by a system of tax rentals that were per-capita grants depending on population and growth of the gross national product.[3] Since tax rentals were equal per-capita grants to the provinces rather than payments depending on the taxes actually collected in the province, they, incorporated implicitly an element of equalization.

In 1957 a major innovation occurred that effectively differentiated the equalizing role of federal-provincial transfers from the purely tax-collecting aspects. Tax rentals, which combined elements of both, were replaced by a system of tax sharing whereby the tax rebated to the province was based on the taxes actually collected in the province. This was done initially by a system of tax abatements, but in 1962 these were superceded by tax-collection agreements whereby the federal government simply acted as a tax-collection agency for the provinces, provided the provinces used the same tax bases (but not necessarily the same rates) as the federal government. This is the system still in existence today.[4] The same act, the 1957 Tax-Sharing Arrangements Act, instituted a system of equalization payments from the federal government to needy provinces. Then, as now, equalization payments were based solely on the tax capacity of the province and not on any differences among provinces in the costs of providing normal services.

Initially, the only tax bases equalized were personal- and corporate-income taxes and succession duties. Equalization was based on the per-capita tax yield of the two highest-yield provinces. The arrangements were to be renegotiated every five years. The first renegotiation resulted in the 1962 Fiscal Arrangements Act, under which equalization was calculated in a way similar to that of the preceding five years except that natural-resources revenues were added. In 1967, the scheme was changed in two fundamental ways. First, the number of tax bases included was expanded from four to sixteen. Second, instead of using the top-two provinces as the level to which needy provinces ought to be raised, the national-average per-capita tax proceeds from each province from each tax source was used. The equalization entitlement of a province for a given tax was calculated as the difference between the national-average tax revenue and the tax revenue that would be collected by applying the national-average tax rate to the province's actual tax base. In 1972, the number of tax sources in the formula was extended to twenty-three, and in 1977 to twenty-nine thereby covering almost all non-debt nongrant sources of revenue to the provinces.

It is worth elaborating on the operation of the present scheme. The equalization formula is calculated on the basis of the following provincial-revenue sources:

1. personal-income tax
2. business-income revenues
3. tobacco tax
4. sales tax
5. gasoline tax
6. diesel-fuel tax
7. motor-vehicle licenses (commercial, noncommercial)
8. alcohol taxes (beer, wine, spirits)
9. health-insurance premiums
10. payroll taxes
11. lotteries
12. succession duties and gift taxes
13. race-track taxes
14. forestry revenues
15. oil and natural-gas revenues (crown-oil revenues, freehold-oil revenues, crown-gas revenues, freehold-gas revenues, sale of crown leases, other oil and gas revenues)

16. mineral revenues
17. water-power rentals
18. miscellaneous taxes and revenues
19. insurance-premium taxes
20. federal-government revenue shared with provinces
21. provincial-property and school-purpose taxes

Each province's equalization entitlement is calculated for each of the revenue sources in the following manner. A common tax base is chosen for each source of revenue, and it is measured for each province and aggregated over provinces to give the national tax base. Total provincial tax collections are aggregated to give national tax revenues. National tax revenues divided by national population gives the national-average per-capita tax revenue, the norm against which a province's equalization entitlement is calculated. The national-average tax rate is obtained by dividing the national tax revenues by the national tax base for each revenue source. This national-average tax rate is then applied to each province's tax base in per-capita terms. The extent to which this falls short of the national-average per-capita revenue from that source is the province's per-capita equalization entitlement from that source. If it exceeds the national average a negative entitlement is recorded. These per-capita entitlements are converted to total entitlements by multiplying by the provincial population. They are then aggregated over revenue sources to give the aggregate equalization entitlement owing to the province. If the sum is positive, the federal government pays that amount to the province out of federal-government general revenues. If it is negative, no sum is paid to the province. In practice, all provinces except Alberta, British Columbia, and Ontario have been recipients of equalization, although Saskatchewan is about to lose have-not status as well.

There are some rather important exceptions to this rule, important because they have precluded Ontario from becoming an equalization recipient, which would have happened had the formula been applied exactly as stated. (These exceptions will also turn out to be important when judged against the analytical results we derive later in the chapter.) Nonrenewable-resource revenues are not treated the same as other revenue sources in the current equalization formula. In particular, only one half of the provincial revenues from these sources is subject to equalization. Furthermore, total equalization payments on their account may not exceed one third of total payments.[5] In practice, it is oil and natural-gas revenues that are preponderant in this category. So great are the increases in these sources, it is expected that the upper ceiling will become binding in 1980-1981. In addition, the federal government announced it would withdraw equalization on account of the sale of crown leases.

It would be rash to attribute a particular motive to the federal government for initiating this downgrading of natural-resource revenues in the equalization formula. Apart from the sheer expense to the federal government of equalizing the unevenly distributed oil and natural-gas revenues, the treatment of these revenues in equalization cannot really be considered in isolation from the more general issue of the sharing of resource rents among the federal government and the provinces. In addition, there is the not unimportant observation that, had resource revenues not been treated in this way, Ontario would have become a recipient of equalization despite its relatively high per-capita income from other sources. Such an outcome would have unpalatable political implications, at least in some quarters. There is a general view in some parts of the nation that Ontario has gained inordinately from the continuing protection initiated by the national policy and that equalization is, in part, a quid pro quo on that account.

The existing scheme expires in 1982, when a new agreement will have to be reached. Given the increased importance of oil and gas revenues as a source of provincial revenues, and given their uneven distribution over provinces, the issues are likely to be contentious. This is especially so because the treatment of natural-resource revenues cannot realistically be separated from the underlying conflict over the jurisdictional claims to resource revenues. This chapter is an attempt to bring economic analysis to bear on the issue.

The existing system comes remarkably close to the type advocated by the Rowell-Sirois Report in 1940. It is designed to bring each province's re-source-raising capacity up to the national average. This allows the provinces to undertake average levels of expenditure at average tax rates if they so wish. It is true that Rowell-Sirois emphasized equalizing the ability to provide public services of average standard rather than simply equalizing the ability to spend. Different provinces, because of differences in cost or need, are able to convert given levels of spending into differing levels of public services. However, given the difficulty in measuring these differences in cost and need, equalizing revenue capacity is probably the best that could be achieved. It is possible to incorporate elements of cost and/or need into equalization, as is done in a crude way in the U.S. revenue-sharing system, but the end result is bound to be very inexact.

It is also rather remarkable how the perceived goals of the present system rely on the rationale first expounded by Rowell-Sirois. For example, compare with Rowell-Sirois the following statement of policy from the Federal-Provincial Tax Structure Committee (1966): "The fiscal arrangement should, through a system of equalization grants, enable each province to provide an adequate level of public services without resort to levels of taxation substantially higher than those of other provinces." Nor has the tenor of the argument changed over the 1970s. Consider the following statement from clause 31, regarding equalization and regional disparities, of the

Liberal Government's Proposed Resolution respecting the Constitution of Canada (1981): "Parliament and the government of Canada are committed to taking such measures as are appropriate to ensure that provinces are able to provide the essential public services referred to in para (1) (c) [i.e., essential public services of reasonable quality to all Canadians] without imposing an undue burden of provincial taxation."

It is uncanny how the objectives of the Rowell-Sirois Report have survived virtually unaltered despite the passage of time and, especially changes in circumstance. After all, the provinces are far from being in the state of financial crisis characterizing the late 1930s. This is partly a reflection of the paucity of attention paid by economists to analyzing in a thorough way the economics of federal systems. One could, of course, argue that the political goal is one that cannot be subject to economic criticism because it involves a basic value judgment about the objectives of policy. We do not take that view. If such a policy goal is justified, it must be so according to the criterion that it makes individuals better off using the usual economic yardsticks of efficiency and equity. Our analysis will show that it is not a sensible goal when judged by these conventional economic criteria.

Although economic analysis of equalization has been somewhat lacking, criticisms of the existing scheme and proposals for reform have not been. At the most fundamental level, some economists would presumably prefer no equalization scheme. Although T.J. Courchene (1978), for example, may not explicitly advocate its abolition, the tenor of his argument is that on economic grounds equalization is harmful. It essentially prevents the natural-adjustment mechanisms of the economy from working by discouraging the mobility of factors of production, especially labor, from depressed regions to more advanced ones. The scheme is seen to cause a misallocation of the nation's resources. A complementary view is that, if redistribution is desired, it is best done by interpersonal transfers rather than intergovernmental ones. Thus, some form of negative income taxation may by more sensible (although even this would result in efficiency costs in reduced mobility). There also exist in the literature several proposals for reforming the existing system. Many authors have suggested converting the system from a so-called gross scheme to a net scheme. That is, provinces whose equalization entitlement is negative should be required to pay sums into the scheme so that, on net, payments to have-not provinces would be balanced by receipts from have provinces. The problem is particularly acute with respect to resource revenues, since these are typically tax sources to which the federal government has only limited access. Thus, if the federal government has to pay large sums on equalizing resource revenues, it has to obtain the financing from its own tax sources. The latter will typically not come geographically from the same source as the resource revenues being equalized. Therefore, the redistributive potential is limited. Partly to correct this deficiency, Courchene (1979) has suggested moving part way to a net system by dividing the tax sources to be equalized into two tiers. The first tier would include personal- and corporate-income taxes and sales taxes and would be equalized in much the same way as at present. The second tier would include all other revenue sources and would be operated on a net bases. It should, of course, be noted that this proposal would not change the principle of equalization, only the mechanics of the way in which it operates.

It has been noted in the literature that there may well be a case for treating resource rents differently from other sorts of tax bases, particularly because the base of resource rents is less mobile among provinces and thereby susceptible to inefficiencies. Not only that, the existence of resource rents can cause misallocation of resources to the extent that labor is induced to migrate to capture its share of the rents (Courchene and Melvin 1980: Flatters and Purvis 1980; Helliwell 1980; and McLure forthcoming; Usher 1977). R.W. Boadway and K.H. Norrie (1980) noted that there may also be some equity reasons for redistributing resource rents. However, these arguments have yet to be incorporated into a more thorough analysis of equalization payments.

Finally, there are several authors who see some merit in simplifying the equalization formula per se. For example, P. Davenport (1979) has suggested basing equalization entitlements on a single broad notion of income per capita, incorporating personal income, corporate income, and natural-resource revenues. This would amount to a complete change in the nature of equalization away from the Rowell-Sirois Report. The economic justification for such a formulation has yet to be made.

Part of our task will be to assess the validity of these arguments once equalization has been analyzed more carefully from an economic point of view. The question of the appropriate role of equalization payments in a system that already has a formal structure of interpersonal transfers will be a fundamental part of our analysis.

Problems of Equity and Efficiency in a Federal System

The advantages of decentralizing economic power to lower levels of government have been widely recognized in the literature. Lower levels of government are said to be both more responsive to the needs and tastes of local residents and more effective at providing public goods and services of a purely local sort. They also reduce the need for a large bureaucracy at the center and induce what some regard as healthy competition with other government units.[6] At the same time, because their constituencies are restricted, there are bound to be some disadvantages to decentralizing power. Inefficient resource allocation can occur as a result of spillovers of costs or benefits of local public-sector activities, the classic cases being manpower training and education and pollution. Local governments may be prone to erecting various barriers to intranational flows of goods and factors of production and to wasteful tax and expenditure competition.[7] These considerations have spawned a substantial literature on the design of the optimal federal constitution, or what is sometimes referred to as the "assignment problem." This literature has stressed that the choice of a constitution must ultimately involve a trade-off between the advantages and disadvantages of decentralization. This chapter is concerned with the issue of whether, once the constitutional decision has been made, there is a useful role for unconditional equalizing grants among lower levels of governments or from the central level to the latter.

We shall adopt what we take to be the existing division of economic powers between the federal government and the provinces in Canada. We shall also abstract from the sort of provincial behavior that attempts to exploit its market power by setting up barriers to trade and mobility, since this is of no consequence for intergovernmental grants. We shall also ignore spillover benefits and costs, since the use of conditional grants to correct for them is well established in the literature. We will argue that even in a federation of so-called well-behaved provinces certain inherent inequities and economic inefficiencies arise solely out of the decentralization of taxing and expenditure decisions to the provinces and that equalization payments have a useful role to play in correcting for these things. The precise form that the equalization payments should take will depend on the way in which the market economy functions, the exact tax and expenditure policies of the provinces (for example, their chosen tax mix and redistributive policies), and the resolution one wishes to make regarding conflicts between equity and efficiency. Our analysis will presuppose particular assumptions in this regard and will indicate how alternative assumptions give rise to different equalization schemes. One of the interesting results is that equity and efficiency considerations tend to work in the same direction and, in certain circumstances, call for precisely the same equalization scheme.

Provincial governments are taken to have broad powers of taxation. In effect, they are able to levy virtually any tax they desire except for protective tariffs. The most important of these taxes are the personal-income tax, the corporate tax, payroll taxes, sales and excise taxes, property taxes, and taxes on natural resources. It will be useful for us to think of corporate taxes, natural-resource taxes, excise taxes on purchases of firms, and property taxes on businesess as being *source-based taxes*; that is, taxes levied at the sources of income generation. The personal-income tax, retail-sales tax, excise taxes on consumption, payroll taxes and residential-property taxes are classified as *residence-based taxes*; that is, taxes levied on the individual's income or use of income in the province of residence. This usage corresponds with that commonly made in the public-finance literature and is a useful distinction in describing the case for equalization payments according to tax base.[8] It is assumed that provinces in principle, can select tax bases and rates independently. However, in practice, they may be more or less constrained to adopt a particular base and/or rate for a particular tax. This may be because of federal-provincial agreement (as in the case of the Canadian Tax Collection Agreements) or because of implicit constraints imposed by economic competition among provinces for resources. The tax revenues so gathered are then used by the provinces to provide benefits to their citizens within the spending powers of the province (education, health, welfare, transportation, and so on). As a prelude to our analysis we shall present a resumé of how the tax and expenditure programs of individual provinces can lead to inequity and inefficiency from a national point of view.

Equity

It is generally agreed that equity should be a primary goal of government policy. In the literature it is conventional to disassemble the notion of equity into two constituent parts—horizontal and vertical equity. Horizontal equity suggests that likes ought to be treated in a like manner. We shall follow the Carter Report (Royal Commission on Taxation 1966) in using real comprehensive income. One must be careful in defining real comprehensive income to include with current consumption and the accretion of wealth current benefits from government-provided public services. This will be critical for equalization payments. The principle of horizontal equity can be viewed in two ways. The ex-post way is to posit that persons with the same real comprehensive incomes in the presence of government ought to pay the same taxes. The ex-ante view is that, if two individuals have the same real income before government policy, after paying taxes they should also have the same.[9] The two may be the same depending on the incidence of taxes and expenditures. These notions of horizontal equity seem to be reasonable requirements of economic policy, although they are not necessary implications of social-welfare-function maximization.[10]

The criterion of vertical equity requires that persons with differing real incomes should be treated appropriately differently. Appropriateness in this context is a matter of judgment and will be dictated by one's implicit notion of the social-welfare function and by the inefficiencies induced by redistributive policies. We need not be precise on that matter here. We take it that the federal government wishes that there be some redistribution from those with higher real incomes to those with lower ones and that the progressive income tax and transfer system is the prime means for attaining it.

A federal system of government gives rise to inequities in the treatment of individuals in different provinces for two related reasons. First, decentralized provincial-government decision making is inequitable from a national perspective, since identical persons living in different provinces get different net benefits from the actions of the provincial governments. For one thing provinces obtain varying amounts of their revenues from taxes that are incident on nonresidents, and this gives rise to differing amounts of benefits to residents of different provinces. As well, if provincial budgets are redistributive, identical persons will be treated differently over different provinces except in fortuitous circumstances. Some particular examples will be given of this in the next section. All this implies that horizontal equity is violated by the independent actions of the provinces no matter to what notion of vertical equity one subscribes.

Second, the federal tax-transfer system compounds these inequities, since the income base of the progressive tax system differs from real comprehensive income. In particular, it does not include as a component of real income the contribution of provincial public services. These are a legitimate source of real income and differ from one province to the next. In addition, if provinces use their power to levy taxes on nonresidents to lower residence-based taxes, this benefit is not captured in the federal tax system. It is these sources of inequity that our equalization scheme is designed to correct.

Efficiency

The other criterion used for resource allocation is efficiency. In the context of the models of the economy we use, the appropriate notion of production efficiency is equality of marginal products of productive resources over uses. Federal systems of government give rise to inefficiencies in the allocation of factors of production over provinces to the extent that they are mobile, since the actions of provincial governments induce the owners of factors to respond in their locational decisions to signals other than differences in marginal product. In the case of capital this arises from provinces levying different taxes on capital income generated in the province. This may not be too great a problem, since, in fact, provincial tax rates on capital do not differ greatly. As regards labor, however, workers will take into consideration the full benefits of residency, which include not only wage payments but also the net benefit from provincial-government activity. We shall refer to these as net fiscal benefits (NFBs). On efficiency grounds differences in NFBs over provinces ought to be completely eliminated. Under certain equity arguments it will turn out that this is the same prescription for equalization called for by equity.

The case for equalization, then, will rest primarily on the existence of differential flows of NFBs to the residents of differing provinces. Naturally, these NFBs, since they arise out of the behavior of provincial governments, would not exist if the state were a unitary one in which the central government legislated a uniform system of taxes and expenditures nationwide—nor would they exist if the flow of NFBs were capitalized into a fixed factor such as land. Further, the flow of benefits would completely be capitalized into the value of the land held by the landowners at the time the future benefits were perceived. However, this requires that residential land be fixed in supply or that the residents not be able to substitute away from it. This case it unlikely in the Canadian context.

The Role of Equalization Payments

In principle, the inequities and inefficiencies arising out of provincial-government activities could be corrected by a system of interpersonal rather than interprovincial grants. Reliance on interpersonal grants would not work both because the requisite system would be very cumbersome indeed and because it would amount to a complete imposition of federal-government standards of equity on the provinces. Properly designed interprovincial grants allow provinces the leeway to follow policies that accord with the federal-government viewpoint regarding equity (and efficiency) if they so wish but permits them to depart from it in accordance with the preferences of their residents if they choose.

The design of an equalization system can be looked at from an equity point of view or from an efficiency point of view. We shall consider each in turn.

Equity and Equalization

The appropriate equalization formula from an equity point of view depends on empirical facts and individual judgment. The former include how the provinces act and how the economy functions (how prices are formed, factors are mobile, taxes are shifted, and so on). We shall make some assumptions in this regard that are intended to capture in an abstract way the stylized facts of the economy.

The view that the federal government should take of horizontal equity in the presence of inequitable provincial-government activity is a matter of individual judgment. There are two views that the federal government might take. The first, what we shall call *broad-based horizontal equity,* is that persons with the same real comprehensive income ought to be treated identically by both federal and provincial governments taken together. Since provincial governments violate this norm, the federal government must take steps to redress the differences in treatment. That will be the task of equalization payments. The second, or *narrow-based horizontal equity*, is that the federal government need only concern itself with the equity of its own actions when deciding on a policy. The real-income levels achieved after the provincial-government policies have been under-taken is regarded as the starting point. The federal government then only ensures that its own actions are equitable. It turns out that there is still some role, if only a restricted one, for equalization payments under narrow-based equity, because the existing federal tax system does not capture all elements of real income—in particular, it misses NFBs of provincial-government activities.

We shall proceed by considering a taxonomy of cases classified according to whether provincial budgets are distributionally neutral and to whether the broad or narrow view of horizontal equity is taken. By distributional neutrality is meant the following: the provincial budget is distributionally neutral if the taxes each resident pays are used to finance public services of an equal value to him.[11] We shall also take it that taxes on nonresidents finance equal per-capita benefits for all residents.

Narrow-Based Horizontal Equity with Provincial Budgets Distributionally Neutral. The need for equalization arises here because, although the federal government wishes to make comprehensive real incomes more equal, its income-tax base does not include all elements of real income. To see this, note that real income can be defined as:

Real Income = factor payments after provincial taxes + per-capita benefits from provincial activities
= factor payments after provincial taxes + per-capita residence-based taxes + per-capita source-based taxes
= factor payments before taxes + per-capita source-based taxes

This assumes that all residents in a province get the same per-capita benefits from source-based taxes. Residence-based taxes are taken here to be income taxes, although consumption taxes can also be included if the economy faces fixed prices and if provincial purchases are all by residents.[12] Since the federal tax base includes only factor payments before taxes, an element of real income is missing—per-capita source-based taxes.

If these per-capita source-based taxes were included in taxes or income, there would be no requirement for equalization under the narrow-based version of horizontal equity. The federal personal-income tax would be perfectly adequate for pursuing whatever degree of real-income redistribution the federal government desired. However, since the base of the federal income tax is too narrow, some supplementary instrument is desired. A scheme of interprovincial-equalization payments can provide a roughly equitable solution. The federal tax base of the representative person in a province falls short of the ideal by an amount equal to per-capita source-based tax revenues in the province. If included in the tax base the person would have been liable for x times the shortfall, where x is the marginal federal tax rate of the representative citizen of the province. Suppose x is roughly the same over provinces. Then an appropriate equalization scheme would be one that equalized a properation x of per-capita source-based tax revenues.

Notice that under this narrow version of horizontal equity and under the assumption that provincial budgets are distributionally neutral, there is no need to equalize personal-income taxes or other residence-based taxes at all, at least on equity grounds. This is a consequence of the assumptions adopted.

Broad-Based Horizontal Equity with Provincial Budgets Distributionally Neutral. Under broad-based equity the federal government wants to ensure that identical individuals are treated identically under the combined policies of the provincial and federal governments. Not only is there an element missing from the federal income-tax base as before but also persons are receiving different NFBs according to their province of residence. An equalization scheme that equalizes NFBs has the potential to solve this problem provided provinces continue to act in a neutral way. With distributional neutrality, provincial taxes incident on residents give rise to no NFB differentials, since, by assumption, their proceeds are spent to provide a pattern of benefits identically distributed. We make the assumption that residence-based taxes are incident fully on residents. There is thus no advantage to be had from equalizing them.

With source-based taxes we would, however, presume that part of their incidence falls on nonresidents of the province, including residents of other provinces. This is because a significant proportion of the nonlabor factors of production are owned by nonresidents and many of the source-based tax revenues are revenues on rent or economic profit (for example, resource taxes, corporate taxes, property taxes). If all source-based taxes were incident upon non-Canadian nonresidents of the provinces, they would give rise to per-capita NFB differentials equal to the differences in per-capita source-based tax collections.[13] To preserve broad equity these differentials would have to be completely eliminated, that is, source-based tax revenues would have to be fully equalized. Of course, full equalization is not practical, since it would remove all incentive for the provinces to collect source-based tax revenues. The best one could do would be to have a formula based on equalizing tax bases rather than actual tax collections.

To the extent that the incidence of source-based taxes was on residents themselves, they should not be fully equalized. Instead, this part of the revenue should be equalized to the entent of a proportion x (the average-federal-marginal-income-tax rate). On the other hand, if the incidence was on nonresidents of another province more than full equalization is called for. In the end a judgment has to be made about the incidence of source-based taxes before the specifics of the ideal scheme are possible. A presumption might favor the idea that a good part of source-based tax revenues might be equalized, and a formula such as the present one, based on tax bases or capacities rather than actual tax collections, may not be a bad one.

To summarize, several differences emerge between this case and the narrow-based equity case. Under the broad notion of equity assumption about the incidence of provincial taxes must be made before settling on a scheme. Assuming residence-based taxes to be incident on residents, no case for equalizing them exists as in the previous case. However, source-based taxes, if they are incident on nonresidents, should be fully equalized (indeed, more than fully if the residents come from another province—they ought to be given fully to that province rather than being shared). But if the taxes are incident on residents, equalization should be only up to a proportion x. Under the previous scheme, all source-based taxes were equalized in the proportion x regardless of their incidence.

One way to view the difference in equity concepts is in terms of property rights. Under the narrow-based concept, property rights to residents of a province are defined specifically to include the rights to the revenues of source-based taxes.[14] Under the broad-based concept that is not the case. The revenues can be redistributed among all citizens of the nation (as would be the case in a unitary system).

Broad-Based Horizontal Equity with Provincial Budgets Redistributive.
Once we allow provincial budgets to be redistributive things become more complicated, since not only can the redistribution take a wide variety of patterns but also provinces can vary in their behavior. For the purposes of illustration we shall work with a relatively simple pattern of redistribution and we shall assume the provinces to behave uniformly. If the provinces did not behave uniformly, we could base the equalization scheme on some average of the provinces' behavior. Such a scheme would have the property that all provinces could conform to some national norm if they wished but would also leave them leeway to pursue their own legitimate redistributive goals.

We continue to assume that expenditures by provinces are used to provide quasi-private goods distributed to residents on an equal per-capita basis. This is obviously a strong assumption but not unrealistic given the nature of public services provided at the provincial (and municipal) levels.[15] With equal per-capita benefits the arguments on source-based taxation are unaltered. We need only consider the redistribution implicit in residence-based taxes (all of which we assume to be incident on residents).

The simplest case to consider is that in which residence-based taxes are proportional to the incomes of provincial residents. This makes the combined tax-expenditure system redistributive from higher- to lower-income groups. It also makes the equalization scheme quite simple. Consider the simple case in which all provinces levy the same rate of tax on residents and use the proceeds to provide equal per-capita benefits within the province. Then all residents of a given income level across the nation will pay the same taxes but will receive different levels of public service according to province of residence. This difference in public services will be the difference in NFB on account of residence-based taxes. It will equal the difference in per-capita average residence-based tax collections (since the same rate is applied to all income and only average-income levels differ). Also, the difference in NFBs will be exactly the same for all income levels. An equalization scheme that fully equalizes differences in per-capita residence-based tax collections will be ideally suited to eliminate these differences in NFBs over provinces. It will enable all provinces to provide the same level of per-capita benefits at the same tax rates to its citizens.[16]

Such a scheme will be equitable in the broad sense, since it will ensure that all citizens are treated identically by the combined actions of provincial and federal governments. The federal government can then pursue whatever redistribution it wishes using its progressive income tax. If the provinces behave differently from one another, full equity cannot be achieved. However, there is nothing more equalization can do in the face of decisions of provincial governments to pursue different distributional goals. Equalization can do no more than make it potentially possible to achieve equity. In the absence of equalization (or its equivalent in interpersonal transfers) equity nationwide would be impossible.

Examples can easily be constructed to show that if provincial budgets were more progressive than assumed above more than full equalization of residence-based tax revenues would be called for. Equivalently, if less progressive, less than full equalization is optimal. Indeed, if provincial budgets were regressive, the equalization on the broad-equity criterion should go from the lower- to the higher-per-capita-income province. In any case, some judgment about the incidence pattern of provincial budgets must be formed before one can settle on the desired equalization formula.

Narrow-Based Horizontal Equity with Provincial Budgets Redistributive. Under narrow-based equity, the benefits of the actions of provincial governments are taken as part of the legitimate real incomes of residents of the province against which federal standards of equity are applied. Once again, we assume equal per-capita benefits so that the arguments regarding source-based taxation are unaltered—a proportion x should still be equalized. As regards residence-based taxation, with redistributive budgets NFBs are generated for various income groups, which differ over provinces, and these ought to be included in the federal tax base but are not. Recall that the NFB differential over provinces is identical for all income levels when residence-based taxes are taken to be proportional to income. However, within a province NFBs will differ from one income group to another. In particular, under redistributive taxation the NFB from residence-based taxation will be positive for low-income persons, negative for high-income persons, and zero for the person of average income.

If one were to aggregate the NFBs from residence-based taxation of all persons over a province, they would net out to zero. That is, they arise from pure redistribution. Furthermore, if the federal marginal tax rate were constant over the relevant income levels, the additional amount of federal tax that below-average-income persons would owe if NFBs were included in income would just equal the amount that would be owing to above-average persons whose real incomes are overstated by the federal tax base. To eliminate the horizontal inequities, what is required is a redistribution of the federal tax burden within each province. In these circumstances, interprovincial redistribution of funds would be to no avail and so equalization of residence-based taxes would be undesirable.

Of course, if the federal marginal tax rate were progressive, this conclusion would not hold. Provinces with above-average incomes should be receiving some equalization. However, unless the marginal rates are sharply progressive, the amounts would likely be relatively small and worth ignoring.

The results of the four classifications considered are summarized in table 3-1. This table assumes that residence-based taxes are incident on residents, source-based taxes are incident on foreigners (or that the amount incident on residents are offset by that incident on other Canadians not resident in the province), benefits of source-based taxes are per capita, redistribution of residence-based taxes is as outlined, and all provinces behave identically ex post.

Table 3-1
Ideal-Equalization Schemes under Various Assumptions

	Narrow-Based Equity	Broad-Based Equity
Provinces distributionally neutral	100x percent of source-based tax revenues only	100 percent of source-based tax revenues only
Provincial budgets redistributive	100x percent of source-based tax revenues only	100 percent of source-based and residence-based tax revenues

Efficiency and Equalization

So far we have simply ignored the possibility that equalization might induce a reallocation of resources over provinces. Efficiency consequences might therefore be expected when adopting any scheme that influences real incomes according to province of residence. Indeed, one of the arguments frequently made against the present equalization scheme is precisely that it interferes with resource allocation, in particular with the migration decisions of individuals. Careful analysis will show that, although the present system undoubtedly does lead to such inefficiencies, a fairly extensive scheme of equalization will be called for on efficiency grounds, and that scheme will accord closely with that satisfying horizontal equity.

The efficiency of ideal-equalization schemes can be easily shown using a simple model. The point is a familiar one and has been made often in the context of the inefficiency of migration in the presence of resource rents.[17] Consider a simple case in which all individuals are identical and receive their income from wage income and property income. Wage income is only obtained from the province of residence whereas property income is obtained from ownership of property and is independent of province of residence (before tax). In the absence of provincial governments, migration only influences wage income received (after federal taxes and expenditures, which we take to be uniform over the nation). Assuming costless migration, workers will therefore migrate until wages are equalized over regions. Under competitive conditions, this implies that marginal products are equalized over regions and efficient interprovincial labor allocation is ensured.

This is shown by the allocation L_e in figure 3-1. This diagram depicts the marginal-value products (MP_A, MP_B) in A and B for various allocations of a fixed labor supply (L_A, L_B). The equilibrium L_e is at the point of intersection of these two curves. The equilibrium allocation corresponds to the efficient allocation of labor over the two regions.

Now introduce provincial governments into A and B. If these governments merely tax residents on, say, their income and use that income to provide private goods that otherwise would have been provided by the market, nothing has changed. The equilibrium allocation of labor is still L_e, since real incomes have not changed. Neither an equity case nor an efficiency case exists for equalization. Of course, in these circumstances if some equalization payments were made from one region to the other efficiency would now be destroyed.

Suppose now that province A levies a tax on rents and uses the proceeds either to displace income taxes on residents or to provide additional public services. There will now be a net advantage to residing in A simply to capture one's share of the provincial public services financed out of the rents. Labor will migrate to A until a wage differential is created that is large

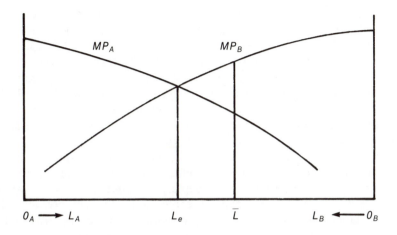

Figure 3-1. Interregional Allocation of Labor

enough to compensate for the net benefits of the provincially collected tax on rents. Labor will now be misallocated, since $MP_A < MP_B$, and thus the provincial rents will have induced an inefficiency into the system. This inefficiency can be eliminated by an ideal scheme that equalizes resource-rent collections over provinces—exactly the same measure called for on equity grounds.

Of course, implementation problems arise here. Full equalization will not be possible because of the incentive effects it would have on provincial governments. If actual tax revenues from a particular source are fully equalized, provinces will have little incentive to raise revenues from that source. The equalization will have to be on tax capacity or some such measure divorced from tax effort. Also, a certain amount of inefficiency will be inevitable if we are to abide by our assumption of allowing provinces to pursue independent tax and expenditure policies. For example, provinces may decide on different tax rates on capital, and this will upset efficiency in its allocation. Nonetheless, as far as taxes on rents or other source-based taxes are concerned, efficiency in the allocation of resources will call for full equalization. This is consistent with the prescription called for on grounds of horizontal equity vis-à-vis the no-government position.

Suppose that provincial governments also engage in some redistribution via their residence-based taxation and expenditures. One might think of the case of proportional taxation and equal per-capita benefits. This intraprovincial redistribution gives rise to NFBs that differ systematically over provinces, being higher in provinces with high average incomes than those with low incomes. Marginal products of labor for a given income group will not be equated over provinces, since workers also respond to differences in NFBs when migrating. From an efficiency point of view, given free migration, the NFBs should be equalized. Thus, in this particular regime of things, efficency calls for full equalization of all provincial tax revenues. Efficiency and equity are fully compatible when equity is interpreted to include the effects of both federal-and provincial-government actions. If the redistributive actions of provinces differ from that assumed here, the exact type of equalization will change, but efficiency and equity (in the sense discussed) will continue to hold simultaneously.

One caveat should be pointed out. We have taken for granted that the flow of rent-tax revenues and NFBs yields benefits to residents as they accrue. However, since these benefits depend on residency, it is possible in principle that they could be capitalized into land values and accrue to the class of landowners who held land at the time the future benefits of the provincial-government actions were perceived. Such capitalization can occur if land for residency is scarce and in inelastic demand by residents. To the extent that capitalization does occur, one can argue that equalization is not necessary on efficiency (or equity) grounds since the fiscal benefits of residency are accruing to landowners rather than to migrants and residents at large. On the other hand, equalization may do no harm, since it will presumably be capitalized to the same extent. A much fuller analysis of the effects of capitalization than we have been able to conduct would clearly be desirable. However, since land is generally not scarce relative to the number of migrants, it is unlikely that the extent of capitalization is such as to negate the arguments for equalization.

Evaluation of the Present System

As discussed in the second section, the equalization formula currently in effect (and due to be renegotiated in 1982) encompasses virtually every revenue source available to the provinces.[18] With one important exception the formula brings up to the national average those provinces that would receive less than the national-average per-capita provincial revenues if they applied the national-average tax rates to their own provincial tax bases. The exception is resource revenues, which are equalized only to one half of the national average. It should also be mentioned that there exist other transfers and policies that have an implicit equalizing component in them and that ought to be taken into consideration in any general appraisal of the system. For example, under the established-programs financing scheme, which replaced federal-provincial conditional grants for hospital and medical insurance and postsecondary education in 1977, grants that are effectively unconditional are made to the provinces on an equal per-capita basis. Since

these grants are financed out of the general revenues of the federal government, and since we presume federal taxes to be progressive to some extent,
there is an implicit equalizing component to the scheme. Some conditional
grants also have equalizing elements in them.[19] One might also argue that
there is a regional bias in federal tax, tariff, and transportation policies,
although the magnitudes are difficult to determine.

If we compare the current system of equalization with the ideal system
derived under the assumptions of broad-based horizontal equity and
provincial-government redistribution of the particular sort considered, we
find several differences. The first is that the formula equalizes tax capacities
rather than actual revenues. We have already mentioned the justification
for this. Any system that equalized actual revenues collected would have
severe disincentive effects. Provinces would be reluctant to raise sufficient
tax revenues on their own if they were guaranteed the national average by
an equalization scheme. An effective system cannot depend so directly on
tax effort, and the existing formula seems a reasonable compromise.

A second difference is that the ideal scheme would require no net contribution from the federal government, since well-to-do provinces would
have negative contributions that just covered the entitlements of the have-
not provinces. The existing system only makes payments to the have-not
provinces and finances them from federal revenues. One unfortunate aspect
of this is that a good part of the funds used to finance equalization comes
from taxes borne by the residents of the have-not provinces. This is especially so if the equalization entitlements are on account of revenue sources
to which the federal government has no access, such as resource royalties.
For example, in the case of oil and gas revenues, equalization increases
from an increase in price will typically involve the federal government raising revenues largely in central Canada to finance increased equalization
payments to Quebec and the Maritime provinces. On economic grounds it is
hard to justify such a system.

Another difference with the ideal system is the deliberate exclusion of
Ontario as a recipient of equalization despite the fact that a positive entitlement is owning according to the existing formula. Ontario's change from a
have to a have-not province is because of the rapid increase in importance
of resource revenues as a source of provincial revenues. Once again there is
no economic rationale for this exclusion.

The other important difference has to do with the treatment of resource
revenues, which are equalized only to one half. There are two ways in which
one can justify the special treatment of resource revenues, one of which is
clearly opportunistic or pragmatic, and the other is more substantial. As to
the first, one can view the leniency afforded resource revenues as a quid pro
quo for the fact that some implicit equalization is already taking place via
the price controls on oil and natural gas in Canada. These price controls

have the effect of spreading potential rents to all oil and gas consumers across the nation (albeit in an inefficient way).[20] More subtly, one could also justify this leniency on the grounds that the implicit rents on hydroelectricity, especially in Ontario and Quebec (again disbursed in the form of lower prices to residents), do not find their way into the equalization formula at all.

The more substantive rationale for treating resource revenues more leniently has to do with the concept of equity used. Apart from the treatment of resource revenues, the equalization formula is consistent with the broad view of equity. On ethical grounds the broad view of equity might seem to be the more reasonable one. As we have seen, efficiency arguments also argue for full equalization of all revenues under the assumptions we have been making. However, in the case of resources the ethical appeal of the broad view of horizontal equity might be overshadowed by the property rights to resource revenues conferred on the provinces by the B.N.A. Act. One might then be justified in applying the broad view of equity to all provincial revenue sources other than resources, and the narrow view to the latter. This would be consistent with equalizing resource revenues to a much lesser extent than other sources. In particular, the equalization of resource revenues should be equivalent to taxing them at the going federal marginal tax rate.

All these arguments hinge on the presumptions that provinical-government budgets are redistributive in the manner postulated and that the incidence of taxes and expenditures is as specified.[21] These are matters on which empirical confirmation is a long, long way off. Any view of these matters must necessarily be judgmental. In our view, the assumptions made are reasonable ones.

Conclusion

There exist sound economic reasons, based on considerations of both equity and economic efficiency, for a system of interprovincial-equalization payments in a federal system of government. The precise form of program that is called for depends on certain ethical and legal-constitutional judgements as well as on empirical assumptions about the operation of the national economy. We have focused on the role of natural resources in the Canadian fiscal system. The importance of these issues is indicated by the magnitude of fiscal effects arising from resource revenues in certain provinces. We have used our framework of analysis to present a view as to the appropriate method of equalizing provincial resource revenues and to point out some major deficiencies in the ad-hoc measures that have been adopted in recent years.

Notes

1. They are as follows: forestry revenues, crown-oil revenues, freehold-oil revenues, crown-gas revenues, freehold-gas revenues, sales of crown leases, other oil and gas revenues, mineral revenues, and water-power rentals.

2. Some observers felt that the Report should have been acted on anyway. (Fowler 1981, p. 101).

3. Quebec never participated in these tax-rental arrangements but received an abatement from 1952 on. For a full description of earlier arrangements, see A.M. Moore, J.H. Perry and D.I. Beach (1966).

4. Quebec is not a participant in the tax-collection agreements, and Ontario collects its own corporation tax but allows the federal government to collect personal taxes on its behalf. Alberta has stated its intention of collecting its own corporate taxes.

5. Oil and natural-gas revenues had begun to be treated differently during the 1972-1977 Agreements following the rapid escalation of world prices. From 1975 onward, full equalization was applicable only to the 1973-1974 level of oil and gas revenues. Those above that amount were only equalized to the extent of one third.

6. A general discussion of the advantages and disadvantages of decentralizing economic decision making to lower levels of government may be found in W. Oates (1972) and A. Breton and A.C. Scott (1978).

7. Cases of this in Canada have been well documented by A.E. Safarian (1979) and J. Maxwell and C. Pestieau (1980).

8. See, for example, P.M. Mieszkowski (1967).

9. This latter view has been enunciated at length by M.S. Feldstein (1976) and R.A. Musgrave (1976).

10. J.A. Mirrlees (1972) has provided an instance in the urban-economics literature in which social-welfare maximization calls for treating otherwise identical persons differently. The same point has been made in the context of federal economics by J.M. Hartwick (1980).

11. Provincial public services are taken to be "private" rather than "public" in nature. We consider this to be an appropriate representation of the services provinces provide (health, education, welfare, transportation, and so on).

12. A more careful analytical discussion of this can be found in R.W. Boadway and F.R. Flatters (1981).

13. Recall that we are assuming that provincial public services yield equal per-capita benefits.

14. Furthermore, one must be able to acquire these property rights simply by acquiring residency. This is the source of the efficiency problem.

15. In all our discussion we subsume municipalities under provinces but ignore the problems of intraprovincial equalization over municipalities.

16. This will be so ex post (that is, in the presence of equalization) even if ex ante they chose not to levy the same tax rates as in the example in the text.

17. See, for example, F.R. Flatters and D.D. Purvis (1980), J.F. Helliwell (1980), T.J. Courchene and J.R. Melvin (1980), or C.E. McLure (forthcoming).

18. The main exception is municipal property-tax revenues, part of which is excluded.

19. A discussion of the existing system of grants may be found in Boadway (1980).

20. Helliwell (1980) has provided estimates of the amount of rents accruing to consumers on this account.

21. See Boadway and Flatters (1981) for a discussion of the implications of alternative assumptions.

References

Boadway, R.W. *Intergovernmental Transfers in Canada.* Toronto: Canadian Tax Foundtion, 1980.

Boadway, R.W. and Flatters, F.R. *The Economics of Equalization Payments.* Report prepared for Economic Council of Canada, Ottawa, 1981.

Boadway, R.W. and Norrie, K.H. "Constitutional Reform Canadian-Style: An Economic Perspective." *Canadian Public Policy,* 6 (Summer 1980): 492-505.

Breton, A. and Scott, A.C. *The Economic Constitution of Federal States.* Toronto: University of Toronto Press, 1978.

Buchanan, J.M. "Federalism and Fiscal Equity." *American Economic Review.* 40 (September 1950):583-599.

Canada. *The Canadian Constitution: Proposed Resolution Respecting the Constitution of Canada.* Ottawa: Publications Canada, 1980.

Courchene, T.J. *Refinancing the Canadian Federation: A Survey of the 1977 Fiscal Arrangements Act.* Montreal: C.D. Howe Research Institute, 1979.

———— . "Avenues of Adjustment: The Transfer System and Regional Disparities." In *Canadian Confederation at the Crossroads,* edited by Michael Walker. Vancouver: Fraser Institute, 1978, pp. 145-186.

Courchene, T.J. and Melvin, J.R. "Energy Revenues Consequences for the Rest of Canada." *Canadian Public Policy,* 6 (February 1980):192-204.

Davenport, P. "Equalization Payments and Regional Disparities." Paper presented at the Canadian Economics Association Meetings, Saskatoon, May 1979.

Federal Provincial Tax Structure Committee. Ottawa: Queen's Printer, 1966.

Feldstein, M.S. "On the Theory of Tax Reform." *Journal of Public Economics* 6 (July-August 1976):77-104.

Flatters, F.R. and Purvis, D.D. "Ontario: Policies for and Problems of Adjustment in the 80's." In Ontario Economic Council, *Developments Abroad and the Domestic Economy,* vol. 1, Toronto, 1980, pp. 129-165.

Fowler, R.M. "The Role of Royal Commissions." *Economic Policy Advising in Canada,* edited by D.C. Smith. Montreal: C.D. Howe Research Institute, 1981, chap. 6.

Grewal, B.S.; Brennan, G.; and Mathews, R.L., eds. *The Economics of Federalism.* Canberra: Australian National University Press, 1980.

Hartwick, J.M. "The Henry George Rule, Optimal Population and Interregional Equity." *Canadian Journal of Economics* 13 (November 1980):695-700.

Helliwell, J.F. "Can Canada Be Insulated from Developments Abroad?" In Ontario Economic Council, *Developments Abroad and the Domestic Economy,* vol. 2, Toronto, 1980, pp. 79-102.

McLure, C.E., Jr. "Fiscal Federalism and the Taxation of Economic Rents." In *State and Local Finance in the 80s,* edited by George F. Break. Madison, Wis.: University of Wisconsin Press, forthcoming.

Maxwell, J. and Pestieau, C. *Economic Realities of Contemporary Confederates.* Montreal: C.D. Howe Research Institute, 1980.

Mieszkowski, P.M. "On the Theory of Tax Incidence." *Journal of Political Economy,* 70 (June 1967):250-262.

Mirrlees, J.A. "The Optimal Town." *Swedish Journal of Economics,* 74 (March 1972):114-135.

Moore, A.M.; Perry, J.H.; and Beach, D.I. *The Financing of Canadian Federation.* Toronto: Canadian Tax Foundation, 1966.

Musgrave R.A. "ET, OT and SBT." *Journal of Public Economics* 6 (1976): 3-16.

Oates, W. *Fiscal Federalism.* New York: Harcourt, Brace, and Jovanovich, 1972.

Royal Commission on Dominion-Provincial Relations. *Report (Rowell-Sirois Report).* Ottawa: Queen's Printer, 1940.

Royal Commission on Taxation. *Report (Carter Report).* Ottawa: Queen's Printer, 1966.

Safarian, A.E. *Canadian Federalism and Economic Integration.* Ottawa: Information Canada, 1979.

Usher, D. "Public Property and the Effects of Migration upon Other Residents of the Migrants' Countries of Origin and Destination." *Journal of Political Economy* 85 (October 1977):1001-1020.

Comments

Thomas J. Courchene

Robin Boadway and Frank Flatters must be congratulated on writing an important as well as a relevant chapter. This is particularly the case in the Canadian context, where we are about to renegotiate our system of equalization payments. Indeed, it must rank as one of the seminal pieces relating to the theory of equalization payments. The role of a discussant of such a chapter can take two directions: to attempt to extend and elaborate on the analysis or to focus on some of the chapter's shortcomings. The highroad is, of course, to follow the former. I shall, perhaps unfortunately, opt for the latter. My comments begin with some reference to the pervasive role that equalization plays in the finances of the have-not provinces. This is followed by a bit of historical perspective, since I believe that Boadway and Flatters have gone too far in the direction of linking the current equalization formula to the Rowell-Sirois Report. The remainder of the discussion focuses in various ways on the relationship between equalization and resources, which is the theoretical core of their chapter.

The Role of Equalization: Some Further Evidence

Boadway and Flatters's discussion of Canada's current equalization formula leaves little to be desired. For an American audience, however, it seems appropriate to augment their description with some evidence relating to the importance of equalization payments for the recipient provinces. This is done in table 3-2.

The first row of the table presents indices of per-capita revenues by province for fiscal year 1977-1978, with the all-province average set at 100. The four Atlantic provinces (Newfoundland, New Brunswick, Prince Edward Island, and Nova Scotia) have indices that range from 55 to 65. Ontario, typically viewed as the so-called fat cat of the federation, had per-capita own revenues of only 95 percent of the all-province average. Alberta's index of 227 reflects the presence of energy revenues, but even this is an underestimate of Alberta's revenue potential. For one thing, Alberta has no sales tax, which in Ontario, for example, is set at 7 percent. More importantly, Alberta's energy revenues were substantially understated in 1977-1978, compared to the more recent period, reflecting the much higher world and domestic energy prices.

Row A.2 reveals how the presence of equalization payments affects the

Table 3-2
Provincial Fiscal Capacity, Tax Revenues, Expenditures, and Personal Income, 1977-1978

	Newfoundland	Prince Edward Island	Nova Scotia	New Brunswick	Quebec	Ontario	Manitoba	Saskatchewan	Alberta	British Columbia	All Provinces
Panel A Fiscal-capacity indices											
A.1 Own-source revenues	59	55	64	65	79	97	79	99	227	115	100
A.2 Own-source revenues plus equalization	85	84	85	85	87	88	88	96	212	107	100
A.3 Own-source revenues plus all federal transfers	92	97	88	89	92	88	90	98	192	104	100
Panel B											
B.1 Equaliztion as a percentage of own revenues (1980-81)	52.4	65.1	51.0	48.7	16.5	0	26.1	1.9	0	0	8.1
B.2 Gross provincial revenue (Row A.3 in dollars per capita for 1980-81)	2,514	2,445	2,176	2,224	2,544	1,973	2,169	2,672	4,422	2,335	2,449
Row C: Indices of expenditures per capita	88	96	86	82	108	94	99	103	118	100	100
Row D: Personal income per capita	69	67	80	75	93	109	93	93	104	110	100

Source: Adapted from Thomas J. Courchene, "A Market Perspective on Regional Disparities," *Canadian Public Policy* 7 (Autumn 1981):506-518.
Note: Indices: national average = 100.

fiscal-capacity indices. Alberta and British Columbia remain above 100. (Note that Canada's system of equalization payments is not an interprovincial revenue-sharing pool. Rich provinces contribute nothing directly to the funding of equalization. It comes out of the consolidated revenue of the federal government.) However, the indexes of all the provinces east of Ontario are brought up dramatically. Row A.3 incorporates other federal transfers to the provinces. The major items here are federal provincial transfers for health and higher education (which are essentially equal per-capita transfers) and the 50-percent federal cost-sharing program for welfare. As a result of these transfers, Ontario's index is 88. All other provinces have at least as large a per-capita revenue! Since Ontario is not only the largest province, but (from row D) the province with one of the highest per-capita incomes, it is difficult to argue that Canada's equalization system has failed to live up to its goal of ensuring that all provinces can afford to provide national-average levels of public services without resorting to unduly high tax rates.

Row B.1 of the table presents an alternate view of just how important equalization transfers are to some of the provinces. The data relate to fiscal year 1980-1981, but the percentages would be similar if they were reported on a 1977-1978 basis. As a percent of own revenues, equalization payments range from 65.1 percent for Prince Edward Island to 1.9 percent for Saskatchewan. For the four Maritime provinces they average over 50 percent of own revenues. In Quebec, these payments equal 16.5 percent of own revenues, a relatively small proportion in comparison with some of the other provinces. Yet, because Quebec's population is so large compared to the other have-not provinces, this province's equalization flows approximate one half of the total. Ontario, British Columbia, and Alberta do not receive equalization payments, and the most recent data indicate that Saskatchewan has now joined the ranks of the have provinces. As Boadway and Flatters have pointed out, Ontario qualifies for payments from the formula but has been excluded, arbitrarily, on the basis of its per-capita income. To provide some actual dollar figures, as distinct from indices or percentages, row B.2 presents per-capita revenues for all provinces, corresponding to the concept in row A.3 (except for 1980-1981). Ontario, with $1,973 per capita provides the lower floor, well beneath the all-province average of nearly $2500.

Finally, row C of table 3-2 presents indices relating to per-capita expenditure by province. These data are very revealing because they indicate that although Alberta has a fiscal capacity that is twice that of any other province (row A.3), its per-capita expenditures on public goods and services are only 18 percent above the national average. The difference, of course, ends up in the Alberta Heritage Fund, which is fast becoming the largest pool of capital on the continent, let alone in Canada.

Historical Perspective of Equalization Payments

Boadway and Flatters unduly emphasize the point that the present system of equalization payments is fully consistent with the report of the Royal Commission on Dominion-Provincial Relations (the Rowell-Sirois Report). This is not a major part of their chapter, but it merits some comments anyway. They note that "the exigencies of wartime finance precluded action on the Report." This is not correct. My interpretation is that the provinces were not in favor of the proposals at the 1941 federal-provincial conference. However, a few months later many of the proposals were implemented (for example, the transferring of the personal- and corporate-income taxes to the federal level) because of the exigencies of war finance. In the words of one commentator: "Patriotism accomplished what financial reasoning could not."[1] It should be noted that this aspect of the Rowell-Sirois Report has now substantialy fallen by the wayside, with three of the largest provinces currently mounting their own corporate taxes (Ontario, Quebec, and Alberta). Thus it is not the case, as Boadway and Flatters assert, that the recommendations of the Report "survived virtually unaltered despite the passage of time and, especially, changes in circumstance."

Boadway and Flatters probably were referring only to the equalization proposals (that is, the national-adjustment grants) of the Report. Even here, however, this statement must be qualified. The national-adjustment grants were originally meant to be once-and-for-all settlements (although there was some provision for adjustment), whereas the current equalization payments are essentially open-ended. Second, the national-adjustment grants were basically designed to ensure that all provinces could mount essentially equivalent programs in the areas of social, educational, and development expenses. Much of the monies required to fund these programs now come from what are known as "established programs financing," and in dollar value they dwarf the equalization scheme. Relatedly, there was no particular formula associated with the proposed adjustment grants. Rather, the calculations appear to have been made on the basis of the fiscal need of each of the provinces. Included in this fiscal need was, I believe, an attempt to assess not only the revenue means of each province but as well the expenditure need (that is, it may cost more in some areas to deliver an equivalent level of public services). The current formula pays no attention to expenditure need: the focus is on the revenue side of the budget. Thus they are not justified in arguing that the formula suggested by Davenport (where equalization would be based on personal income augmented by business-income revenues and natural-resource revenues) would "amount to a complete change in the nature of equalization away from the Rowell-Sirois Report." Depending on the pay-out ratio utilized with such a tax base, one can generate either more equalization or less than Canada currently has.

Moreover, the scheme could be a full-blown interprovincial revenue-sharing pool or it could be financed along current lines. It would be hard to argue that all versions of such a scheme would violate the Rowell-Sirois Report.

Boadway and Flatters are correct to note that the philosophy underlying the adjustment grants has survived virtually intact to the present, and indeed it is now about to be embodied in the constitution. But to argue that this philosophy is closely linked with the present formula is not appropriate. For example, nowhere in the current formula (nor any that Boadway and Flatters provide) do we find any definition of an essential public service. Nor is there any precise definition of what constitutes an undue burden of provincial taxation. In short, although the underlying philosophy is enduring and appealing, there exists no monopoly on the manner in which it should be implemented.

Finally, one point that Boadway and Flatters should have noted about the national-adjustment grants is that they were designed to be unconditional grants, as have been all equalization flows in the Canadian context since that time.

Resources and Equalization

The following is a discussion of a few points at the heart of the chapter that leave me somewhat uncomfortable, although overall I remain very impressed with their contribution.

The Broad versus Narrow Horizontal-Equity Distinction

Boadway and Flatters make an important distinction between broad-based horizontal equity (where the federal government acts to ensure that identical individuals are treated identically under the combined policies of the federal and provincial governments) and narrow-based horizontal equity (where the federal government is concerned only with maintaining horizontal equity with respect to its own actions). This makes their chapter far more policy relevent, since the reader is free to impose his or her own view of the appropriate role of the federal government and to focus on the resulting conclusions. My own view is that they should have introduced a similar concept with respect to efficiency. National efficiency is not an obvious assumption to apply to a federation, since almost by definition the provinces are going to enact policies that will violate geographical Pareto optimality. As Musgrave noted: "The very purpose of a fiscal federalism . . . is to permit different groups living in various states [provinces] to express different preferences for public services; and this inevitably leads to differences in the levels of taxation and public services. The resulting differentiation in tax levels may interfere with the most efficient allocation of resources and location of industries . . . such is the cost of political subdivision be it on an intranational or international basis.''[2] Provinces do provide different expenditure and tax packages, and even with identical resource endowments that can lead to very different NFBs across provinces by, say, income class. Boadway and Flatters essentially disregard this issue and argue that with equalization payments provinces have the potential for providing equal NFBs. This is a bit problematic, because provinces could use these monies to generate their own NFB distortions, which could be every bit as serious as those that the equalization payments are designed to rectify. More generally, if efficiency is utilized as the guiding principle in reallocating revenues and particularly resource revenues, then should it not be the case that this efficiency criterion be carried over to the production or expenditure side of public services as well? This leads to the broader issue of whether equalization payments are an obvious implication of their analysis.

Does Equalization Follow from the Model?

Under the assumption of narrow-based horizontal equity and distributionally neutral budgets, Boadway and Flatters argue that problems arise because source-based taxes are not included in the definition of personal income. If the definition of the federal income-tax base were comprehensive enough, no equalization would be required in terms of satisfying horizontal equity. Presumably what they have in mind is that the resource rents become privatized on a once-and-for-all basis (that is, all residents in Alberta as of a certain date are issued a share for present and future royalties). The yearly dividends would then enter personal income and be taxed at the federal marginal rate. Rent-seeking or fiscal-induced migration would be substantially reduced, since newcomers would not be eligible to share in the windfall. There still might be some inmigration if these rents were large enough, since the general level of taxation could then be reduced because the province would get considerable income-tax revenue from the large increase in incomes.

However, since this provision does not exist, the other options are:

1. A system of interpersonal transfers to residents of other provinces, which would probably have to be differentiated by province. This, the authors point out, would be cumbersome and politically unacceptable (in the United States it would also be unconstitutional). However, since this model does build on individual maximization it is the theoretically correct solution to the problem.

2. Transfers to Ottawa equal to the federal marginal rate times the resource-based taxes, which would then be used to fund federally provided

equal-per-capita expenditures across the country or could be used to reduce other taxes. This option is not addressed in the Boadway-Flatters chapter, but it seems to be fully consistent with the analysis.

3. Equalization transfers from the rich to the poor provinces equal to the federal marginal tax rate times the provincial per-capita source-based tax revenues. This has the potential for removing the horizontal inequity, although the actual result will depend on how the recipient provinces spend these funds. The difference between items 2 and 3 is that under the former the potential exists for a lower overall size of the public sector, since it is more likely that the federal government would follow the lower-tax route than would the provinces.

In any event, equalization is only one of the possibilities that flow from the Boadway-Flatters model. And it is not even clear just how such a solution would square with the preferred comprehensive income-tax solution. Consider the following scenario. All resource rents are included in personal income on an equal-per-capita basis. Ottawa now gets its marginal-tax-rate share. Suppose the province then applies a confiscatory tax to the remainder of the resource rents allocated to persons. This is one way of viewing what actually occurs in Alberta. (Under the new Alberta-Ottawa energy agreement the federal government will get a much larger share of the energy rents. For convenience, let us call this the marginal-rate share. Alberta can be viewed as transferring this amount to Ottawa on behalf of its citizens and taxing the remainder at a 100-percent rate.) A strict reading of the Boadway-Flatters proposal might suggest that no equalization is required, since Ottawa now has its marginal-rate share of the energy rents. But what I believe they are saying is something different, namely that whatever share of overall energy rents Ottawa may receive, it is still the case that any residual provincial revenues from resources ought to be equalized at the federal marginal rate times those provincial revenues.[3] I have trouble with this both on its own grounds and in comparison with what would flow from the notion of a comprehensive income-tax base. It seems to me what might be eligible for equalization is the amount of revenue that would arise if the province taxes these rents at its provincial marginal-tax rate (which is less than one half the federal marginal rate). Any excess revenues collected are the result of greater tax effort on the part of the Alberta government and should not be eligible for equalization. In any event, their analysis in this section is not as clear as it might be.

Rent-Seeking Migration and the Efficiency Issue

Boadway and Flatters are correct to point out that the existence of provincially collected resource rents have the potential for encouraging rent-seeking migration into the resource-rich provinces. In equilibrium in the

Boadway-Flatters model, workers would move to Alberta until the point where they drive the nominal wage down sufficiently in this province to offset the net fiscal benefits arising from taxing resource rents. In other words, factor-price equalization would not hold within the country. This is questionable, since in their model they do not allow capital to move as well. What is likely to happen is that too much labor and too much capital would move to Alberta. This would continue until the resource rents in Alberta relative to capital and labor were in rough equality with the situation in the rest of Canada, that is, factor-price equalization might hold throughout if one assumes that capital is more mobile than labor.

In terms of the policy implications arising from the efficiency issue, the fall of the nominal wage in Alberta below that of, say, Ontario would be cause for concern. However, the opposite is now occurring: wages are rising in Alberta relative to Ontario. In part this may reflect the rising cost of living, particularly the housing component, in Alberta, which in turn may be a result either of congestion costs or of capitalization of some of the Heritage Fund into land values. In any event, although the theoretical point is surely valid, its immediate policy relevance is questionable.

Much more relevant in terms of current policy and equally important in theory is the existence of a distortion in the manner in which factor incomes are taxed in the public and private sectors in Canada. Section 125 of the BNA Act in effect states that the crown cannot tax the crown (that is, the federal government cannot tax the provincial government). What this means is that there exists a tremendous incentive for the provinces to "provincialize" or "nationalize" the resource sector, because any income would escape federal tax. As important, Alberta's Heritage Fund will soon be earning over a billion dollars of interest annually, all of which will escape federal tax. This entire issue is discussed in more detail in the context of John Whyte's chapter (chapter 6). Nevertheless, it seems imperative that pressure be put on all levels of government so that factor incomes (particularly profits, rents, and interest) are treated in the same manner whether they arise in the public or private sectors. This would be important in its own right. It would provide Canada with a firm basis on which to mount an effective equalization program, since the problem areas of the present program are precisely those associated with provincial revenues that are in effect factor incomes.

Conclusion

Boadway-Flatters conclude their analysis by focusing on the degree to which Canada's equalization system is consistent with their model. This is no doubt valuable. It is worth pointing out however that there is now a new proposal for the equalization program. Very briefly, the scheme proposes to maintain roughly the same list of tax sources as Boadway-Flatters outline (with the addition of all property taxes, rather than only those related to school-purpose expenditures). Unlike the present system, which essentially equalizes revenues to the national-average level, the proposed scheme would equalize revenues to the Ontario average. Since Ontario has effectively a zero base for the important resource revenues (oil and natural gas), this means that no province will receive equalization from the fossil-fuel tax sources. This will not mean that equalization payments will fall relative to the current system, because the Ontario average is higher than the national average for virtually all the remaining tax sources.

This proposed scheme in some ways runs completely counter to the Boadway-Flatters analysis, because there will essentially be no equalization flows arising from the fossil-energy sector, whereas under some assumptions Boadway-Flatters assumed that only these sorts of revenues ought to be equalized. Although there are problems with this proposed system, it seems to me that it is easy to make the argument that it is at least as consistent with the Rowell-Sirois dictate that all provinces should have access to revenues such that they can mount the average level of public services without resorting to unduly high tax rates. Surely, bringing all provinces' revenues up to the Ontario average would satisfy this.

Notes

1. Comment made by R.M. Burns, appearing in J.C. Strick, *Canadian Public Finance* (Toronto: Holt, Rinehart and Winston, 1973), p. 101.

2. R. A. Musgrave, *The Theory of Public Finance* (New York: McGraw-Hill, 1959), pp. 179-180.

3. This chapter would appear to be consistent with their recommendation in a more recent paper "Revenue Sharing and Equalization of Natural Resource Revenues," Queen's University, Fall 1981, mimeo.

4 Legal Constraints on State Taxation of Natural Resources

Walter Hellerstein

A little more than three years ago, I began a paper (whose title bears a striking resemblance to that of this chapter) with the following observations:

> The subject of my paper—constitutional constraints on state and local taxation of energy resources—is, it might be suggested, somewhat of a mystery. Examination of the two recently published treatises on constitutional law reveals only a brief allusion to the subject. If one turns to the Reports of the United States Supreme Court, one must wade through a half-century of volumes before discovering an opinion that seriously addresses the issue. And contemporary commentary on state and local taxation of energy resources seldom deems the constitutional questions worthy of more than a paragraph or two.[1]

It is testimony to the dramatic developments in the field of state taxation of natural resources that none of these statements is true today. Both constitutional-law treatises now include discussions of state taxation of natural resources.[2] During its past term, the U.S. Supreme Court handed down two significant decisions involving state taxation of natural resources.[3] And contemporary commentary on state and local taxation now contains a healthy sampling of articles addressed to constitutional and related legal issues raised by state natural-resource taxation. Indeed, as Charles McLure has aptly put it, events are moving so rapidly in this area that writing about it is very much like trying to hit a moving target.[4]

The first section of this chapter considers the application of the federal constitutional restraints on state taxation to particular types of state levies that have been, or may plausibly be, characterized as taxes on natural resources. The second section examines current controversies involving alleged federal-legislative preemption of state natural-resource taxation in the context of cases that have raised the issue. The final section focuses on the role of Congress in imposing legislative restrictions on the states' power to tax natural resources.

**Constitutional Restraints on State Taxation
of Natural Resources**

Severance Taxes

Severance taxes—by which I mean all excises levied on the severance or.production of natural resources and measured by the quantity or value of the resource severed or produced—are the most prevalent form of state taxes imposed specifically on natural resources. The first such tax was imposed by Michigan in 1846, and today there are thirty-three states imposing such taxes. Revenues from these taxes have increased from $1.2 billion or less than 2 percent of state tax revenues in 1974 to $4.2 billion or nearly 5 percent of state tax revenues in 1980.[5] The constitutional limitations on the power of the states to impose severance taxes have been shaped in essential respects by the Supreme Court's recent decision in *Commonwealth Edison Co.* v. *Montana,* which sustained over constitutional objections Montana's 30-percent severance tax on coal.[6]

The Commerce Clause. The commerce clause by its terms is no more than an affirmative grant of power to Congress "to regulate Commerce with foreign nations, and among the several States, and with the Indian Tribes."[7] Nevertheless, from the beginning of our constitutional history the U.S. Supreme Court has elaborated the view that "became central to our whole constitutional scheme: the doctrine that the Commerce Clause, by its own force and without national legislation, puts it into the power of the Court to place limits upon state authority."[8]

The Traditional Analytical Framework. The commerce-clause criteria by which the validity of state severance taxes had traditionally been measured were established in the 1920s by three decisions of the Supreme Court. The first and most significant of these decisions was *Heisler* v. *Thomas Colliery Co.*[9] The case involved a challenge to a Pennsylvania tax on "each and every ton of anthracite coal . . . mined, washed, screened, or otherwise prepared for market" in the state.[10] Nine northeastern states joined the plaintiff, a stockholder in the Thomas Colliery Company, in seeking to enjoin Pennsylvania from enforcing and the company from complying with the taxing scheme on the grounds that the statute was unconstitutional. The commerce-clause claim, which was pressed most vigorously by the states, rested on the contention that the levy on anthracite coal discriminated against interstate commerce because in design and effect the exaction fell on a commodity destined primarily for out-of-state shipment and consumption, with the ultimate tax burden being borne by residents of other states. Thus the states argued:

Pennsylvania has a natural monopoly of anthracite coal in this country. That coal is a prime necessity of life, especially in the northeastern States. Eighty per cent of such coal is shipped out of Pennsylvania. . . .

The declared intention at the time this act was passed was so to use the natural monopoly which Pennsylvania possesses as to compel the inhabitants of other States to pay a tax to Pennsylvania by collecting a special tax from the colliery which would inevitably pass such tax on to the consumer. . . .

As this coal has already borne its full share of ordinary, non-discriminatory property taxes, . . . to sustain this additional and discriminatory tax imposed upon anthracite coal alone would permit the holder of a natural monopoly to use the channels of interstate commerce to tax persons in other States to the extent of about $6,000,000 a year. . . .

The question at issue extends far beyond the validity or invalidity of the particular tax in question. It will establish a far reaching principle for good or ill. If the tax be upheld, it is inevitable that every State which possesses natural resources essential to other States will impose similar taxes in order to make those whom it cannot directly and constitutionally tax contribute to its exchequer through the channels of commerce. Indeed, several States may combine so as to create absolute monopolies by the enactment of uniform laws exacting taxes similar to this. Such a situation would bring back the commercial conflicts between the States which the commerce clause was enacted to prevent. A result so absolutely repugnant to both the letter and the purpose of the commerce clause ought not to be permitted.[11]

The Supreme Court's rejoinder, which must be viewed in light of the then-prevailing doctrine that interstate commerce enjoyed an absolute immunity from state taxation,[12] was unequivocal:

The reach and consequences of the contention repel its acceptance. If the possibility, or, indeed, certainty of exportation of a product or article from a State determines it to be in interstate commerce before the commencement of its movement from the State, it would seem to follow that it is in such commerce from the instant of its growth or production, and in the case of coals, as they lie in the ground. The result would be curious. It would nationalize all industries, it would nationalize and withdraw from state jurisdiction and deliver to federal commercial control the fruits of California and the South, the wheat of the West and its meats, the cotton of the South, the shoes of Massachusetts and the woolen industries of other States, at the very inception of their production or growth, that is, the fruits unpicked, the cotton and wheat ungathered, hides and flesh of cattle yet "on the hoof," wool yet unshorn and coal yet unmined, because they are in varying percentages destined for and surely to be exported to States other than those of their production.[13]

The Court concluded that the coal Pennsylvania sought to tax was "too definitely situated to be misunderstood" and that no claim predicated on the commerce clause could properly be made, since the coal had not yet entered the stream of commerce.[14]

The position taken by the Court in *Heisler* was reinforced by two decisions that followed on its heels, *Oliver Iron Mining Co.* v. *Lord*[15] and *Hope Natural Gas Co.* v. *Hall.*[16] In each case the Court rejected a commerce-clause attack similar to that leveled in *Heisler,* holding that a tax on the mining of iron ore or on the production of natural gas was, like the tax on the severance of coal in *Heisler,* an exaction on a local activity that imposed no burden on interstate commerce.

The Court's disposition of the commerce-clause objections raised in *Heisler, Oliver Iron Mining,* and *Hope Natural Gas* may, in retrospect, seem highly formalistic and essentially unresponsive to the underlying claim of discrimination. These cases nevertheless established the fundamental principle that laid the cornerstone for commerce-clause adjudication of state severance taxes for the next fifty years: The imposition of a facially nondiscriminatory excise tax on the severance or production of natural resources in the state fell outside the pale of commerce-clause protection, despite the fact that a substantial portion of the resources would be shipped and consumed beyond the state's borders, because the activities taxed were deemed to occur before their entry into the stream of commerce. Objections based on subsequent events were deemed to be immaterial. Later decisions elaborated on and extended the principles set forth in these early cases, but no explicit modification of doctrine or undermining of holding occurred. And, although the Court struck down excise taxes on natural resources when the incidence of the tax was found to fall on interstate rather than local activity and drew lines between interstate and local activity that could not be characterized as bright, it was an enduring article of faith for the next half-century that a severance tax on natural resources was invulnerable to attack on commerce-clause grounds.

Commonwealth Edison Co. v. *Montana.* In June 1978, a number of coal companies and their out-of-state utility customers filed suit in the state district court in Montana alleging, among other things, that Montana's 30-percent severance tax on coal violated the commerce clause.[17] The substance of their commerce-clause claim was little different from the contentions advanced in *Heisler* more than fifty years earlier. They alleged that "[a]t the time each Coal Producing Plaintiff extracts coal from its mines in Montana, the ultimate destination of such coal is fixed and is known to be a destination outside Montana"[18]; that "[f]rom at least the time of severance from the earth until arrival and delivery of such coal at an ultimate destination outside Montana, such coal is and continues to be in and to substantially affect interstate commerce"[19]; that "[t]he ultimate burden of [severance] tax payments . . . falls upon the Utility Plaintiffs and upon their customers in [other] states"[20]; and that "[t]he Coal Severance Tax is not fairly related to the services and protection provided by Montana,"[21] "discriminates against interstate commerce,"[22] and "unduly burden[s] interstate commerce."[23] The state district court, relying on *Heisler* and its progeny, dismissed the plaintiffs' commerce-clause claim,[24] and the Supreme Court of Montana affirmed, although on somewhat broader grounds.[25] When the U.S. Supreme Court noted probable jurisdiction of the case in the fall of 1980, however, it was apparent that a commerce-clause defense predicated on *Heisler* alone would face rough going and that the objections to Montana's severance tax were likely to be evaluated on grounds more in keeping with the Court's contemporary commerce-clause jurisprudence.

In *Commonwealth Edison,* the Supreme Court had few qualms about abandoning the rationale of *Heisler* as a tool of commerce-clause analysis.[26] *Heisler* had been decided, after all, during an era when the commerce-clause doctrine controlling state taxes affecting interstate commerce was markedly different from the commerce-clause doctrine that prevails today. When *Heisler* was decided interstate commerce was thought to enjoy an absolute immunity from state taxation. Consequently, any determination that a state tax was imposed directly on an activity in interstate commerce completely removed that activity from state tax power. Indeed, in *Heisler* the Court's holding that a severance tax falls on a local activity preceding interstate commerce was motivated, at least in part, by its concern that the opposite conclusion would "withdraw from state jurisdiction" subjects of taxation that were traditional components of the states' tax base.[27]

The constitutional ground rules for determining the validity of a state tax affecting interstate commerce had substantially changed, however, since *Heisler* was handed down. The Court had repudiated the notion that interstate commerce was immune from state taxation and had embraced the principle that such commerce must pay its way. The Court had likewise eroded the doctrine that state taxes or regulations affecting interstate commerce were not subject to commerce-clause scrutiny merely because they were imposed on a local or intrastate event. In the place of the older, formalistic approach to state taxes, the Court had developed the "consistent and rational method of inquiry," which looked to "the practical effect of a challenged tax" on interstate commerce.[28] The Court thus concluded in *Commonwealth Edison* that

> a state severance tax is not immunized from Commerce Clause scrutiny by a claim that the tax is imposed on goods prior to their entry into the stream of interstate commerce. Any contrary statements in *Heisler* and its progeny are disapproved. We agree with appellants that the Montana tax must be evaluated under *Complete Auto Transit*'s four-part test. Under that test, a state tax does not offend the Commerce Clause if it "is applied to an activity with a substantial nexus with the taxing State, is fairly apportioned, does not discriminate against interstate commerce, and is fairly related to services provided by the State."[29]

There has never been much doubt that a state severance tax would satisfy the first two prongs of the Court's commerce-clause standard, and the taxpayers in the Montana severance-tax case did not even raise the issue. The Court in *Commonwealth Edison* nevertheless observed in passing that "there can be no argument here that a substantial, in fact, the only nexus of the severance of coal is established in Montana."[30] It likewise remarked that there can be no question of unfair apportionment, and consequently, of an unconstitutional risk of multiple taxation, because " 'the severance can occur in no other state' and 'no other state can tax the severance.' "[31]

The claim that Montana's severance tax discriminated against interstate commerce did not fit neatly within the Court's proscription against discriminatory levies. Severance taxes, after all, are generally nondiscriminatory on their face, applying to every ton of coal or barrel of oil or cubic foot of gas extracted in the state. No distinction is drawn in such taxing schemes between local and out-of-state interests: the burden of the tax is borne according to the amount or value of the coal, oil, or gas produced or, if the tax is shifted forward, according to the amount or value consumed, without regard to the residence of the producer or the consumer. Montana's tax was no exception.

The claim that Montana's severance tax discriminated against interstate commerce, however, was predicated on two interrelated propositions that arguably brought the case within the Court's doctrine forbidding discriminatory levies. First, it was contended that the burden of the tax was in fact borne largely by out-of-state consumers, which depended on whether the tax was exported along with the resource. Second, it was alleged that the amount of the tax exceeded the costs imposed on and benefits provided by the state in connection with the extraction of the resource. The second contention was a necessary element of the commerce-clause argument because the states do not violate the commerce clause when they demand from those consuming their resources reimbursement for a fair share of such costs and benefits.

The argument, as I have stated it elsewhere, thus boils down to the proposition that:

> a State in a position to exact a levy on its energy resources that is passed on to out-of-state consumers violates the Commerce Clause when it imposes a tax greater than that necessary to recoup the costs associated with the extraction of that resource from the State. As thus narrowed, the argument has considerable force. Putting aside for the moment the formidable evidentiary problems involved in proving such a case, one may fairly contend that the State's effective selection of a class of out-of-state taxpayers to shoulder a tax burden grossly in excess of any costs imposed directly or indirectly by such taxpayers on the State places an unconstitutional burden upon interstate commerce. For the Court has made it clear that facially nondiscriminatory taxes which by their practical operation discriminate against interstate commerce are vulnerable to attack on Commerce Clause

grounds. While the States need not fine-tune the exercise of their taxing power to accord with a precise accounting of the costs imposed by and benefits provided to the taxpayer, they should not be permitted to single out the nonresident taxpayer to bear the brunt of a demonstrable imbalance on this score, at least if it can be shown that other levies with a less selective impact do not suffer from such an imbalance.[32]

Obviously, it was the dissenting opinion in *Commonwealth Edison* that relied on this excerpt from my article. The majority found the argument unpersuasive for several reasons. First, it adverted to the difficulties involved were it confronted with the task of "judging the validity of a state tax by assessing the State's 'monopoly' position or its 'exportation' of the tax burden out of the State."[33] Second, it observed that the premise underlying its commerce-clause decisions was that state borders are irrelevant and that to "invalidate the Montana tax solely because most of Montana's coal is shipped across the very state borders that ordinarily are to be considered irrelevant would require a significant and . . . unwarranted departure from the rationale of our prior discrimination cases."[34] Third, the Court was unwilling to characterize as discriminatory a tax that treated residents and nonresidents alike, even if its effect was to deny nonresidents access to another state's resources at reasonable prices.[35] Finally, and most importantly, the Court recognized that the

appellants' discrimination theory ultimately collapses into the claim that the Montana tax is invalid under the fourth prong of the [Court's] test: that the tax is not "fairly related to the services provided by the State." Because appellants conceded that Montana may impose *some* severance tax on coal mined in the State, the only remaining foundation for their discrimination theory is a claim that the tax burden borne by the out-of-state consumers of Montana coal is excessive. This is, of course, merely a variant of appellants' assertion that the Montana tax does not satisfy the "fairly related" prong of the [Court's] test.[36]

The fourth prong of the Court's commerce-clause test—that a tax be "fairly related to services provided by the State"—has ostensibly been the most powerful predicate of a commerce-clause challenge to state severance taxes. If the commerce clause requires that there be a reasonable quantitative relationship between a state tax and the services provided to the taxpayer by the state and if severance-tax payers can prove their allegations that severance taxes far exceed any benefits provided or costs incurred by the state, then severance-tax payers have indeed raised a substantial commerce-clause issue.

As the Court held in *Commonwealth Edison,* however, the major premise of the taxpayers' commerce-clause syllogism was false. The so-called fairly related test does not impose a requirement that the amount of a tax bear some quantitative relationship to the value of services provided by the state to the taxpayers. It requires only that "the *measure* of the tax must be reasonably related to the extent of the [taxpayer's] contact [with the State], since it is the activities or presence of the taxpayer in the State that may properly be made to bear a 'just share of state tax burden.' "[37]

In light of this reading of the fairly related criterion, the Court in *Commonwealth Edison* had little difficulty in concluding that Montana's severance tax satisfied it.

> The "operating incidence" of the tax is on the mining of coal within Montana. Because it is measured as a percentage of the value of the coal taken, the Montana tax is in "proper proportion" to appellants' activities within the State and, therefore, to their "consequent enjoyment of the opportunities and protections which the State has afforded" in connection to those activities. When a tax is assessed in proportion to a taxpayer's activities or presence in a State, the taxpayer is shouldering its fair share of supporting the State's provision of "police and fire protection, the benefit of a trained work force, and 'the advantages of a civilized society.' "[38]

The Court justified its narrow construction of the fairly related test on a number of grounds. It distinguished cases involving user charges imposed as compensation for specific state-provided services, in which it had required that the fees in question be commensurate with the services provided, from an exaction like Montana's which was "imposed for the general support of government."[39] It recited its long-standing rule, articulated in the due-process context, that

> A tax is not an assessment of benefits. It is, as we have said, a means of distributing the burden of the cost of government. The only benefit to which the taxpayer is constitutionally entitled is that derived from his enjoyment of the privileges of living in an organized society, established and safeguarded by the devotion of taxes to public purposes. Any other view would preclude the levying of taxes except as they are used to compensate for the burden on those who pay them, and would involve abandonment of the most fundamental principle of government—that it exists primarily to provide for the common good.[40]

The Court saw no reason why the salutary principle loses its force

> merely because the taxed activity has some connection to interstate commerce. . . . To accept appellants' apparent suggestion that the Commerce Clause prohibits the States from requiring an activity connected to interstate commerce to contribute to the general cost of providing governmental services, as distinct from those costs attributable to the taxed activity, would place such commerce in a privileged position.[41]

Moreover, the Court found nothing in its prior cases to suggest that the relevant inquiry under the fairly related test is "the *amount* of the tax or the *value* of the benefits allegedly bestowed as measured by the costs the State incurs on account of the taxpayer's activities."[42]

In the end, however, it was not the language or holdings of its precedents that, in my judgment, led the Court to reject the taxpayers' contention that the fairly related test should be construed to require "a factual inquiry into the relationship between the revenues generated by a tax and the costs incurred on account of the taxed activity, in order to provide a mechanism for judicial disapproval under the Commerce Clause of state taxes that are excessive."[43] Rather, it was the Court's view of its proper role in adjudicating state tax controversies that was the motive force in its decision. The taxpayers had conceded, after all, that Montana's severance tax would have passed constitutional muster at some unspecified lower rate. By arguing that the tax at its existing rate violated the fairly related criterion of the commerce clause, the taxpayers were inescapably seeking a judicial determination of the appropriate rate of a state tax. The Court's response to the taxpayers' efforts was unequivocal:

> The simple fact is that the appropriate level or rate of taxation is essentially a matter for legislative, and not judicial resolution. In essence, appellants ask this Court to prescribe a test for the validity of state taxes that would require state and federal courts to calculate acceptable rates or levels of taxation of activities that are conceded to be legitimate subjects of taxation. This we decline to do.[44]

Court Adjudication under the Commerce Clause. The Court's opinion in *Commonwealth Edison* makes it clear that a typical state severance tax will survive commerce-clause scrutiny regardless of the extent to which the resource (or the tax) is exported and regardless of its rate or amount. The central meaning of the Court's opinion, however, has less to do with doctrinal considerations than with the institutional considerations that seem to be guiding the Court in delineating the scope of state tax power under the commerce clause. The Court has made it plain, especially in recent years, that its role in adjudicating state tax controversies is a limited one. The Court's adoption of a narrow role in this area is attributable to two critical institutional considerations. First, the Court is institutionally incapable of prescribing broad solutions to the vexing problems of state taxation of interstate commerce. As Justice Frankfurter has stated:

> At best, this Court can only act negatively; it can determine whether a specific state tax is imposed in violation of the Commerce Clause. Such decisions must necessarily depend on the application of rough and ready legal concepts. We cannot make a detailed inquiry into the incidence of

diverse economic burdens in order to determine the extent to which such burdens conflict with the necessities of national economic life. Neither can we devise appropriate standards for dividing up national revenue on the basis of more or less abstract principles of constitutional law, which cannot be responsive to the subtleties of the interrelated economies of Nation and State.[45]

As the Special Subcommittee on State Taxation of Interstate Commerce of the House Judiciary Committee observed over fifteen years ago: "The inadequacy of the judicial process to deal with the problems of multistate taxation has long been recognized by members of the Supreme Court. In recent years, jurists with such varied philosophies as Justices Jackson, Rutledge, Black, Frankfurter, Douglas, and Clark, have all subscribed to this view."[46]

Second, the Court is well aware that in our constitutional scheme its decisions under the commerce clause are tentative accommodations of state and national interests that are ultimately subject to revision by Congress. The Court has consistently reaffirmed its view of the broad power of Congress to draw whatever lines it believes are appropriate with respect to matters affecting interstate commerce. Indeed, in many of its recent decisions refusing to invalidate state tax legislation under the commerce clause, the Court has invited Congress to act if it is unhappy with the results flowing from the Court's hands-off attitude in this domain.

The Court's opinion in *Commonwealth Edison* relied heavily on these institutional considerations in refusing to strike down Montana's tax:

> In the first place, it is doubtful whether any legal test could adequately reflect the numerous competing economic, geographic, demographic, social, and political considerations that must inform a decision about an acceptable rate or level of state taxation, and yet be reasonably capable of application in a wide variety of individual cases. But even apart from the difficulty of the judicial undertaking, the nature of the factfinding and judgment that would be required of the courts merely reinforces the conclusion that questions about the appropriate level of state taxes must be resolved through the political process. Under our federal system, the determination is to be made by state legislatures in the first instance and, if necessary, by Congress when particular state taxes are thought to be contrary to federal interests.[47]

In short, the Court's decision in *Commonwealth Edison* does not reflect a judgment that the taxing scheme it sustained comports with its view of sound national policy. Rather it reflects a determination that the state, in the exercise of its essential taxing power, has not transcended any of the specific limitations that the commerce clause imposes on state taxation and that the Court is institutionally incapable of going beyond such a judgment in adjudicating the constitutionality of such a measure. Moreover, the Court knows in adopting such a posture that there is another branch of the federal government—the Congress—that is institutionally equipped and constitutionally empowered to forge more systematic and restrictive limitations on the power of the states to tax interstate commerce, if Congress is so minded.

The Due-Process Clause. Broadly speaking, the due-process clause of the Fourteenth Amendment has been construed by the Supreme Court to limit the territorial reach of the states' taxing powers.[48] This general restraint has been applied in essentially two situations. First, when a state seeks to tax an out-of-state taxpayer whose connections with the state are insubstantial, the due-process clause has been invoked to forbid the exercise of state tax power, because the state lacks a sufficient nexus with the taxpayer. Second, even if the taxpayer is concededly within the state's tax jurisdiction, the due-process clause requires that the measure of the tax fairly reflect the taxpayer's activities in the state. For example, a tax levied on or measured by the property of an interstate railroad will violate the due-process clause if the railroad property subject to the tax is not reasonably apportioned to the taxing state.

As the discussion of commerce-clause restraints on state severance taxation suggests, the nexus and apportionment requirements embodied in the due-process clause have little impact on state severance taxes. It is worth observing, however, that the due-process clause would forbid the states from imposing a confiscatory severance tax, a limitation that takes on significance in light of the taxpayers' assertion in *Commonwealth Edison* that adoption of Montana's position would leave the states free of constitutional restraint to impose taxes "equal to 100%, or even 1,000% or 2,000%, of the value of the coal."[49] The taxpayers did not actually allege that the Montana tax was an uncompensated taking of property in violation of the due-process clause, nor could they reasonably have done so. Nevertheless the Court, although abjuring any inquiry into the appropriate level or rate of taxation under the commerce clause, noted that a taxing statute "may be judicially disapproved" if it amounts to the "confiscation of property."[50] Although this restriction may not substantially limit state taxing power, it demonstrates the lack of substance in the imaginary horribles conjured up by the taxpayers in attempting to persuade the Court in *Commonwealth Edison* to adjudicate taxes for excessiveness under the commerce clause.

The Equal-Protection Clause. The equal-protection clause of the Fourteenth Amendment generally prohibits the states from making unreasonable classifications.[51] The same cases that established the traditional analytical framework governing commerce-clause challenges to state severance taxes also established the controlling principles governing equal-protection challenges to such taxes. In *Heisler*[52] it was alleged that the imposition of a tax upon anthracite coal but not upon bituminous coal created an arbitrary and unreasonable classification in violation of the equal-protection Clause.[52] Relying on a substantial body of precedent that had permitted the states broad leeway in making classifications for tax purposes, the Supreme Court concluded that the state possessed the power to distinguish between anthracite and bituminous coal in its taxing scheme. The Court observed that the two types of coal differed in their physical properties, in their uses as fuel, and in their alternative uses. Such differences provided the state with a rational basis for according the coals distinct tax treatment. It was of no consequence that the coals shared common characteristics and were sold in competition for fuel purposes. So long as there was some reasonable basis for the classification, it could withstand constitutional scrutiny under the equal-protection Clause.

In *Oliver Iron Mining,* the Court likewise rejected the taxpayers equal-protection claim.[53] It adverted to the "wide discretion" the state may exercise in selecting the subjects of taxation and declined to disturb the state's taxing scheme over the objections that it failed to include within its scope certain mine owners, lessees, and contractors engaging in operations related to mining and that it discriminated between taxpayers in the determination of the measure of the tax.[54] Finally, in *Hope Natural Gas,*[55] the Court summarily disposed of the taxpayers' equal-protection objections with the remark that "[n]othing indicates a purpose to extend different treatment to those of the same class."[56]

Unlike the commerce-clause doctrine embraced by *Heisler* and its progeny, the equal-protection doctrine articulated in these cases remains good law today. Although there have been significant developments in the law of equal protection, these developments have not narrowed the broad latitude the Court has accorded the states in drawing lines for tax purposes. The equal-protection clause therefore generally will not provide a taxpayer with a substantial basis for challenging a classification embodied in a state severance tax.

Privileges-and-Immunities Clause. The privileges-and-immunities clause of Article IV of the Constitution provides that "[t]he citizens of each State shall be entitled to all of the Privileges and Immunities of Citizens in the several states."[57] The clause has generally been construed to forbid state regulations and taxes that impose greater burdens on nonresidents than on residents. Because state severance-tax schemes do not distinguish between residents and nonresidents, there is no basis for a claim that such measures violate the privileges-and-immunities clause.

Other Taxes

Although plainly the most characteristic, severance taxes are by no means the only levies considered as taxes on natural resources. Other special exices directed at a natural-resource industry may be viewed as a species of natural-resource tax. So may *ad-valorem* property taxes levied on natural resources or even a corporate-income tax with provisions for income derived from natural-resource production. Indeed, at some level of generality, any tax that includes within its base a natural resource or the income or receipts it generates could be considered a tax on natural resources. Thus a personal-income tax imposed in part on an individual's dividends from the Exxon Corporation might be so considered.

Although we should not be mesmerized by the labels state legislatures append to their taxing schemes, some lines have to be drawn to keep the discussion of natural-resource taxation meaningful. The balance of the discussion of the constitutional restraints on state natural-resource taxation will therefore examine those levies that make some special provision for taxation of a natural resource. Whether it be the formal subject of the tax or the way an otherwise-general tax is measured or apportioned, the universe of levies considered embraces only those directed exclusively at natural resources or that treat natural resources differently from other subjects included in the tax base. I shall focus on the additional constitutional problems that may be encountered in the context of nonseverance taxation of natural resources.

Special Excises. Special excises other than severance taxes imposed on the natural-resource industry are common features of state tax systems. Many states, for example, impose special excises on natural-gas pipelines or utilities, usually measured by the gross receipts derived from the services rendered in the state. Lately oil companies have been the target of special excises imposed on their downstream operations by states in no position to exact severance taxes on their upstream operations. And West Virginia, which produces far more coal than Montana, taxes coal primarily through its business-and-occupation tax, measured by the gross receipts from the sale of the coal.

The Commerce Clause. Many excises of the type described once raised substantial issues under the commerce clause because they allegedly violated the prohibition against direct taxes on interstate commerce, especially if imposed on the privilege of carrying on business in the state. With the demise of the direct-indirect distinction as a means for determining the validity of state taxes under the commerce clause and with the repudiation of the doctrine that a tax on the privilege of doing interstate business is per se unconstitutional under the clause, these levies would today be evaluated under the familiar four-prong test the Court has enunciated in its recent commerce-clause opinions.

The absence of a sufficient nexus between the taxpayer's activity and the taxing state could give rise to a substantial commerce-clause claim if the levy were imposed on a natural resource that was merely in transit through the state. Thus a levy imposed on some activity incident to the interstate transmission of natural gas might be challenged on the ground that it failed to satisfy the Court's nexus criterion. Given the Court's generally permissive approach to the nexus requirement, however, the limitation is not likely to loom large as a commerce-clause restraint in this context.

When a special excise is imposed on an interstate natural-resource enterprise, its tax base will in some cases be apportioned by a formula designed to attribute to the taxing state a portion of the base commensurate with the intrastate activities of the taxpayer. Thus a privilege tax on an interstate pipeline company, measured by its gross earnings, may be apportioned to the state by the ratio of the mileage of the lines in the state as compared to the entire mileage of lines in all states. In other cases, the levy will include no provision for formulary apportionment of the tax base, but the Court's fair-apportionment requirement will nevertheless be satisfied because the measure of the levy will include only values associated with activities in the taxing state. Thus West Virginia's gross-receipts tax on coal and other products generally is measured by the "value of the products in the condition or form in which they exist immediately before transportation out of the State."[58] As the Supreme Court has declared, "[w]hen a general business tax levies only on the value of services performed within the State, the tax is properly apportioned and multiple burdens logically cannot occur."[59]

Sometimes, however, there may be a serious question whether a special excise imposed on the natural-resource industry meets the Court's fair-apportionment criterion. In *Michigan-Wisconsin Pipe Line Co.* v. *Calvert*, Texas levied a tax on the occupation of "gathering gas" as applied to an interstate natural-gas pipeline company.[60] The tax was measured by the entire volume of gas to be shipped in interstate commerce. Although the Court's decision striking down the tax rested largely on the now-discredited theory that the tax was imposed "directly" on "interstate commerce itself,"[61] the Court has recently explained its decision in the following terms: "This Court declared the tax unconstitutional because it amounted to an unapportioned levy on the transportation of the entire volume of gas. The exaction did not relate to the length of the Texas portion of the pipeline or to the percentage of the taxpayer's business taking place in Texas."[62] Although the Court has not always insisted that an excise tax imposed on a nominally local event be measured only by values reflecting the intrastate activities of the taxpayer, its recent remarks suggest that it intends to police this requirement with some care in the context of state taxation of natural resources.

Special excises other than severance taxes imposed on natural resources may raise issues of discrimination against interstate commerce. We need look no further than the Court's 1980-1981 term to find a classic illustration of such a tax. In *Maryland* v. *Louisiana,* the Court considered a challenge to Louisiana's tax on the "first use" within Louisiana of any natural gas that was not subject to a severance or production tax imposed by Louisiana or any other state.[63] The broad definition of a taxable *use* contained in the statute was all-encompassing and was clearly intended to embrace any palpable connection that natural gas conceivably could have with Louisiana. At the same time, the exclusion of gas already subject to state severance or production taxes from the scope of the first-use tax exempted virtually all gas produced in other states inasmuch as every state in the country with significant natural-gas production imposes severance or production taxes on such gas. The actual incidence of the first-use tax was therefore confined to natural gas that was produced on the Outer Continental Shelf (OCS), where no state has tax jurisdiction, if such gas was subsequently "used" in Louisiana.

The limited practical impact of the first-use tax was no accident of statutory draftsmanship. Its sponsors explicitly declared that the target of the exaction was OCS gas extracted outside Louisiana's territorial limits but subsequently brought within them. In their view, such gas was not bearing its fair share of Louisiana taxes because gas produced in Louisiana was subject to the state severance tax, which gas produced offshore escaped. Because both types of gas ultimately imposed similar costs on and derived similar benefits from the state, it was thought that both types of gas should bear similar tax burdens. The first-use tax was allegedly designed to achieve this result by imposing on the first use in the state of previously untaxed natural gas a levy equal (7 cents per 1,000 cubic feet) to that imposed by the Louisiana severance tax on natural gas.

Liability for first-use taxes was imposed on the owner of the gas at the time the first taxable use occurred within Louisiana. In most cases, the burden would fall on pipeline companies, since about 85 percent of the OCS gas brought ashore is owned by such companies, who purchase the gas from the producers at the wellhead. Exemption from and credits for first-use-tax liability were provided in a number of instances. First-use taxes could be used as a credit against Louisiana severance taxes on gas and other natural resources. Credits against other Louisiana taxes were likewise provided to municipal or state-regulated electric-generating plants and natural-gas distributing services located within Louisiana, as well as any direct purchaser of gas used for consumption directly by that purchaser, if the fuel costs involved had been increased by the first-use tax. Exemption from first-use-tax liability was provided for imported natural gas used for drilling for oil or gas within the state.

In addressing the commerce-clause challenge to the levy, the Court found it necessary to consider only "the fundamental principle . . . that no State, consistent with the Commerce Clause, may 'impose a tax which discriminates against interstate commerce . . . by providing a direct commercial advantage to local business.'"[64] In the Court's view, "the Louisiana First-Use Tax unquestionably discriminates against interstate commerce in favor of local interests as the necessary result of various tax credits and exclusions."[65] The Court observed that exemption from first-use-tax liability of gas dedicated to certain instate uses favored local over out-of-state users of such gas. It noted that the severance-tax credit for first-use taxes favored those who both own OCS gas and engage in Louisiana production. "The obvious economic effect of this Severance Tax Credit is to encourage natural gas owners involved in the production of OCS gas to invest in mineral exploration and development within Louisiana rather than to invest in further OCS development or in production in other States."[66] The Court further pointed out that the credits for electric utilities, gas distributors, and direct purchasers against Louisiana taxes for increased costs attributable to first-use taxes substantially protects local consumers from the impact of the first-use tax, but out-of-state consumers receive no comparable protection.

Although the special master to whom the case had been assigned was not oblivious to the argument that the first-use tax favored local over out-of-state interests, he nevertheless denied the plaintiffs' motion for judgment on the pleadings on the ground that further evidentiary hearings might demonstrate that the levy was "a proper 'compensating' tax intended to complement the state severance tax as the use tax complemented the sales tax in *Henneford* v. *Silas Mason Co.*"[67] The Court found the analogy unpersuasive. "The common thread running through the cases upholding compensatory taxes," declared the Court, "is the equality of treatment between local and interstate commerce."[68] Thus the use tax was upheld over commerce-clause objections in *Silas Mason* because, when considered in conjunction with the sales tax, "the stranger from afar is subject to no greater burdens as a consequence of ownership than the dweller within the gates."[69] But, as the Court had already demonstrated, the pattern of credits and exemptions in the first-use tax effectively destroyed the equality the levy was purportedly designed to establish between gas extracted offshore and gas extracted in Louisiana. The scheme of exemptions and credits created a favored category of OCS gas—namely, gas owned by producers with Louisiana severance-tax liability or gas consumed in the state. Although the statute may have created equality in some instances between OCS gas and Louisiana gas dedicated to the interstate market, this was not enough to save the tax. As the Court concluded: "We need not know how unequal the Tax is before concluding that it unconstitutionally discriminates. . . . [T]he

First-Use Tax is unconstitutional under the Commerce Clause because it unfairly discriminates against purchasers of gas moving through Louisiana in interstate commerce.''[70]

An instructive contrast may be drawn between the Court's decision in *Maryland* v. *Louisiana* and its decision in *Commonwealth Edison Co.* v. *Montana. Maryland* suggests that the Court will continue to scrutinize with great care claims that a state tax on natural resources discriminates against interstate commerce and that the Court's decision in *Commonwealth Edison* should not be interpreted as a relaxation of its traditional vigilance in this domain. *Commonwealth Edison* suggests, however, that the concept of discrimination is not so unlimited as to embrace any alleged differential impact that a tax may have within and without the state and that only when it is asserted that a tax favors or provides a competitive advantage to instate over out-of-state interests will the Court treat it as an issue of discrimination.

As indicated, the meaning of the Court's fairly related test was somewhat of a mystery before the Court in *Commonwealth Edison* finally settled on its content. The Court summarized its holding on this issue by observing "when the measure of a tax bears no relationship to the taxpayers [*sic*] presence or activities in a State, a court may properly conclude under the fourth prong of the *Complete Auto Transit* test that the State is imposing an undue burden on interstate commerce.''[71] Although we do not yet have any decisions other than *Commonwealth Edison* that have applied this criterion, it is worth noting that the Court cited *Michigan Wisconsin Pipe Line Co.* v. *Calvert* as an example of a case that might violate the standard. In that case, it will be recalled, the subject of the tax was the "gathering of gas," and the measure was the entire volume of gas shipped in interstate commerce. How the measure might be adjusted to satisfy the Court is not intimated nor is the distinction, if any, between the fairly related test and the fair-apportionment criterion in this context suggested. Indeed, the *Calvert* case in recent years seems to have been employed by the Court as a whipping boy for all the evils that a tax is capable of perpetrating under the commerce clause.

The Louisiana first-use tax may be another example of a tax on natural resources that would fail to meet the Court's fairly related standard. Although the Court did not reach the issue in condemning the levy, it observed in passing that "the Tax is imposed on each use as a function of the volume of the gas subject to the use, without attempting to tailor the amount of the Tax depending on the nature or extent of the actual use of the gas within Louisiana.''[72] Although future decisions of the Court will fully elucidate the meaning of the fairly related test, it would appear that the Court will scrutinize the relationship between the subject and the measure of a tax somewhat more closely than it has in the past, even though it will not undertake any inquiry into the quantitative relationship between the amount of a tax and the value of benefits bestowed on the taxpayer by the state.

Due-Process, Equal-Protection, and Privileges-and-Immunities Clauses.
There appear to be no discrete problems associated with due-process, equal-protection, or privileges-and-immunities limitations on special excises on natural resources that warrant extended comment. A special excise on natural resources might under some circumstances be held confiscatory, in which case the due-process clause would, of course, bar the levy. There do not appear to be any equal-protection problems peculiar to special excises, and the criteria discussed earlier would apply to such levies. Finally, the privileges-and-immunities clause would bar any special excise discriminating against nonresident taxpayers in favor of resident taxpayers. Such a levy would in all likelihood be vulnerable to attack under the commerce clause as well, if not under the equal-protection clause.

Property Taxes. The *ad-valorem* property tax may be considered a significant state tax on natural resources, although it is predominantly administered at the local level and provides the primary source of local-government tax revenues. The property tax, to be sure, is not directed exclusively at natural resources. Indeed, natural-resource properties are, in principle, no different from other property subject to *ad-valorem* taxation. Depending on a state's procedures, a state or local assessor examines the resource and places a value on it for tax purposes. The local millage rate is then applied to the assessed value to determine the appropriate tax. In practice, however, natural resources are frequently classified or valued differently from other properties for *ad-valorem* tax purposes, and this separate treatment justifies inclusion of the *ad-valorem* property tax in the scope of this inquiry.

Although the *ad-valorem* property tax is the principal means of taxing natural resources in some states, its use and importance have gradually declined, largely because of administrative problems associated with fair and accurate assessment of the natural-resource properties by local assessors who are ill-equipped to deal with the complex valuation issues involved. I have been unable to locate data breaking down the source of local property-tax revenue so that a comparison of the revenue generated by local *ad-valorem* and state severance taxes on natural resources could be made. Severance taxes appear, however, to be the more important source of revenue Indeed, a number of states that have adopted severance taxes have provided that such taxes are imposed in lieu of all other *ad-valorem* taxes that might otherwise have been imposed on the resource in question. (In such cases, provision is ordinarily made to distribute some of the severance-tax revenue to the localities whose *ad-valorem* tax bases have been thus limited.) In other states, however, severance and property taxes on natural resources coexist.

Although the economic implications of imposing an *ad-valorem* property tax versus a severance tax on natural resources may be quite different, the constitutional attacks that could be leveled against the two types of levies are virtually indistinguishable and, in light of *Commonwealth Edison,* equally unavailing. Indeed, the Supreme Court observed in *Commonwealth Edison* that "[i]n many respects, a severance tax is like a real property tax."[73] In short, property taxes on natural resources seem no more vulnerable to constitutional challenge than severance taxes.

Income Taxes. Income taxes have been identified (along with severance and property taxes) as one of three tax instruments available to states wishing to generate revenue from natural resources. For reasons set forth previously, taxes imposed on income derived from natural-resource exploitation as part of a general scheme taxing income from all economic activity lie outside the scope of this chapter. There is, however, one recent—some would say flagrant—example of special treatment of a natural-resource industry for state-income-tax purposes that is peculiar to state taxation and merits some consideration.

Prior to 1978, Alaska taxed the income of oil and gas corporations in the same way that it taxed the income of most other corporations doing business in the state. Employing a federally based definition of taxable income, Alaska apportioned a share of such income to the state by means of the three-factor formula of property, payroll, and sales typically used by the states in apportioning corporate income.[74] In 1978, however, Alaska enacted the Oil and Gas Corporate Income Tax.[75] The statute established a special regime for taxing the income of oil and gas companies that, among other things, required such companies to determine their Alaska income by separate accounting rather than by formulary apportionment. The statute also denied them deductions available to other corporate taxpayers. The result was to attribute to Alaska substantially more income than had been attributed to the state by the prior statute. Under the shadow of litigation challenging the constitutionality of the Oil and Gas Corporate Income Tax, Alaska has quite recently further modified its corporate-income tax by providing, among other things, for apportionment of the income of oil and gas companies under special rules applicable only to such companies and for a graduated tax rate on corporate income.[76]

The constitutional issues raised by the various configurations of Alaska's attempts to tax the income of the oil and gas industry are too numerous and complex to cover in this chapter. We will, however, take a brief look at some of the critical issues the courts will have to confront in resolving the controversy over the constitutionality of the Alaska taxing scheme.

There are two principal commerce-clause issues raised by the Alaska legislation: whether it meets the Court's fair-apportionment criterion and whether it discriminates against interstate commerce. Disposition of the first issue depends on how one reads the Court's recent decisions dealing with state income apportionment, decisions that are susceptible to more than one reading on the central questions raised by the Alaska legislation. One might argue that the Court's preference for formulary apportionment over separate accounting reflected in its recent opinions amounts to a constitutional mandate to the states to apportion rather than to separately account for the income of a unitary enterprise conducted in part within the state. Even if such an argument would lack force as an abstract proposition, the claim might become more compelling in the face of other states' statutes apportioning the income of such enterprises, which would create the risk or, indeed, the actuality of multiple tax burdens when considered in conjunction with a separate-accounting approach. Although the subsequent version of the Alaska statute with its special apportionment provisions for oil and gas income might satisfy the Court's penchant for apportionment over separate accounting, it could well suffer from the same constitutional infirmities as a separate-accounting approach if the Court were to focus on the possibility of multiple taxation rather than on the methodology employed by the state to avoid it.

Despite these sorts of objections, it must be kept in mind that the Court has consistently emphasized the leeway the states possess in their choice and implementation of division-of-income methods. When forced to choose between two methods—because the methods, taken together, necessarily exposed a taxpayer's income to duplicative taxation—it is true that the Court expressed a preference for apportionment. But separate accounting and formulary apportionment will not necessarily lead to taxation of more than 100 percent of a taxpayer's tax base. Both methods recognize that more than one state may legitimately tax a share of a multistate enterprise's income, although they employ different techniques for determining that share. The Court's unwillingness to constitutionalize state division-of-income rules and its apparent tolerance for some overlap in the taxation of income resulting from the states' choices of different approaches in this area suggest that the vulnerability of Alaska's taxing scheme to constitutional attack on fair-apportionment grounds is hardly a foregone conclusion.

As to the claim that Alaska's taxing scheme discriminates against interstate commerce, *Commonwealth Edison* would appear to have substantially undermined such a contention. Alaska may have singled out for special treatment an industry whose tax burden is borne largely out of state (either by nonresident consumers or by nonresident shareholders), but such an argument carries little weight after the Montana severance-tax case. Furthermore, there is nothing in the Alaska taxing statute that appears to favor local over out-of-state interests. In short, although Alaska's corporate-income tax may discriminate against the oil and gas industry, the discrimination is not of the kind that the Court has been willing to characterize as discrimination against interstate commerce under the commerce clause.

This brings us finally to the claim that, even if not discriminatory under the commerce clause, Alaska's oil and gas tax should be stricken as an invalid classification under the equal-protection clause. Here, of course, the taxpayers run into the broad latitude the Court has permitted the states in classifying for tax purposes. That the oil and gas industry is not permitted to apportion its income as other industries are, that it is denied certain deductions allowed to others, or that it is peculiarly subject to the highest bracket of a progressive rate schedule would not seem to raise serious equal-protection problems. Nevertheless, we should not be too quick to conclude that these equal-protection allegations lack substance. Taken jointly rather than severally, considered against the history of Alaska's efforts to tailor its apportionment provisions to its own interests, viewed in light of the fact—noted by Justice Blackmun dissenting in *Commonwealth Edison*—that "[n]inety percent of Alaska's revenue derives from petroleum taxes and royalties,"[77] Alaska's corporate-income tax on the oil and gas industry might well violate the norms of fiscal balance that were troubling some of the justices in *Commonwealth Edison* and lead the Court to invalidate the tax.

Federal Preemption of State Taxes on Natural Resources

General Principles of Preemption Analysis

Aside from the broad constitutional principles considered in this chapter's first section, the states are restrained in their power to tax natural resources by any federal legislation that limits such power.[78] The rub, of course, is to determine whether a particular tax is preempted by a particular federal statute or group of statutes. As anyone familiar with the cases and commentary on federal preemption of state law well knows, general principles of adjudication are of little aid in determining the outcome of a specific preemption controversy. The Court itself has frequently made this point:

> There is not—and from the very nature of the problem there cannot be—any rigid formula or rule which can be used as a universal pattern to determine the meaning and purpose of every act of Congress. This Court, in considering the validity of state laws in the light of treaties or federal laws touching the same subject, has made use of the following expressions: conflicting; contrary to; occupying the field; repugnance; difference, ir-

reconcilability; inconsistency; violation, curtailment; and interference. But none of these expressions provides an infallible constitutional test or an exclusive constitutional yardstick. In the final analysis, there can be no one crystal clear distinctly marked formula. Our primary function is to determine whether, under the circumstances of th[e] particular case, [the state's] law stands as an obstacle to the accomplishment and execution of the full purposes and objectives of Congress.[79]

The peculiarly ad-hoc quality of adjudication in the preemption field stems from the fact that every preemption case involves the consideration of at least two statutory schemes whose relationship must be evaluated against the broad decision-making criteria quoted. Indeed, the challenge to Montana's coal severance tax on preemption grounds was predicated on no less than ten federal enactments; the claim that Louisiana's first-use tax was preempted by federal legislation was rooted in four statutory schemes. The question here, then, is what type of state taxing measure is susceptible to a claim of federal preemption?

Preemption and State Taxation of Natural Resources

General Considerations. The Supreme Court has rarely found a state tax preempted by federal legislation except in cases involving the federal government's own tax liability or that of its special wards, the Indian tribes. The relative infrequency with which state taxes, as distinguished from state regulations, directed at the private sector are found to conflict with federal legislation stems from several factors that have a significant bearing on federal preemption of state taxes. First, the states' power of taxation has always been regarded as essential to their independent existence and thus to the federal scheme created by the framers of the constitution. State tax power may not be unique in this regard, but it nevertheless constitutes a discrete aspect of state authority that has consistently been viewed as an indispensable attribute of state sovereignty. Second, the exercise of state tax power has traditionally been regarded as compatible with the exercise of federal power. A state tax statute may, of course, be incompatible with a federal regulatory scheme. Nevertheless, the strong tradition of concurrent federal and state taxation is not a characteristic shared by many other forms of state legislation.

A third distinguishing feature of state tax legislation is that its effect in the ordinary case is simply to impose an increased cost on the person, property, or activity subject to taxation. In this respect, it is different from other forms of state legislation that prescribe specific rules of conduct for engaging in particular activities. One might argue, however, that the suggested distinction is specious because the ultimate effects of both types of legislation are the same, namely, to impose increased costs on engaging in the activity in question. Even conceding the point insofar as costs are concerned, the distinction between a state tax and a state regulation is significant for purposes of preemption analysis. A state tax, in contrast to a state regulation, prescribes no mode of conduct in an area in which Congress has adopted rules of its own. Hence, the impact of a state tax on whatever substantive policies are embodied in these federal rules is likely to be more attenuated than the impact of a state regulation prescribing rules regarding the same subject matter.

Specific Applications. In *Commonwealth Edison,* the Court rejected the taxpayers' claims that the various federal statutes on which they relied preempted Montana's coal severance tax. The gravamen of the taxpayers' preemption claim was that Montana's 30-percent tax on coal substantially frustrated national energy policy as reflected in a welter of federal statutes that were allegedly intended to foster the use and production of coal and, particularly, low-sulphur coal like that found in Montana. Although the Court agreed with the taxpayers that many federal enactments did indeed encourage the use of coal, the Court refused to accept the taxpayers' "implicit suggestion that these general statements demonstrate a congressional intent to pre-empt all state legislation that may have an adverse impact on the use of coal."[80] Despite frequent statements in other cases suggesting that a state law was preempted because it conflicted with a general policy embodied in a federal statute, the Court in *Commonwealth Edison* declared that "[i]n cases such as this, it is necessary to look beyond general expressions of 'national policy' to specific federal statutes with which the state law is claimed to conflict."[81]

In *Maryland* v. *Louisiana,* the Court struck down Louisiana's first-use tax in part on the ground that it was preempted by federal legislation. In addition to the provisions of the tax described previously, the Louisiana Legislature had sought to ensure that imposition of the levy's economic burden fell on the owners of the natural gas, or their customers, by stipulating that the "tax shall be deemed a cost associated with uses made by the owner in preparation of marketing of the natural gas."[82] The statute further provided that "any agreement or contract by which an owner . . . claims a right to reimbursement or refund of such taxes from any other party in interest other than a purchaser of such natural gas is . . . declared to be against public policy."[83] In substance, these provisions forbade the statutory owners of natural gas, who were generally the pipeline companies, from passing back the burden of the first-use tax to producers and compelled the pipelines either to absorb the burden of the tax themselves or to pass it on to their customers, who would ordinarily be out-of-state consumers.

In addressing the claim that these provisions of the first-use tax were preempted by the Natural Gas Act, the Court identified the purpose of the Natural Gas Act as being "to assure that consumers of natural gas receive a fair price and also to protect against the economic power of the interstate pipelines."[84] In accord with this purpose, "the Gas Act was intended to provide the FPC, now the FERC, with authority to regulate the wholesale pricing of natural gas in the flow of interstate commerce from wellhead to delivery to consumers."[85] As noted, however, several provisions of the first-use tax attempted to limit the ability of the pipelines to shift the burden of the tax back to the producers. The Court therefore concluded:

> The effect of [these provisions] is to interfere with the FERC's authority to regulate the determination of the proper allocation of costs associated with the sale of natural gas to consumers. . . . By specifying that the First-Use Tax is a processing cost to be either borne by the pipeline or other owner without compensation, an unlikely event in light of the large sums involved, or passed on to purchasers, Louisiana has attempted a substantial usurpation of the authority of the FERC by dictating to the pipelines the allocation of processing costs for the interstate shipment of natural gas.[86]

Once again, an instructive contrast may be drawn between *Commonwealth Edison* and *Maryland* v. *Louisiana*. In *Commonwealth Edison* the Court refused to hold that a tax was preempted merely because it imposed an increased cost on activity favored by federal legislation. The Court's decision was no doubt motivated in part by the general consideration that every tax, after all, imposes increased costs on the person, property, or activity subject to the levy. Elementary economics teaches that such a cost will ordinarily reduce the demand for the goods or services taxed. To the extent that federal legislation reflects policies designed to encourage the production of specified goods and services or the participation in certain activities that a state seeks to tax, the tax tends to frustrate federal policy. Yet to allow such frustration to be a predicate for preemption of state tax legislation runs counter to traditional views regarding the appropriate place of state taxation in the federal system. There can be little quarrel with the abstract proposition that the states in pursuit of their fiscal objectives should not be permitted to frustrate federal policies, but that frustration must ordinarily amount to more than a higher price tag on federally encouraged activities before a conflict between state and federal legislation will be found.

Maryland v. *Louisiana,* on the other hand, raised preemption issues quite distinct from the objection that a state tax imposed an additional cost on a federally favored activity. The first-use tax was not merely a revenue-raising measure, it was also a price-control scheme. By attempting to ensure that only the pipeline companies or their out-of-state customers bear the burden of the tax and that producers and Louisiana consumers escape its impact, the state was indeed prescribing a "mode of conduct in an area in which Congress ha[d] adopted rules of its own." The Court therefore was uninhibited in *Maryland* v. *Louisiana* by the considerations that would ordinarily constrain it from holding a state tax preempted by federal legislation, because the tax in effect was a substantive regulation.

The suggested distinction for purposes of federal-preemption analysis between a true tax and a tax masquerading as (or having characteristics of) a regulation finds support in two recent cases in the lower federal courts involving state taxation of the oil industry. In 1980, New York and Connecticut each imposed a tax on oil companies at the rate of 2 percent of their gross receipts derived from or allocated to the state.[87] Each taxing scheme contained an anti-pass-through provision forbidding or limiting the right of the companies to pass the burden of the tax on to consumers in the state. In each case, the oil companies conceded that the taxes themselves were valid and indicated their willingness to pay them when due. They challenged the anti-pass-through provisions, however, on the ground that they were preempted by federal legislation.

In each case, a federal district court sustained the oil companies' claims.[88] After lengthy analyses of the elaborate federal schemes involved, the courts concluded that the anti-pass-through provisions conflicted with federal legislation relating to the pricing of petroleum products. In the New York case, which involved products that were both subject to and exempt from federal price control, the court found that the efforts of New York to insulate its citizens from the impact of a local tax frustrated federal price-control policy to ensure equitable prices among all regions and to allow local taxes to be passed through to customers in the taxing jurisdiction. The court in the New York case also agreed with the conclusion of the court in the Connecticut case, which involved only products that were exempt from price control, that the anti-pass-through provision frustrated federal energy policy:

> Because it subjects to price regulation petroleum products that federal authorities have decided should be free of price regulation, the [Connecticut statute] "stands as an obstacle to the accomplishment and execution of the full purposes and objectives of Congress" in enacting the [Emergency Petroleum Allocation Act].[89]

Whether the courts' ultimate conclusions in these cases are sound is not important for present purposes. The critical point is that the courts treated the issue as a typical preemption controversy. The considerations that usually justify special deference to the exercise of state tax power were inapposite because the states in these cases were seeking to accomplish traditional regulatory objectives—to wit, price control—through their taxing schemes.

The court of appeals reviewing these cases disposed of them on jurisdictional grounds without reaching the merits. Its decisions nevertheless reinforce the distinction between the state's exercise of its taxing power and its regulatory power. In holding that the actions in question were not barred by the statute preventing federal courts from enjoining state taxes,[90] the court observed that the New York anti-pass-through provision is "not an exercise of a taxing power but a police power affecting the price structure of petroleum products"[91] and that the Connecticut anti-pass-through provision is a "price control system even more complex than the New York provision."[92]

The Role of Congress in Limiting State Taxation of Natural Resources

Congress has seldom limited state tax power. Recently, however, there has been a flurry of legislative activity over proposed federal limitations on state taxation, much of which has focused on state severance taxes. Legislation has been proposed imposing a percentage limitation (12.5 percent) on the rate at which severance taxes could be levied on specified resources. These proposals raise the question of the appropriate role of Congress in dealing with the issues raised by state taxation of natural resources.

There is—or at least there should be—no dispute over the power of Congress to act in this area. Whatever doubts might once have existed have been removed by the Court's recent decisions affirming the broad power of Congress to act under the commerce clause and inviting Congress to mediate the controversy over state severance taxes if "such taxes are thought to be contrary to federal interests."[93] The real questions with respect to Congress's role in this area have to do with the wisdom of its intervening and the precise form its intervention should take if it decides to act.

It is not my task here to evaluate the merits of these questions. There are already volumes of congressional testimony devoted to them, and we have only begun to address the complex and sensitive issues involved. I would, however, like to suggest some general considerations that should inform the congressional determination of whether and how to make law in this area.

First, just as the Court's decision sustaining Montana's severance tax should not be taken as an endorsement of the tax as a matter of sound national policy, neither should the existence of congressional power to limit such taxes be taken as a mandate for Congress to act in this area. As Chief Justice Marshall recognized, the states' "power of taxation is indispensable to their existence," and any efforts to limit this power should be treated as a matter of the greatest delicacy.[94]

Second, if Congress does decide to legislate with respect to state severance taxes, it should do so in an even-handed manner. If consumers are in fact bearing the burden of state severance taxes, an issue that is hardly free from doubt, and if Congress is concerned about this burden, then Congress should forge a solution that is responsive to the general problem. Although the Constitution may not limit Congress's power to single out coal, for example, as the focus of a rate limitation, if Congress is concerned about the burden of energy taxes on energy consumers, it would be hard as a matter of interstate equity to ignore severance taxes on oil or gas, which may impose equivalent cost burdens on the consumers of such energy. Moreover, if Congress is concerned generally about state tax exportation, then perhaps Congress should focus on a wide variety of levies (such as Nevada's taxes on gambling or New York's tax on stock transfers) before settling on an appropriate legislative solution to the problem.

Finally, if Congress wants to limit the power of the states to exploit their resource position through taxation of natural resources by imposing a restraint on severance taxes, it is not at all clear that Congress will have accomplished its purpose. From the preceding discussion it is apparent that state tax structures have diverse and protean characteristics which may be resistant to congressional efforts at controlling them. As noted, several states already tax natural resources largely through the real property tax, a number that would no doubt increase if Congress were to limit state severance taxes. Other states tax natural resources through general business and occupation taxes, which provide the states with another alternative for escaping the impact of a severance-tax limitation. Indeed, even a corporate-income tax may be made to serve as a special levy on the natural-resource industry. In short, if Congress is serious about restraining the power of the states to tax natural resources, it has a much more thorny problem on its hands than merely determining the rate at which the states should be permitted to impose severance taxes.

Conclusion

The legal constraints on state taxation of natural resources in the American federal system are not substantial. Except for a few narrowly defined limitations, the states may generally tax natural resources without fear of constitutional restraint. There is, moreover, no federal legislation explicitly limiting state power to tax natural resources, and courts will not interpret broad national policies embodied in federal legislation as circumscribing the scope of state tax power. Although Congress may see fit in the future to limit the states' power to tax natural resources, the states are largely free, for the moment at least, to go their own way in this domain subject only to the constraints of the marketplace and the collective wisdom of their legislatures.

Notes

1. Hellerstein, *Constitutional Constraints on State and Local Taxation of Energy Resources,* 31 Nat'l. Tax J. 245 (1978) footnotes omitted. Reprinted with permission. In preparing this chapter, I have drawn freely from this work and my earlier work in this area, especially *State Taxation in the Federal System: Perspectives on Louisiana's First Use Tax on Natural Gas,* 55 Tul. L. Rev. 601 (1981); and Testimony of Walter Hellerstein, *The Commerce Clause and Severance Taxes: Hearings Before the Subcomm. on Intergovernmental Relations of the Senate Comm. on Governmental Affairs,* 97th Cong., 1st Sess. (July 15, 1981). See also Hellerstein, *Constitutional Limitations on State Tax Exportation,* 1982 Am. B. Found. Research J., pp. 1-71, which was prepared at the same time as this chapter and which contains a similar discussion of some of the issues addressed here, although with a somewhat different focus. I would also like to disclose that I consulted with the State of Montana in connection with Commonwealth Edison Co. v. Montana, 101 S. Ct. 2946 (1981), which is discussed in detail in the chapter. The views expressed here, of course, are entirely my own and do not necessarily represent those of Montana.

To reduce the length of the original version of this chapter as presented at the TRED Conference, many of the footnotes typically found in scholarly legal writing have been shortened or eliminated. Likewise, much of the background discussion of the case law not bearing directly on state taxation of natural resources has been cut. Copies of the original version of the chapter are available from the author.

2. J. Nowak, R. Rotunda, & J. Young, Handbook on Constitutional Law (Supp. 1981); L. Tribe, American Constitutional Law (Supp. 1982).

3. Commonwealth Edison Co. v. Montana, 101 S. Ct. 2946 (1981); Maryland v. Louisiana, 101 S. Ct. 2114 (1981).

4. Letter from Charles E. McLure, Jr., to Walter Hellerstein, 20 March 1981.

5. Statement of Shirley Kallek, associate director for Economic Fields, Bureau of the Census, U.S. Department of Commerce, *The Commerce Clause and Severance Taxes: Hearings before the Subcomm. on Intergovernmental Relations of the Senate Comm. on Governmental Operations,* 97th Cong., 1st Sess. 1-2 (1981).

6. 101 S. Ct. 2946 (1981).

7. U.S. Const. art. I, sec. 8, cl. 3.

8. F. Frankfurter, The Commerce Clause under Marshall, Taney, and Waite 18 (Quadrangle Paperback ed. 1964).

9. 260 U.S. 245 (1922).

10. 1921 Pa. Laws 479.

11. 260 U.S. at 251-53.

12. *Id.* at 259-60.

13. 260 U.S. at 259-60.

14. *Id.* at 261.

15. 262 U.S. 172 (1923).

16. 274 U.S. 284 (1927).

17. Mont. Code Ann. sec. 15-35-101 *et seq.* (1979). The tax is imposed "on each ton of coal produced in the state." *Id.* sec. 15-35-103. It is measured by the value or "contract sales price" of the coal, which means "the price of coal extracted and prepared for shipment F.O.B. mine, excluding the amount charged by the seller to pay taxes paid on production." *Id.* sec. 15-35-102(1). The rate of the tax varies from 3 to 30 percent depending on the value and energy content of the coal and the method of extraction. *Id.* sec. 15-35-103. Substantially all the coal involved in the case was alleged to be subject to the 30-percent rate. In fact, however, the effective rate of the tax is lower than the statutory rate because taxes paid on production to federal, state, and local governments are excluded in computing the value of the coal to which the severance tax applies. Taxes on production would include not only the severance tax but also such levies as the State Resource Indemnity Trust Fund Tax, the local *ad-valorem* property tax, the Federal Abandoned Mine Reclamation Fee, and the Federal Black Lung Tax. See *id.* sec. 15-35-102(6). Hence a nominal rate of 30 percent would amount to an effective rate closer to 20 percent.

18. Complaint of Commonwealth Edison Co., et al., para. 21, Commonwealth Edison Co. v. Montana, No. 42657 (Dist. Ct. of Lewis and Clark Cty., 1st Jud. Dist. of Montana, June 20, 1978).

19. *Id.,* para 22.

20. *Id.,* para 18.

21. *Id.,* para 26.

22. *Id.,* para 27.

23. *Id.,* para 28.

24. No. 42657 (Dist. Ct. of Lewis and Clark Cty., 1st Jud. Dist. of Montana, July 27, 1979).

25. 615 P.2d 847 (1980).

26. 101 S. Ct. 2946 (1981).

27. 260 U.S. at 259.

28. Mobil Oil Corp. v. Commissioner of Taxes, 445 U.S. 425, 443 (1980), quoted in Commonwealth Edison Co. v. Montana, 101 S. Ct. 2946, 2953 (1981).

29. 101 S. Ct. at 2953.

30. *Id.,* quoting Commonwealth Edison Co. v. Montana, 615 P.2d 847, 855 (1980).

31. *Id.,* quoting Commonwealth Edison Co. v. Montana, 615 P.2d 847, 855 (1980).

32. Hellerstein, *Constitutional Constraints on State and Local Taxation of Energy Resources,* 31 Nat'l Tax J. 245, 249 (1978). Reprinted with permission.

33. 101 S. Ct. at 2954.

34. *Id.*

35. *Id.* at 2955.

36. *Id.*

37. *Id.* at 2958.

38. *Id.* at 2958-59.

39. *Id.* at 2956, quoting Commonwealth Edison Co. v. Montana, 615 P.2d 847, 856 (1980).

40. *Id.* at 2956-57, quoting Carmichael v. Southern Coal & Coke Co., 301 U.S. 495, 521-22 (1937).

41. *Id.* at 2957.

42. *Id.* at 2958 (emphasis in original).

43. *Id.* at 2959.

44. *Id.*

45. Northwestern States Portland Cement Co. v. Minnesota, 358 U.S. 450, 476 (1959) (Frankfurter, J., dissenting).

46. Special Subcomm. on State Taxation of Interstate Commerce of the House Comm. on the Judiciary, State Taxation of Interstate Commerce, H.R. Rep. No. 1480, 88th Cong., 2d Sess. 13 (1964).

47. 101 S. Ct. at 2959.

48. U.S. Const. amend. XIV, sec. 1 ("nor shall any State deprive any person of life, liberty, or property without due process of law").

49. Brief for Appellants at 24, Commonwealth Edison Co. v. Montana, 101 S. Ct. 2946 (1981).

50. 101 S. Ct. at 2959, n. 17, quoting Magnano Co. v. Hamilton, 292 U.S. 40, 44 (1934); *see also* City of Pittsburgh v. Alco Parking Corp., 417 U.S. 369 (1974).

51. U.S. Const. amend. XIV, sec. 1 ("nor [shall any State] deny to any person within its jurisdiction the equal protection of the laws").

52. 260 U.S. 245 (1922).

53. 262 U.S. 172 (1923).

54. *Id.* at 179.

55. 274 U.S. 284 (1927).

56. *Id.* at 289.

57. U.S. Const. art IV, sec. 2. The Fourteenth Amendment to the Constitution also contains a privileges-and-immunities Clause, which provides that "[n]o State shall make or enforce any law which shall abridge the privileges or immunities of citizens of the United States." Five years after the amendment was adopted, however, the Supreme Court held that this provision created no new rights of national citizenship, but merely furnished an additional guarantee of rights which citizens of the United States already possessed. The Slaughter House Cases, 83 U.S. (16 Wall.) 36 (1873). It therefore has no independent significance as a limitation as state tax

powers. *See* Madden v. Kentucky, 309 U.S. 83 (1940) *overruling* Colgate v. Harvey, 296 U.S. 404 (1935).

58. W. Va. Code sec. 11-13-2 (1981 Supp.).

59. Department of Revenue v. Association of Washington Stevedoring Cos., 435 U.S. 734, 746-47 (1978).

60. 347 U.S. 157 (1954).

61. *Id.* at 166-70.

62. Department of Revenue v. Association of Washington Stevedoring Cos., 435 U.S. 734, 749 n. 18 (1978).

63. 101 S. Ct. 2114 (1981).

64. 101 S. Ct. at 2133, quoting Northwestern States Portland Cement Co. v. Minnesota, 358 U.S. 450, 458 (1959).

65. *Id.* at 2134.

66. *Id.*

67. 101 S. Ct. at 2135.

68. *Id.*

69. Henneford v. Silas Mason Co., 300 U.S. 577, 584 (1937).

70. 101 S. Ct. at 2136.

71. 101 S. Ct. at 2960.

72. 101 S. Ct. at 2133 n. 27.

73. 101 S. Ct. at 2957.

74. Alaska Stat. secs. 43.19, 43.20.021 (Supp. 1980).

75. *Id.* sec. 43.21.010 *et seq.*

76. Alaska Laws Ch. 116 (S.B. 524), reported in 42 St. Tax Rev. (CCH), pp. 3-7 (Aug. 3, 1981).

77. 101 S. Ct. at 2968 n. 11.

78. "This Constitution, and the Laws of the United States which shall be made in Pursuance thereof . . . shall be the Supreme Law of the Land . . . any thing in the Constitution or Laws of any State to the contrary notwithstanding." U.S. Const. art. VI, cl. 2.

79. Hines v. Davidowitz, 312 U.S. 52, 67 (1941).

80. 101 S. Ct. at 2962.

81. *Id.*

82. La. Rev. Stat. Ann. sec. 47:1303(c) (West. Supp. 1980).

83. *Id.*

84. 101 S. Ct. at 2129.

85. *Id.* at 2130.

86. *Id.*

87. N.Y. Tax Law sec. 182 (McKinney Supp. 1980); Conn. Pub. Act No. 80-71 (1980).

88. Mobil Oil Corp. v. Tully, 499 F. Supp. 888, 892 (N.D.N.Y. 1980), *dismissed in part,* 639 F.2d 912 (2d Cir.), *cert. denied,* 101 S. Ct. 3123

(1981); Mobil Oil Corp. v. Dubno, 492 F. Supp. 1004, 1006 (D. Conn. 1980), *dismissed in part and affirmed in part,* 639 F.2d 919 (2d Cir.) *cert. denied,* 101 S. Ct. 3122 (1981).

89. 492 F. Supp. at 1014; *accord,* 499 F. Supp. at 907.

90. 28 U.S.C. sec. 1341 (1980).

91. Mobil Oil Corp. v. Tully, 639 F.2d 912, 918 (2d Cir.), *cert. denied,* 101 S. Ct. 3123.

92. Mobil Oil Corp. v. Dubno, 639 F.2d 919, 922 (2d Cir.), *cert. denied,* 101 S. Ct. 3122 (1981).

93. 101 S. Ct. at 2959.

94. Gibbons v. Ogden, 22 U.S. (9 Wheat.) 1, 199 (1824).

Comments

Oliver Oldman

Commonwealth Edison Co. v. *Montana* certainly demonstrates how little the underlying commerce-clause questions facing the Supreme Court have changed in the past twenty-five years. My reaction to it could be described by a statement in the 1957 article by Ernest J. Brown.[1] Commenting on state taxation of interstate transportation, Brown wrote, "If the Court is nevertheless prepared to sanction such taxes, the decision would be cast in more reassuring form if . . . it acknowledged that it was consciously giving warrant to the taxing jurisdiction to exploit its geographical position at the cost of consumers and producers outside." Brown identified an "open economy" as the goal of the commerce clause. This case seems to me to move the Court a step away from this, again without acknowledgment that its decision sanctions state exploitation of a strategic position.

Most troubling is the Court's refusal to consider economic data. As Justice Blackmun's dissenting opinion points out, the complexity of the issues does not justify a dismissal of the case, the more so because Congress could by legislation step in to change a result it found unacceptable. Brown wrote, "[T]he Court might the more readily intervene against state legislation under a commerce clause challenge, since it would at most make what it believed a proper allocation of power, tentative and subject to reallocation by Congress."[2] By declining even to hear economic evidence, the Court has left the problem entirely in the hands of Congress—and the evidence of the past quarter-century strongly suggests that no action can be expected from that body. At the very least, if the Court will provide no forum for such a case, it should openly renounce the new realism it proclaimed in its 1977 *Complete Auto Transit* decision and admit that formalism is still the guide.[3] The permissive formalism at work here is a sharp contrast to the formalism expounded by Justice Frankfurter, but it is formalism nonetheless.[4] One need only consider what has become of the fourth prong of the *Complete Auto Transit* tests to realize that.[5]

I do not mean to suggest that a trial on the merits would necessarily have overturned the tax, for I do not know what evidence might have been offered as to, for example, the environmental damage produced by coal mining. A 30-percent tax on coal may well turn out to be comparable in this respect to a 3-percent tax on oil. The point is that some trial should have been permitted. If it proved only that the fourth prong of the *Complete Auto*

These comments would not have been converted from my notes for the oral remarks at the TRED meeting but for the skilled cooperation of my colleague, Joan M. Youngman, with whom I have been jointly teaching in this field this year and who was present at the meeting.

167

Transit tests was impossible to apply, a revision of those tests would be in order. But the fourth prong survives now in words only, rendered almost meaningless by this practical application.

What does a decision like this mean for economic federalism? It certainly contradicts Brown's notion of an open economy—not necessarily a free-trade zone, subject to no taxes, but neither a region within which monopoly advantage permits exploitation of markets and consumers. In the private sector, antitrust laws work toward this goal, but the Court has refused to apply the Sherman Act to "state action or official action directed by a state."[6] Against this background, the *Commonwealth Edison* decision invites a state to export its taxes, recovering far more in revenue from a given enterprise than it contributes by way of costs.[7] The effect of such "centrifugal forces of localism" on a federal system must be detrimental.[8] Perhaps the difficulties thus produced will finally induce congressional action. The history of the past few decades, however, does not provide much cause for anticipation in that regard.

Notes

1. Brown, *The Open Economy: Justice Frankfurter and the Position of the Judiciary*, 67 Yale L. J. 219, 230 (1957).

2. *Id*. at 221.

3. Complete Auto Transit, Inc. v. Brady, 430 U.S. 274 (1977).

4. The resort to formalism in each case being motivated by the "inherent limitations of the judicial process"—only the result being different. See Brown, *supra* note 1, at 221.

5. Will Louisiana now reimpose its first-use tax, merely removing the preference for the small portion (only 2 percent) consumed within the state? Revenues from the tax could easily be used to compensate Louisiana consumers indirectly.

6. Parker v. Brown, 317 U.S. 341, 351 (1943).

7. Surely the fact that 50 percent of the Montana severance-tax revenues were placed in a trust fund suggests an overcompensation. I realize that the facts might prove otherwise, but this just reaffirms the need for an examination of the economic data if the test under the commerce clause is whether the tax is "fairly related to the services provided by the State"—the fourth prong of *Complete Auto Transit*.

8. Brown, *supra* note 1, at 222, quoting Justice Jackson in Duckworth v. Arkansas, 314 U.S. 390, 400 (1941).

5

Tax Exporting and the Commerce Clause

Charles E. McLure, Jr.

The appellants in *Commonwealth Edison Co.* v. *Montana* argued, among other things, that the 30-percent severance tax levied on coal by Montana imposed a burden on interstate trade proscribed by the commerce clause, because much of the tax would be exported to consumers residing outside of Montana. In the majority opinion written by Justice Marshall, the Supreme Court gave short shrift to this argument, noting that

> appellants' assertion that Montana may not "exploit" its "monopoly" position by exporting tax burdens to other states, cannot rest on a claim that there is need to protect the out-of-state consumers of Montana coal from discriminatory tax treatment. As previously noted, there is no real discrimination in this case; the tax burden is borne according to the amount of coal consumed and not according to any distinction between in-state and out-of-state consumers (pp. 2954-2955).

> [N]or do we share appellants' apparent view that the Commerce Clause injects principles of antitrust law into the relations between the States by reference to such imprecise standards as whether one State is "exploiting" its "monopoly" position with respect to a natural resource when the flow of commerce among them is not otherwise impeded. The threshhold questions whether a State enjoys a "monopoly" position and whether the tax burden is shifted out-of-state rather than borne by in-state producers and consumers would require complex factual inquiries about such issues as elasticity of demand for the product and alternate sources of supply. Moreover, under this approach, the constitutionality of a state's tax could well turn on whether the in-state producer is able, through sales contracts or otherwise, to shift the burden of tax forward to its out-of-state customers (n. 8, p. 2955).

It then quoted with approval (also in note 8) the Montana Supreme Court, which had said, "It would be strange indeed if the legality of a tax could be made to depend on the vagaries of the terms of contracts."[1]

Justice Blackmun, joined by justices Powell and Stevens in the dissenting opinion, disagreed with the majority view on both the relevance of tax exporting for determination of constitutionality under the commerce clause

At the time this paper was prepared the author was vice-president of the National Bureau of Economic Research. The opinions expressed here are solely the author's, and not those of the Hoover Institution or the National Bureau of Economic Research. Several comments made at the TRED conference, especially by Martin Zimmerman, have been incorporated in this chapter.

169

and the ability of the court to base such a determination on estimates of tax exporting. Quoting earlier commentators, Blackmun noted,

> "like a toll gate lying athwart a train route, a severance or processing tax conditions access to natural resources." Thus, to the extent that the taxing jurisdiction approaches a monopoly position in the mineral, and consumption is largely outside the State, such taxes are "economically and politically analogous to transportation taxes exploiting geographical position."
>
> [T]he mere fact that the burden of a severance tax is largely shifted forward to out-of-state consumers does not, standing alone, make out a Commerce Clause violation. But the Clause *is* violated when, as appellants allege is the case here, the State effectively selects "a class of out-of-state taxpayers to shoulder a tax burden grossly in excess of any costs imposed directly or indirectly by such taxpayers on the State" (p. 2971).

Blackmun agrees with the majority opinion when he states, "It is true that a trial in this case would require 'complex factual inquiries' into whether economic conditions are such that Montana is in fact able to export the burden of its severance tax." But he concludes by saying, "I do not believe, however, that this threshold inquiry is beyond judicial competence."[2]

This chapter appraises the conflicting contentions found in the majority and dissenting opinions about the feasibility of basing findings of constitutionality under the commerce clause on the results of incidence analysis. The conclusion is, in brief, that the analysis of tax exporting is sufficiently complicated that attempting to base constitutionality on estimates of tax exporting is fraught with danger, especially in times of rapid economic and institutional change. This does not, of course, mean that the Congress should not consider the likely incidence of taxes on natural resources in deciding whether to limit state use of such taxes. Whether the degree of tax exporting would be an appropriate basis for the appraisal of either the constitutionality of state tax provisions or the desirability of congressional limits on state taxes, if the degree of tax exporting could be quantified with ease and certainty, is not addressed here.

In *Commonwealth Edison* the Court was dealing with the narrow issue of whether the Montana severance tax on coal was levied at a rate so high as to burden interstate commerce unconstitutionally. Much of this chapter deals with severance taxes, and many examples are drawn from institutional experience in the coal market. But the question that must be examined here goes well beyond this narrow case. First, severance taxes are only one of many ways in which natural resources can be taxed by producing states.[3] Obvious alternatives that have been widely used for similar purposes are property taxes and corporate-income taxes. Moreover, producing states are not the only ones attempting to play the tax-exporting game. Gross-receipts taxes imposed by consuming states in combination with statutes intended to

prevent the taxes from being passed forward to consumers, if constitutional, might also entail tax exporting, but to nonresident owners of oil
companies. Some in consuming states appear to believe that adoption of the
unitary approach to the taxation of the net income of oil companies would
have the same effect.

Most popular discussion of tax exporting, and all that in the *Commonwealth Edison* case, focuses on exporting to nonresident consumers.
But tax exporting occurs just as surely when rents received by nonresident
owners of resources are reduced by a tax. Again, how this kind of tax exporting should be viewed in adjudication of the constitutionality of state
taxes under the commerce clause is not considered here, but it is well to keep
in mind that determination of a tax burden on rents often implies tax exporting to nonresidents.[4]

Although it is true that all taxes levied on natural resources by producing states bear a general resemblance, there are important differences in
likely outcomes, depending on the particular type of tax (severance, property,
or income tax) as well as the conditions under which it is levied. The latter
result from differences in the degree of geographic concentration, the
mobility of various factors or industry, cartelization by taxing states, international competition or price-umbrella effects, natural substitutability,
government regulation, the prevalance of long-term contracts, the importance of transportation costs and the way in which such costs are determined, unionization, and market structure as well as the more mundane
attributes of long- and short-run elasticities of supply and demand.[5]

It is, of course, very difficult to allow for all these factors simultaneously
in one simple analytical model, especially if the primary exposition of the
model is verbal. The exposition therefore begins with the relatively simple
case of a severance tax levied in a competitive market that is free of non-
fiscal government intervention that would significantly affect the outcome
of the analysis. Market dominance and collusion by producing states play
an important role in this analysis. Various other complications are then considered. Following that, property taxes and corporate-income taxes levied in
producing states are considered briefly. This discussion of taxation of
natural resources by producer states is augmented by brief consideration of
the incidence of taxes that could be used by consumer states to try to tap
rents from natural resources.

Severance Taxes in a Free-Market Setting

Figure 5-1 provides a useful starting point for the analysis of tax exporting.
In it, panel A shows the production situation in state A, the one levying the
tax to be examined. That is, curve S_A is the supply curve of the natural

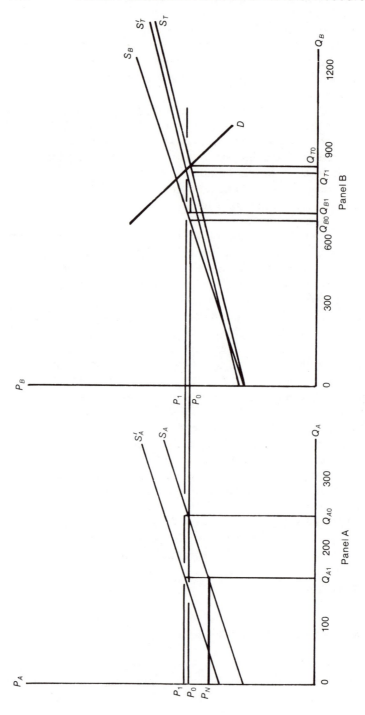

Figure 5-1. Possibility of Tax Exporting by State *A*

resource in question, based on costs prevailing in the state. Panel B shows the analogous information for production in the rest of the country, indicated by curve S_B. For convenience, different horizontal scales (in the ratio of 3 to 1) are used in the two panels. Curve S_T in panel B represents the aggregate-supply curve for the nation as a whole. It is derived by summing horizontally the supply curves for the two individual states, S_A and S_B. The way these curves are drawn implies that state A provides only a relatively small part (approximately one fourth) of the entire national output of the commodity in question.[6] The demand curve for the nation as a whole is indicated in panel B by curve D, and its intersection with S_T determines the equilibrium price, P_0, and national output of the commodity in question, Q_{T0}. Since, by assumption, there are as yet no taxes in the model, this price prevails in both markets, and the output produced in each of the two states (Q_{A0} and Q_{B0}) is indicated by the intersection of the relevant state supply curve with this price line.

Imposition of a severance tax in state A can be illustrated by an upward shift in curve S_A by the amount of the tax, to S_A'.[7] This shift is also reflected in an analogous shift in S_T to S'_T. The new equilibrium price is given by P_1. At this price national output has been reduced somewhat, from Q_{T0} to Q_{T1}. The fall in national output is not greater, given the elasticity of national demand, because the relatively elastic production outside the taxing state rises (from Q_{B0} to Q_{B1}) in response to the higher price and partially offsets the lost output in the taxing state that has been choked off by the tax. This reduction in output resulting from the tax is indicated by the shift in the quantity produced in state A from Q_{A0} to Q_{A1}. Because of the increase in market price, resource rents increase in the state not imposing the tax (by the vertical difference between P_1 and P_0, per unit of output, at least for the quantity produced in the absence of tax). Those in the taxing state fall, per unit of output, by the vertical distance between the price net of severance tax, P_N, and the initial price, P_0.[8]

Tax exporting to nonresident consumers occurs to the extent that the tax induces an increase in the price of the commodity and the good is bought by nonresidents.[9] As is suggested by this diagram, if a state producing only a small fraction of the national output of a given commodity levies a severance tax, there will be little effect on the national price of the commodity and therefore hardly an exporting of the tax to out-of-state consumers, even if virtually all the state's output of the taxed commodity is exported. If, however, the taxing state were the only producer, the analysis of tax incidence would be identical to that for a nationwide tax, and the likelihood that the tax would be reflected in higher prices and exported to consumers would be substantially greater. (Such a case could be examined in figure 5-1 by assuming state B to be the only producer and examining a tax levied there, that is, by ignoring panel A and considering only curves S_T, S'_T, and D in panel B.) Realistic cases that are of interest in the context of the present policy debate are, of course, intermediate between these two. That is, interest is strongest from a policy point of view where there is substantial market dominance by one state or a few states; but rarely is dominance complete.

Figure 5-1 can be employed to examine the incidence of a tax levied by a state with substantial market dominance. One need assume only that the tax that causes the aggregate-supply curve to shift is imposed by state B rather than state A. Clearly, for a given configuration of elasticities of supply and demand and percentage of out-of-state consumption, tax exporting is greater if the tax is imposed by state B than by state A.[10] Indeed, it can be shown (McLure 1981*a*) that the degree to which a severance tax is reflected in higher prices is directly related to the degree of market dominance by the taxing state. In the extreme case in which all supply curves are perfectly elastic and the aggregate-demand curve is totally inelastic—the conditions under which a national severance tax would be shifted forward completely—the percentage of the tax that is reflected in higher prices is exactly equal to the taxing state's share in national output of the commodity. This conclusion will be employed further.[11]

Understanding the role market dominance plays in the analysis of tax exporting makes it easy to appreciate the importance of cartelization by producing states. Suppose that only two states with equal output produce the entire national output of a natural resource but consume very little of it. If only one levies a severance tax on the commodity, ordinarily at most one half of the tax will be reflected in higher prices and possibly exported to nonresident consumers. The remainder will simply reduce resource rents originating in the state. (Note, in addition, that because of the nationwide rise in price, the nontaxing state will also export half the tax, per unit of output sold to nonresidents, levied by the taxing state. Its economic rents, per unit of output, will rise by half of the tax.[12]) If, however, the two states agree to levy identical severance taxes, market dominance by taxing states will be complete, and shifting to consumers, most of whom are presumed to be nonresidents, will be much more nearly complete. In the polar cases of either completely elastic supply or completely inelastic demand, all the tax will be shifted to consumers in this case, and the rents will be unaffected.

Consider now the situation in which one of the producing states imposes a severance tax and then the second imposes an identical tax, acting independently and perhaps after the passage of a substantial amount of time. This might occur, for example, if the resource were discovered in the second state long after it had been discovered, exploited, and taxed in the first. To simplify matters assume that supply is equally elastic in the two states and demand is completely inelastic. If we consider imposition of the two taxes as independent actions, we are forced to conclude that one half of each tax would be shifted forward to consumers, even though the entire tax would be shifted forward if it were imposed simultaneously and, perhaps collusively in both states. These apparently inconsistent results are easily reconciled. Recall that when the tax is imposed in one state the price rises throughout the nation by half the amount of the tax, and per-unit rents fall in the taxing state and rise in the nontaxing state, in both cases by one half the amount of the tax. If the same tax is imposed sequentially in both states the total price rise equals the tax, and effects on rents cancel. But the tax of either state, considered by itself, only raises the price by 50 percent of the tax.[13] (This anomalous result plays an important part in the discussion of table 5-1 and in the discussion of the ability of energy-rich states to thrive under the rent-increasing umbrella of OPEC.)

It takes little imagination to see the relevance of this analysis to concrete situations occurring in the United States. Montana alone accounts for a significant percentage of the nation's output of low-sulfur soft coal, and with Wyoming and North Dakota it produces an even greater percentage of the low-sulfur coal used in the midwestern area defined by the economics of transportation. Moreover, the market share of these three states is projected to grow rapidly. All three states export virtually all their coal, either directly or through electricity generated within the state for transmission to other states. Acting alone, Montana might be able to export a substantial fraction of any severance tax it imposed. But if it were to act in collusion with one or both of its two neighboring states to raise taxes, the degree of exporting would be even greater.[14]

From the discussion of the previous paragraphs it can be seen that important questions of interpretation of facts can arise. Suppose that three states completely dominate the national market for one resource. To simplify the analysis assume that each state supplies one third of the market, that supply in all three states is equally elastic, that aggregate demand is totally inelastic, and that no consumption of the resource in question occurs within any of the three producing states. (The last assumption implies that any tax that is shifted to consumers is also exported.) Suppose now that the three states impose severance taxes of 10 percent, 20 percent, and 30 percent and that consumers of the taxed resource question the constitutionality of one or more of the severance taxes under the commerce clause, on the grounds of tax exporting. Our objective is to attempt to help the Court to determine how much of any tax under challenge is exported in this hypothetical case.

The answer to this question depends on exactly how the factual situation just described is interpreted. First, suppose that only one of the state taxes is under constitutional challenge, but it is asserted that this tax was set with the collusion of the other two producing states.[15] Since the state tax rates are set at different levels, by assumption, collusion must be interpreted as complete at the 10-percent level, as involving only two of the states at the 20-percent level, and as nonexistent at the 30-percent level, at which one of the states is "going it alone." The result of an analysis under these assumptions is given in the top part of the second group of four columns in table 5-1. (The bottom of these columns just repeats information contained in the top and is therefore ignored.) The 10-percent tax can be exported entirely to nonresident consumers, because dominance by colluding states is complete at that level. The same is true of the first 10 percentage points of the 20-percent tax. But only two thirds of the second 10 percentage points of the 20-percent tax can be exported. This raises the interesting question of whether the courts should be concerned with this marginal export rate of 67 percent or with the average export rate of 83 percent. Finally, by analogy to the results for the first two rates, we see that 67 percent of all revenues resulting from the 30-percent tax can be assumed to be exported to nonresidents. But at the margin only 33 percent can be exported.

Collusion between the states is, of course, only one possible analytic scenario. Any state defending the constitutionality of its severance tax against a charge of exporting would naturally deny that it had acted in collusion with its sister states in choosing its tax rate.[16] This denial would probably be especially convincing if all the taxes under examination had not been imposed at their existing rates within a short period of time.[17] Under this description of events, taxes levied in other states would be of no direct analytical relevance—they would be of no more relevance than geologic overburden or the weather, regardless of their levels. Under this independence description of the process of setting tax rates, each state would export one third of its tax, both on average and at the margin, as indicated by the top

Table 5-1
Percentage of Taxes Exported under Alternate Conceptual Experiments

Tax under Challenge (percent)	Independent				In Collusion			
	First 10 Percent	Second 10 Percent	Third 10 Percent	Total	First 10 Percent	Second 10 Percent	Third 10 Percent	Total
10	33			33	100			100
20	33	33		33	100	67		83
30	33	33	33	33	100	67	33	67
10 and	67			67	100			100
20	67	33		50	100	67		83
10 and	67			67	100			100
30	67	33	33	44	100	67	33	67
20 and	67	67		67	100	67		83
30	67	67	33	55	100	67	33	67

Note: Captions indicate whether taxes in other states not under challenge are assumed to be set independently of those under challenge or in collusion. Where two taxes are challenged, it is assumed that they are set in collusion but independently of the tax in the third state.

part of the first four columns in table 5-1. This rate is, of course, well below any of the export rates in the collusion columns of table 5-1, except for the marginal export rate on the last 10 percent of the 30-percent tax. Thus it matters a great deal whether the courts believe severance taxes are set independently or through collusion.

Even the difficulties arising from the ambiguities described thus far are compounded if more than one tax is challenged in a particular suit. Suppose, for example, that both the 10- and 20-percent taxes are challenged under the independence assumption. (That is, it is argued that the 10- and 20- percent rates are set collusively, but independently of the 30-percent rate.) Since these two states account for two thirds of the total output, 67 percent of the first 10 percent of the taxes could be exported. But only 33 percent of the next 10 percent of the 20-percent tax could be exported. Thus we have an export rate for the 10-percent tax (67 percent) that differs from both those previously determined (100 percent under total collusion and 33 percent under total independence). The 33-percent marginal export rate for the 20-percent tax equals the export rate for the 20-percent tax challenged alone under the independence assumption. But both it and the 50-percent average export rate differ substantially from the marginal and average rates under the collusion assumption (67 and 83 percent, respectively). Even worse, contrast this situation with the case in which the 20- and 30-percent tax rates are challenged, under the assumption that they are set collusively, but independently of the 10-percent rate. Here the marginal and average export rates for the 20-percent tax are both 67 percent, a figure found in several other cases, and for the 30-percent tax considered under these circumstances the marginal rate is 33 percent, as is always the case for this tax. But the average export rate of 55 percent is found in no other case, including that in which the 10- and 30-percent rates are challenged simultaneously, under the assumption that they are set independently of the 20-percent rate (where it is 44 percent).

This simple example suggests the difficulty of the "complex factual inquiries" needed to determine whether an unconstitutional degree of tax exporting occurs. In this case the basic economic analysis is relatively straightforward, being severely circumscribed by the simplifying assumptions underlying the example.[18] But the degree of tax exporting one finds depends crucially on (1) which of the three taxes is being examined; (2) whether a given tax is being examined alone or in conjunction with a suit questioning the constitutionality of the tax levied by one or more other states; (3) whether it is assumed that the tax (or taxes) under challenge is set independently or in collusion with one or more other states; and (4) whether one is interested in the average or marginal rate of tax exporting. It is difficult to know whether these questions can generally be answered satisfactorily in judicial proceedings, given that, except for the third, independence versus collusion, none of them has ever been explicitly asked. Certainly, one might want to agree in principle with Justice Blackmun that " 'the complexity of a properly presented federal question is hardly a suitable basis for denying federal courts the power to adjudicate' " (n. 17, p. 2971). But probably one should not be overly sanguine about the outcome of such adjudication, in part because it is so difficult to know when the question is presented properly.

Substitution, Regulation, and Transportation

Discussion to this point has been entirely in terms of "a commodity" or "a natural resource." To focus on the role played by market dominance, we have generally assumed that aggregate national demand for that commodity is totally price inelastic. But aggregate demand for virtually all commodities tends to have at least some price elasticity over some range of price, especially in the long run, if only because of the existence of substitutes of various degrees of perfection. Thus aluminum can be substituted for steel in the production of automobile engines; glass and aluminum are substitutable in the packaging of beer and soft drinks; for some uses electrical wiring can be made of either aluminum or copper; and coal, gas, oil, nuclear power, hydroelectric power, solar energy, and even sweaters and blankets are actual or potential substitutes. Cutting the other way is the fact that coal can be either high or low in sulfur. The two are not perfect substitutes, and the Great Plains states come much closer to complete dominance of the market for the preferable low-sulfur variety. Moreover, the degree of potential substitution changes over time, as new technology evolves, in part in response to shifts in relative prices. This, alone, makes it difficult to make estimates of tax exporting that are immutable as well as accurate when made.

Any state attempting to export taxes on natural resources must recognize these possibilities for substitution between commodities in designing its tax system, as must any court attempting to determine the extent to tax exporting by a given state. Of particular interest in the context of *Commonwealth Edison* is the potential for substitution between coal and various alternate sources of energy, particularly in the generation of electric power. A simple relabeling of figure 5-1 will allow us to examine this situation. Suppose that panel A describes the supply of steam coal and panel B that for oil and gas used in generating electricity, as well as the aggregate supply and demand for fuels used for this purpose. (It would be necessary to rescale the horizontal axes in terms of Btu's and the vertical axis in terms of price per Btu.)

Suppose, now, that the prices of oil and (indirectly) gas are determined outside the model, say through the actions of OPEC. (The role of federal agencies responsible for the regulation of the prices and uses of oil or gas will be considered later.) If coal were sold in spot markets, an increase in

this externally determined price for oil or gas would be reflected in a corresponding increase in the price at which coal could be sold and therefore in
the economic rents received by owners of coal. This increase in rents is
much like that resulting in a nontaxing state when a tax is imposed by one
producing state. Some observers conclude from this induced rise in the price
of coal that a severance tax levied on coal would be shifted forward to consumers. This would, of course, be erroneous, unless one believes that the
higher taxes on coal were enacted in collusion with the members of OPEC.
In a sense, the higher price for the competitive fuel acts like an umbrella
over owners of coal, allowing them to raise their price. But it is the OPEC
umbrella, not the tax on coal, that would cause the price of coal to rise.[19] To
see this, we need only consider what would happen if the tax were imposed
(or raised), in the absence of OPEC action. The analysis presented thus far
indicates that in this situation, where the taxing states do not dominate the
relevant market (in this case the market for fuel for generation of electricity),
the severance tax on coal cannot be exported to nonresident consumers.

Coal has a very high ratio of bulk and weight to value. Thus, transportation costs loom large in the price of coal delivered to electric utilities in
Texas and the Midwest. But the demand for transportation of coal is also
extremely price inelastic, especially in the short run, since coal that cannot
be taken to market has little immediate value. (Of course, coal can be left in
the ground; over the longer run electric-generating plants can be built nearer
the coal mines so that electricity, rather than coal, can be transported.) To
the extent that railroads have monopolies in the transportation of coal and
are not hindered by rate regulation, they can capture some of the increased
rents resulting from higher market prices for coal by raising freight rates.[20]
Indeed, in a situation in which coal is sold in spot markets and aggregate
resource rents are determined by the price umbrella being held by OPEC,
the states and the railroads may compete to capture the available rents.
Which is more successful probably depends on the relative abilities of the
states to collude and play off railroads against one another and of the railroads to whipsaw the states.[21] In any event, if either taxes or freight rates
were raised, rents would be captured by the states or the railroads. Neither
kind of increase in cost could be shifted forward to consumers, since an attempt to raise the delivered price of coal above the umbrella price would
cause conversion to alternative fuels, at least in the long run.[22]

There is, of course, considerable difficulty in pretending that coal is
sold on spot markets. As is well know, the great majority of coal being produced is sold to public utilities under long-term contracts. The price received
for coal under such contracts would generally not be directly affected by the
actions of OPEC. But if the contracts provide for the pass-through of severance taxes, prices would rise by the full amount of any increases in taxes, up
to the level equivalent to the new price for oil and gas.[23] That is, the existence

of such contracts would greatly modify the spot-market result, by providing that the creation of rents through increases in price could occur if, and only if, the rents were taxed away! Under these circumstances it is clearly more natural to think of the increase in severance tax as being borne by the consumer than by the recipient of rents, since in the absence of the tax the rents that are taxed away would not exist.

Government regulatory activities have tended recently to accentuate the ability of coal-producing states to export severance taxes.[24] First, the decontrol of the price of oil would have freed economic forces that would have created the kind of price umbrella described earlier; this would have facilitated tax exporting via price increases sanctioned under long-term contracts. A similar effect might have occurred if natural gas had been decontrolled. In fact, however, regulatory activity has gone even further than merely allowing the umbrella prices of oil and gas to rise to the level set by OPEC. Prohibition of the use of oil and gas in new electric-power plants segments the market for hydrocarbon fuels and makes the umbrella price set by OPEC largely irrelevant.[25] The coal-producing states do, of course, enjoy substantially greater dominance of the market for coal than of the market for all fuels potentially used in generating electricity. The only important remaining potential competition for coal comes from nuclear power, hydroelectric power (especially imported from eastern Canada), and eventually perhaps solar energy. Government regulation of nuclear power, which could even take the form of a moratorium on future installations, further segments the market and reduces the constraining influence of power from this alternative source.

As suggested, freight rates for the shipment of coal resemble taxes. If coal is sold under long-term contract, increases in freight rates are likely to be borne by consumers, until the umbrella price is reached. If the discipline provided by the world price of oil is removed by government regulation or the actions of OPEC, the only limit that would remain on the ability of states and railroads to tax consumers would appear to be joint maximization of the sum of severance taxes and railroad profits. A study by Martin Zimmerman and Christopher Alt (1981) suggests that if Montana and Wyoming were to act collusively, but as the residual supplier of coal, the tax rate that would maximize joint tax revenues, given present freight rates, would be 62.5 percent, or more than double Montana's present rate. This would represent an increase of about $3 per ton over the present tax. Zimmerman and Alt (1981, p. 20) also note that increases in freight rates since 1975 that cannot be explained by various determinants of costs amount to over $2 per ton.

The discussion of this section indicates that in addition to the considerations described in the previous section, it is important to know the extent of potential substitution between various natural resources to predict the degree of tax shifting and exporting. By itself, this may be a tall order, especially for a commodity such as aluminum. Moreover, the existence and nature of long-term contracts can be important. Finally, changes in government regulations can make it either more or less difficult to export a tax, and railroads may vie with states for the economic rents potentially available from natural resources. Considerations such as these add to the "formidable evidentiary difficulties" encountered in estimating the degree to which taxes on natural resources would be exported in a given situation.

Moreover, analytical results might well be capricious or at least transitory. For example, one could easily construct an example in which nothing differed between two situations except the extent to which sales were made under long-term contracts. Should a tax be held constitutional in one case but not in the other? Might a natural evolution of contracts that did not depend on influences of taxes result in a change in the finding of constitutionality? Would private parties really be allowed to rewrite contracts to provide that any new tax would be passed through and therefore be found unconstitutional? What if contracts allowed pass-through for some taxes but not others? It is not unusual for constitutionality of a tax to depend on the exact way in which statutes are written rather than on substance. But should the constitutionality of a tax depend on the degree of tax exporting, if that, in turn, were to depend on possibly subtle differences in the wording, not of the tax statutes, but of private contracts? Should the constitutionality of a severance tax on coal ride on the actions of OPEC or on whether a moratorium on the construction of nuclear-power plants or other government regulation eliminates a potential constraint on the ability to shift taxes forward, especially when regulations such as these may depend on the occurrence of accidents such as that at Three Mile Island?

Other Producer Taxes on Natural Resources

To some extent, the incidence of property taxes and income taxes is more difficult to assess than is that of severance taxes. This is true, in part, because the incidence of those taxes depends on how they are assessed on natural resources, details that are not necessarily revealed by these generic terms. Beyond that, the theoretical literature on the incidence of excises, of which a severance tax is one variant, shows less recent "churning" than does the analogous literature on these two taxes. It does, however, generally appear that such taxes imposed by producer states are less likely to be shifted forward and exported to nonresident consumers than are severance taxes levied under similar circumstances.

Producing states are likely to attempt to use a net-income tax to tap rents from natural resources in one of two ways.[26] The most effective way would be to employ separate accounting, under which the firm or group of firms operating in the state would be required to treat their activities in the taxing state, or those functions that are particularly profitable, such as production, as separate entities. Thus, for example, Alaska has required that separate accounting be used to measure the taxable income of oil and gas companies resulting from production and pipeline transportation, although it uses formula apportionment to tax other industries.[27] If the deductions allowed in calculating net income under this approach are set arbitrarily, as they are in Alaska, so that they vary little with expenses actually incurred, a tax that is described as being levied on net income may actually resemble fairly closely a peculiar form of severance tax with a fixed deduction or credit. In that instance the analysis of the previous sections applies. (But pass-through of such taxes may not be allowed under long-term contracts.) If, however, actual expenses are used in measuring net income, the tax is more likely to resemble a true income tax and to be borne by recipients of rents. Certainly there is little reason to expect much shifting to consumers, except in the case of economic rents that are modest, relative to normal return to capital, combined with substantial market dominance by the taxing state.

Most states actually employ formula apportionment, rather than separate accounting, to determine the part of the total income of a nationwide firm on which to levy tax. That is, the state taxes a fraction of the firm's total income equal to a weighted average of the firm's fractions of nationwide payroll, property, and sales occurring within the state. (Usually these three factors are accorded equal weight.) I have argued elsewhere that a tax such as this should be interpreted as economically equivalent to three separate taxes, levied on payroll, property, and sales, at rates equal to the product of one third the statutory tax rate and the firm's nationwide profit margins on payroll, property, and sales.[28] Incidence and other economic effects would be relatively difficult to untangle completely, because the effective rate of tax applied to payroll, property, and sales differs between firms, depending on their rate of profitability throughout the nation. But the portion of the corporate tax related to property is likely to have incidence much like that of a property tax, the effects of the payroll-related part of the tax are likely to resemble those of a payroll tax, and the incidence of the sales-related part of the corporate tax can be expected to resemble that of a tax on sales.

States generally base the sales factor on sales at destination. But a substantial producing state interested in exporting its income tax (or, indeed, gaining substantial income from it) would define sales at origin rather than at destination. (For example, before moving to separate accounting for the oil industry, Alaska had employed sales at the wellhead in its sales factor for that industry.) Only this case seems worth considering in the present context. (The use of formula apportionment by consuming states in an attempt to tax resource rents is considered in the next section.) An income tax on a resource sector based on sales at origin is, of course, roughly equivalent to a severance tax.

It seems unlikely that the parts of the income tax of a producing state that are related to property or to payroll would result in much exporting of burden to nonresident consumers. Both would probably be borne largely by recipients of rents originating in the state.[29] The conditions under which the sales-related part of the corporate tax could be exported would seem to resemble those for the severance tax. There is generally little reason to expect much shifting to consumers, in the absence of market dominance.

There are a number of ways of valuing deposits of natural resources for the purpose of levying property taxes. These do, however, tend to reduce to setting an assessed value on property based on the present value of the stream of future income.[30] If that is a stream of net income, the analysis of the incidence of a property tax resembles that of the incidence of an income tax. (Presumably the similarity is to an income tax levied under separate accounting, not formula apportionment.) If, as is more common, a stream of gross receipts is being discounted, the propery tax tends to resemble a severance tax. In either event the analysis presented earlier should be generally applicable.[31]

Tax Exporting by Consuming States

Apparently spurred on by widespread publicity of the image of "blue-eyed Arabs," consuming states have been considering, and even enacting, legislation that they probably hope would allow them to cut themselves in on the increased rents from natural resources that have resulted from the actions of OPEC and from shortages of various natural resources. The likely distributional effects of two such efforts by consuming states deserve special attention.

Several states, among them New York and Connecticut, have passed gross-receipts taxes on petroleum companies operating within their boundaries, coupled with provisions intended to prevent the companies from raising prices of products sold in the state in response to the tax. The intended effect can be examined using figure 5-2 and is easily understood. The supply curve S faced by any individual consuming state is almost completely elastic.[32] Imposition of a gross-receipts tax implies that the state's demand curve, as seen by the industry, D', would lie below the actual demand curve D by the amount of the tax. In the absence of the limitation on price increases, the price in the taxing state would rise by the full amount of the gross-receipts tax, or from P_0 to P_1, and the equilibrium quantity of petroleum products

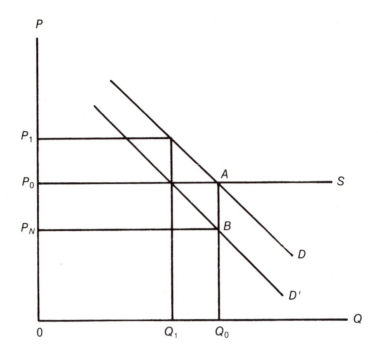

Figure 5-2. Incidence of State Tax on Gross Receipts, with and without Price Control

sold in the state would shrink from Q_0 to Q_1. Needless to say, such a tax that would simply be borne by resident consumers would not be a very popular measure in states already burdened by high and rising costs of energy.

The prohibition on raising price in response to the tax is intended to change the nature of the demand curve faced by the oil companies in the taxing state. The price ceiling implies that to the left of point A the demand curve becomes horizontal at price P_0. As seen from the vantage point of the consumer, it appears that nothing would be changed by imposition of the tax; the price would remain at P_0 and the consumer would be in equilibrium at Q_0. Rents of the oil companies would simply be reduced by the vertical distance between P_0 and P_N. Note, however, that the oil companies would not be in equilibrium in this situation, at least in the long run. As seen by them, the demand curve (net of tax) would be $P_N BD'$. The attempt to combine the gross-receipts tax with price controls would result in diversion of petroleum products to other markets; if the supply curve were as elastic as shown here, diversion would be complete, because $P_N BD'$ lies below the supply curve at every point. Thus in long-run equilibrium the goal presumably envisaged in this legislation would not be realized.

Of course, rents could be captured in the short run. Although the long-run supply of petroleum products might be almost as elastic as shown in figure 5-2, in the short run supply is less elastic than is indicated here. In particular, service stations cannot be converted instantaneously to other uses, and long-term contracts of various kinds exist. Depending on the exact nature of contractual arrangements and other rigidities, the short-run effect of a policy of this type might very well be a substantial reduction in rents or quasi-rents.[33] Note, however, that this burden might very well be borne in large part by resident owners of service stations rather than by oil companies, depending on contractual arrangements.

Finally, if the tax and price ceiling described here were imposed in the context of federal allocation of energy among states, the consuming states would find even long-run exportation of their tax to owners of oil companies substantially easier. This combination of policies would have the effect of imposing on the oil companies a totally inelastic supply curve and confronting them with a totally elastic demand curve at the prevailing retail price. Under these conditions the tax would reduce rents, but it would not cause diversion of products to other markets. The imposition of state ceilings on prices has, however, been found to conflict with federal regulation of prices of energy and therefore to be illegal.[34]

It appears that a movement is underway in many consuming states to attempt to use the so-called unitary method of taxing corporate income to capture part of the rents of the oil companies. This movement can be traced to two recent Supreme Court cases.[35] In *Exxon Corp.* v. *Wisconsin Department of Revenue* the company had used functional separate accounting to argue that only its production activities were profitable. (It claimed that both exploration and development and marketing were not profitable.) It therefore argued that Wisconsin should tax none of its income, since only marketing occurred there. The Supreme Court rejected this argument, noting that Exxon carried on a "unitary business" extending from exploration and development through production to marketing. In such a case, the Court ruled, a state was justified in using formula apportionment of the entire income of the corporation and that separate accounting could not be used to insulate production income from the tax net of the consuming state.

In *Mobil Oil Corp.* v. *Commissioner of Taxes*, a case decided shortly before *Exxon*, the Court went even farther in ruling that states could constitutionally include dividends, including those paid from income earned abroad, in income to be apportioned by formula, so long as a unitary business was involved. Consuming states may see in the unitary-business approach the opportunity to apportion to themselves income of the oil companies that they would not be able to tax under separate accounting. (Naturally they define sales, the factor of interest, on the basis of destination.) This, they apparently think, will allow them to take a share of the rents of the petroleum companies.

The analysis of the incidence of the corporate-income tax suggests that these expectations may not be realized, at least in the long run. Where any one state is concerned, the corporate-income tax is best considered a composite of taxes levied on whatever enters the state's apportionment formula. This being the case, it appears that the sales-related part of the state corporate-income tax should have incidence very much like that of a state sales tax. We would not, of course, ordinarily expect this to be borne by rents, in the absence of successful measures to prevent pass-through of the tax, such as those discussed earlier. Similarly, to the extent that property and payroll are required to provide distribution of energy within the taxing state, we would expect the burden to be on consumers rather than on rents.[36]

Note, however, that once again the incidence of a particular tax depends on the exact question being asked. Suppose all consuming states were to impose corporate-income taxes using the same rate and apportionment formula. In such a case the aggregate of all such taxes would, indeed, be just a corporate-income tax, not a composite of taxes on the factors in the formula. Such a tax would probably be borne largely by rents. Thus we are faced again with the question of whether taxes are set independently by consuming states or in concert. In this case independence would imply a burden on resident consumers, and collusion would imply incidence on (and, to a large degree, exporting to) recipients of rents.

Concluding Assessment

Despite the venerable position the analysis of tax incidence has occupied in the history of microeconomic thought, much work remains in establishing the principles that determine the ability of states to export taxes and in gaining general understanding of, and agreement on, those principles. Often the results of analysis depend crucially on exactly what question is asked and how it is framed, something that is not generally recognized. Moreover, even if there is widespread understanding and agreement of the principles of tax incidence and the proper questions are asked, extremely complex factual inquiries may be required in some instances to determine the extent to which taxes are likely to be exported. These involve careful investigation of the considerations discussed in this chapter and the impact they have. Even worse, economic considerations are not constant over time, as tastes, technological opportunities, and known availability of resources change. Beyond that, institutional change can bring with it changes in the extent of tax exporting. It seems extremely difficult to gain sufficient and permanent agreement on the likelihood of exporting of various taxes to provide the basis for adjudication. Basing legislation on estimates of tax exporting, is, of course, somewhat more practical, since congressional hearings provide a forum in which to consider such estimates—although it is not one particularly conducive to the determination of truth.

Notes

1. Page references are to 101 S. Ct. 2946 (1981). Throughout this chapter references made by the Court in quoted material are omitted.

2. Blackmun's dissent goes on to say, "if the trail court were to determine that the tax is exported, it would then have to determine whether the tax is 'fairly related' within the meaning of *Complete Auto Transit*." The Blackmun dissent also disagrees with the majority's interpretation of the important fourth prong of the *Complete Auto Transit* test of a commerce-clause violation. As Blackmun noted (p. 2968), the majority interpretation "emasculates the fourth prong." Under Blackmun's interpretation of the fourth prong, substantial additional evidentiary burdens would arise (see Hellerstein 1978). These issues are not discussed further here. Nor do I consider the extent to which taxes can be considered payments for benefits received; indeed, benefits of public services are ignored completely in the discussion of incidence analysis that follows.

3. Taxation of energy is only one source of potential conflict in a nation that suddenly believes it is running short of natural resources. As noted by many observers, other natural resources, Florida sunshine, the historical advantage of the New York stock exchange, and various other instances of geographically concentrated production have the potential of raising constitutional challenges akin to those in *Commonwealth Edison*. On the general question of constitutional limits on the exporting of state taxes, see Hellerstein (1982). Nor do I consider taxes on processing of natural resources, such as oil refining in Texas or generation of electricity in the coal states, but see McLure (1980b).

4. Gillis and McLure (1975, p. 391) distinguish between the legal owner of resources and the economic owner, the distinction being that the focus in incidence analysis is on who bears the burden of taxes that reduce resource rents. Note that this can be taxpayers, throughout the nation, when taxes reduce royalties on federal lands.

5. A careful reader will note that the elasticities of supply and demand cannot really even be specified until the various factors mentioned in this sentence are considered. The somewhat imprecise wording of the text is used simply to emphasize that in the analysis of geographic-tax incidence one must be particularly careful to consider such factors, rather than simply drawing a diagram containing the supply and demand curves for the entire nation, as is sometimes done. Elaboration on this point is the purpose of

much of the remainder of this chapter, as well as McLure (1982). Unionization and market structure, factors that can significantly affect incidence even in closed economies, are not considered here to allow focus on determinants of incidence that are particularly important in a geographic context.

6. One fourth probably should not be considered to be a "relatively small" part of national output for the purpose at hand, which is to show the role played by market dominance in the analysis of tax exporting. But a tax levied by a state that really produced only a very small share of national output would have such a small impact on price that the effect could not be shown clearly in this diagram.

7. This exposition treats severance taxes as simple per-unit levies on output. Consideration of a similar tax based on value of output would change little. But more complicated forms of taxation could render the analysis substantially more difficult and—to stress a major theme—determination of the degree of tax exporting more uncertain.

8. This reduction in rents per unit of output applies, strictly speaking, only to the quantity produced in the situation with the tax in place. Producer surplus is also lost over the range between Q_{A0} and Q_{A1}. But because the supply curve is upward-sloping, the average per-unit loss of surplus over this range is only about one half that on the units that are produced when the tax is imposed.

9. A careful statement of the second requirement should probably be in terms of net exports of the taxed good. No net exporting of the tax would occur if state A bought from state B as much (or more) of the taxed commodity as it sold to state B. This complication is ignored here, as elsewhere. See also note 12 for further consideration of this interpretation of tax exporting.

10. One way to see this is to realize that to produce a given shift in S_T a higher tax is required in state A than in state B. Thus a given tax-induced increase in price represents a greater fraction of the tax if B is the taxing state.

11. The fraction of a production tax that is reflected in higher prices given by $F = S/(S + D)] \cdot \{\alpha s_t/[\alpha s_t + (1 - \alpha)s_n]\}$ where S and D are nationwide elasticities of supply and demand for the taxed product, s_t and s_n are the elasticities of supply in the taxing and nontaxing states, respectively, and α is the taxing state's share in national output. Strictly speaking the result given in the text occurs if either all supply curves are equally elastic and demand is totally inelastic or all supply curves are perfectly elastic, regardless of the elasticity of demand. The second condition is rather misleading, since the slightest effort to tax output would price the taxing state completely out of the market. For convenience the discussion that follows employs the first of these weaker conditions. Of course, to the extent that demand has some elasticity, the degree of tax shifting is overstated.

It may be worth emphasizing that the analysis of market dominance presented here is concerned only with attempting to determine how much of the tax levied by one state or by several states acting in concert is shifted to consumers. Thus, if demand is inelastic and all supply elasticities are constant and equal over the relevant range, as is assumed for simplicity, the question of primary interest is simply what fraction of national output is produced by the taxing state or states.

12. This conclusion can, of course, be generalized to any number of producing states. In the extreme case of completely inelastic demand consumers would pay an additional amount for the taxed commodity (including quantities bought from nontaxing states) that is exactly equal to the tax revenues collected by the one state levying the tax. As noted earlier, the extra amount paid by consumers that does not find its ways into the public coffers of the taxing state raises land rents in the nontaxing states. This has led Peter Mieszkowski to suggest in his comments that perhaps the entire tax should be deemed to be shifted to consumers and therefore exported. I believe my interpretation to be more in accord with prior literature and intuitive understanding of tax exporting. Moreover, the implication that tax exporting would always be complete under these conditions, and not dependent on the degree of market dominance, seems misleading as well as counterintuitive.

13. Analysis similar to that of figure 5-1 can be employed heuristically to see this. When the tax is imposed in the first state, it does not exist in the second. Thus 50-percent forward shifting is our standard result. If, now, the second state imposes a tax, we do our analysis with a supply curve for the first state that includes its tax. Again, 50-percent forward shifting and exporting occurs.

14. The following statements quoted from Zimmerman and Alt (1981, pp. 20-21) are worth note: ". . . Montana and Wyoming have considerable market power. It would be in the interest of Montana and Wyoming to raise taxes above the currently high levels. The only effective break [sic] on the market power of these states is interregional competition. . . . Clearly, concerted action among states or among railroads could remove the limits on market power."

15. The relevance of this assumption is seen by noting that the dissenting opinion contains the following quotation from Church (1978, p. 278): " '[t]ax leadership' in western states appears to be an emerging reality." Similarly, it notes that "the 1974 Montana Subcommittee on Fossil Fuel Taxation was directed by the Montana legislature 'to investigate the feasibility and value of multistate taxation of coal with the Dakotas and Wyoming, and to contract and cooperate joining with these other states to achieve that end' " (note 5, p. 296).

16. This raises the interesting question of how "conscious parallelism" in setting state tax rates should be treated.

17. Suppose, however, that the three rates had previously been 0, 10 percent, and 20 percent. A uniform 10-percent increase in tax rates would be completely reflected in higher prices under the conditions assumed.

18. Note that the possible variation in export rates is reduced somewhat in this example by the simplifying assumptions that (1) there are only three producing states; (2) output is split evenly between the three states, (3) tax rates differ by 10 percent; and (4) all production is exported.

19. Martin Zimmerman has noted in his comments on this chapter that this result would hold only if both fuels continued to be competitive in the Btu-equivalent equilibrium prevailing after the increase in oil prices by OPEC. Under these conditions the OPEC price constitutes a ceiling as well as an umbrella. If the members of OPEC priced themselves out of the market for generating fuel, oil would cease to be an effective substitute for coal in that market, the OPEC price would not be a ceiling, at least initially, and the ease of shifting and tax exporting in spot markets would simply be given by the basic free-market analysis. In this respect, beyond the price at which oil became noncompetitive, the result would be quite similar to that for regulatory segmentation of the market. Shifting and exporting would be much more likely than if the OPEC price effectively constituted a ceiling price as well as an umbrella.

20. For more on this point, see Zimmerman and Alt (1981).

21. Presumably the coal companies would not act as disinterested bystanders in this conflict; given their desire to protect their own interests, they can be expected to attempt some whipsawing of their own.

22. In the situation described in note 19, increases in freight rates might be partially reflected in consumer prices.

23. The price could, of course, go even higher for coal already under contract, depending on whether taxes were set at rates greater than needed to capture all increases in rents, if contracts specified quantities to be bought, as well as allowing pass-through of taxes; see also McLure (1982) for further development of this point.

24. An earlier federal policy that helped energy-rich states was the import quotas imposed on crude oil during the 1960s. This raised domestic prices and created greater pools of rents for the states to tap, as did the prorationing activities of the Texas Railroad Commission and the complementary actions of the Interstate Oil Compact.

25. Martin Zimmerman has noted that given present levels of OPEC prices these regulations have little such effect; OPEC has, in effect, priced itself out of this market. See also note 19.

26. On the general nature of state corporation-income taxes, see McLure (1981b) and McLure, "State Corporate Income Taxes" (forthcoming).

27. Alaska has recently gone back to a more conventional tax based on formula apportionment.

28. For an analysis of the incidence and other economic effects of state corporation-income taxes, especially those levied using formula apportionment, see McLure (1980a, 1981c).

29. In an industrial context it might be more likely that the part of the corporate tax related to payroll would be borne by labor, since the latter might be relatively immobile, geographically. But given the need to bring in large amounts of capital and labor to exploit natural resources, it seems unlikely that in the long run either the payroll or property-related parts of the tax would not be borne by rents, except perhaps where rents are relatively unimportant and taxing states dominate the national market.

30. For more on this, see chapter 2 of this book.

31. The point is not that the incidence and other economic effects of a property tax are identical to those of an income or severance tax. Substantial differences in the speed and efficiency of exploitation can be induced by differences in these taxes. But tendencies for tax exporting may be quite similar, despite these differences. Mieszkowski and Toder in chapter 2 note that in several states assessed value is based directly on the value of current output, making the similarity to a severance tax even greater. For more on how various kinds of taxation (including expected changes therein) affect decisions on exploitation of natural resources, see Dasgupta, Heal, and Stiglitz (1980) or Conrad and Hool (1981).

32. By analogy to the discussion of taxes levied by producing states, we can note that most consuming states are far from dominating national (let alone world) consumption of petroleum products.

33. This could be shown by drawing an upward sloping short-run supply curve passing through point A and intersecting $P_N BD'$. The short-run price increase in the absence of the price control would, of course, be less than shown in figure 5-2.

34. On this and other cases involving constitutional challenges of state taxes on energy, see chapter 4 of this book.

35. For an excellent discussion of these two cases, see Hellerstein (1980).

36. These tendencies might, of course, not be fully realized in the short run, when there are many contractual obligations and other rigidities that would prevent escaping the burden of the tax.

References

Church, Albert M. "Conflicting Federal, State and Local Interest Trends in State and Local Energy Taxation Coal and Copper—A Case in Point." *National Tax Journal* 31 (September 1978):269-283.

Conrad, Robert F. and Hool, Bryce. "Resource Taxation with Heterogeneous Quality and Endogenous Resources." *Journal of Public Economics* 16 (August 1981):17-33.

Dasgupta, P.; Heal, G.M.; and Stiglitz, J.E. "The Taxation of Exhaustible Resources." In *Public Policy and the Tax System*, edited by G.A. Hughes and G.M. Heal. London: George Allen and Unwin, 1980, pp. 150-172.

Gillis, Malcolm and Charles E. McLure, Jr. "The Incidence of the World's Taxes on Natural Resources with Special Reference to Bauxite." *American Economic Review* 65 (May 1975):389-396.

Hellerstein, Walter. "Constitutional Constraints on State and Local Taxation of Energy Resources." *National Tax Journal* 31 (September 1978):245-256.

_____ . "State Income Taxation of Multijurisdictional Corporations: Reflections on *Mobil, Exxon,* and H.R. 5076." *Michigan Law Review* 79 (November 1980):131-171.

_____ . "Constitutional Limitations on State Tax Exportation." *American Bar Foundation Research Journal.* Winter 1982, pp. 1-77.

McLure, Charles E., Jr. "The State Corporate Income Tax: Lambs in Wolves' Clothing." In *The Economics of Taxation*, edited by Henry J. Aaron and Michael J. Boskin. Washington: Brookings Institution, 1980a, pp. 327-346.

_____ . "The Economic Effects of a Texas Tax on the Refining of Petroleum Products." *Growth and Change* 11 (July 1980b):2-8.

_____ . "Market Dominance and the Exporting of State Taxes." *National Tax Journal* 34 (December 1981a):483-485.

_____ . "Toward Uniformity in Interstate Taxation: A Further Analysis." *Tax Notes* (13 July 1981b):51-63.

_____ . "The Elusive Incidence of the Corporate Income Tax: The State Case." *Public Finance Quarterly* 9 (October 1981c):395-413.

_____ . "Incidence Analysis and the Courts: An Examination of Four 1981 Cases." *Supreme Court Economic Review* 1 (1982):128-212.

_____ . "Fiscal Federalism and the Taxation of Economic Rents." In *State and Local Finance in the 80s*, edited by George F. Break. Madison, Wis.: University of Wisconsin Press, forthcoming.

_____ . "State Corporate Income Taxes." In *State and Local Finance in the 80s*, edited by George F. Break. Madison, Wis.: University of Wisconsin Press, forthcoming.

Zimmerman, Martin B., and Christopher Alt. "The Western Coal Cartel." Hoover Institution Working Papers in Economics No. E-80-9, 1981.

Comments

Martin Zimmerman

The Supreme Court ruling in *Commonwealth Edison* is a victory for practicality. As Charles McLure clearly points out, the difficulties are legion in attempting to show to what degree an excise tax constitutes any burden on interstate commerce, let alone an "undue burden." The majority opinion wisely fears to tread in these murky waters.

However, the minority viewpoint bears discussion, since it raises a number of issues of public-policy interest. The majority opinion is a rule of practicality. The minority opinion is a rule of reason. They recognize that monopoly power exists in many resource markets. They realize that state legislatures are well positioned to exploit this market power. And finally, they know that severance taxes can be the instrument the states use to raise the price of the resource. The minority further feels that evidentiary difficulties should not be a bar to dealing with and adjudicating an issue.

How does this opinion stack up against the facts of the coal industry in general and Montana, in particular? In regard to the existence of monopoly power, the indication is that Montana and Wyoming together do possess a degree of market power. They control a large supply of low-cost low-sulfur coal. Their position in the coal market is somewhat analogous to OPEC's. There are high-cost alternatives to Montana and Wyoming coal, just as there are high-cost alternatives to OPEC oil. The state legislatures, by setting taxes, are in a position to exploit the inelasticity of their residual-demand curves. If monopoly power exists and is used, there is a public-policy issue. The minority said that this issue could be dealt with by the courts.

This raises the second point. Are evidentiary issues too complex for the courts? McLure puts forth a host of reasons why this is the case. First, he argues, it is important to know whether states acted in isolation or in concert. Montana has a 30-percent severance tax, but Wyoming has only an 18-percent tax. Given the almost perfect substitutability between Monatana and Wyoming coal, only the 18 percent can be exported. Is Montana to be held liable for 30 percent or for 18 percent? How much of that 18 percent was, in fact, exported? McLure shows how the answer depends on geographic concentration, mobility of resources, the prevalence of long-term contracts and transportation costs, as well as issues of substitution in the long and short runs.

To anyone familiar with the U.S. antitrust laws, this list is familiar. In any antitrust case similar issues arise. Was there a conspiracy? What is the relevant market? Do transportation costs provide market protection? What is the collective liability? What is the liability of a single participant? All these issues arise and are dealt with in antitrust cases. It is clear then that courts deal with these issues and Congress had mandated that they do so in the area of antitrust.

What then is unique in the severence-tax cases? Why can we not deal with this issue of public policy in the courts? The problem is that the Montana severance tax case was not a Sherman Act case. The issue was not monopoly but the constitutional issue of undue burden on interstate commerce. In a monopoly case, liability can be separated from damages. First it is established whether the law was broken; then the court decides who was damaged and by how much. In the case at hand, whether the constitution was violated depends on who was damaged and by how much. Some damage is constitutional, undue damage is not. It is this aspect of treating severance tax cases under the Constitution that makes the issue difficult. In the constitutional issue of undue burden, a damage assessment is necessary from the outset.

Since Congress had determined that in antitrust suits courts must deal with the issue of monopolization, they do. The Court in this case faced no congressional mandate and therefore decided not to deal with complexities they were not compelled to consider. It should be noted that even with antitrust law, the courts have chosen not to deal with the issue of whether a price is monopoly price. They deal only with monopoly behavior.

Where does that leave us? First, the minority is right in that there is a potentially important issue. Second, the majority and McLure are right in that a constitutional remedy is infeasible. What then do we do? There are two possibilities. Congressional action could limit severance taxes. Indeed, there are several proposals now before Congress to limit coal severance taxes.

Severance-tax caps as now proposed do not fully preclude the potential for monopoly behavior. State legislatures are not the only parties able to exploit their market position. In the case of Powder River Basin Coal, the railroads share similar advantages. Only one railroad, the Burlington Northern, currently can ship Powder River Basin coal. One other rail link is under construction, but the railroads will continue to have market power. If the states are prohibited from exploiting market power, more is left for the railroads. That means a tax cap will have distributional implications but will not solve the monopoly problem. The Staggers Act has, in essence, removed regulatory authority over most coal rates. We could, of course, couple tax caps and railroad regulation of coal rates. Given the past history of regulation of coal rates, this is not likely to work. Railroads setting point-to-point rates, even in a regulated environment, had a great deal of discretion.

There is one other way to encourage competition in western coal. Slurry pipelines could compete effectively with unit trains. Slurry pipelines, however, need the right of eminent domain so they may cross railroads. Congress is currrently considering legislation to grant this right over the objections of the railroad industry.

In summary, the judicial remedy is unavailable. Some remedy is necessary. Legislative remedy is feasible, but an approach based solely on tax limitation will not reach the goal. Any legislative remedy must look at the entire market. With a more competitive transport sector, a maximum tax makes some sense. Without transport competiton, a maximum tax serves only to redistribute profits.

Comments

Peter Mieszkowski

What is the importance of dominance—or the size of the state imposing the tax? Clearly if a state with 80 percent of output imposes a 10-percent tax it will collect much more tax and distort energy markets more significantly than will a state with 1 percent of output imposing the same tax. Consequently as a practical matter the court or the policymaker has to pay close attention to market shares. Related to this is whether there is likely to be collusion between producing states on the setting of taxes. The policymaker should respond differently if he believes that a high tax imposed by a Montana is likely to be followed by the imposition of taxes in exporting competing states or if he believes that the tax is an isolated event. But what constitutes collusion? If a number of states all impose high rates of tax—is this collusion or is this simply the outcome of decentralized decisions made by individual states where each makes the trade off between either raising its tax to collect more revenue and running the risk of lower output or setting lower rates of tax to enhance output and possibly tax revenues through output effects. To my knowledge there is no definite analysis of the type of equilibrium that is likely to result from noncollusive, decentralized tax determination. Presumably general competitive arguments would imply that the more fragmented production is the lower will be the equilibrium level of tax in the nation. But this is really an article of faith more than anything.

As a practical matter high taxes by one producer might be struck down (even if the producer is not especially large)—even if there is uncertainty as to whether the other states will follow suit, or whether a common set of high tax rates were determined by explicit collusion or through an equilibrium process that is quite decentralized, where each producing state expects other states to impose high taxes.

There may be a "tipping phenomenon" at work here—where, if a sufficient number of states impose high taxes, the rest will follow suit—although if taxes are low to begin with, it will be hard to "swim against the current." Of course dominance and size are important in this process, since a large producer may be much more likely to break out of a low tax equilibrium. Having said this I am uncertain as to how I am to interpret McLure's assertion that it matters a great deal whether severance taxes are set independently or through collusion. The main issue is whether shifting of the tax or exporting should be tied to the change in the price in the taxing state.

Consider the extremes—if the producing state's share is 100 percent, price will rise by 100 percent (assuming perfectly inelastic demand). If the

197

production share is 50 percent, prices will go up by 50 percent. But because of the umbrella effects the price goes up in the nontaxing state, and thus the total cost of coal goes up by the full amount of tax revenues and there is the redistribution of rents between producing states. The same point generalizes to ten states or to one hundred. So from an incidence or burden standpoint we conclude that the change in price multiplied with the total quantity produced will equal tax revenenues collected. We conclude also that to a first-order approximation total land rents remain unchanged.

The opposing point of view—which will emphasize dominance—is to key on differences between the size of the taxing region relative to the market as a whole. Thus the model is not to analyze two identical regions or ten or one hundred but instead to ask what is the difference between a tax imposed by a region that produces 70 percent of the output relative to the effects if a 30-percent producer imposes the tax. In one respect, given certain simplifying assumptions, there is no difference from the case where there are a number of regions of equal size. The change in the prices times the total quantity produced is equal to total tax revenues in the tax-imposing state, and total land rents remain unchanged. But the extent that price changes relative to the tax and the extent to which rents in the taxing jurisdiction change relative to tax collections are very different. If the large jurisdiction imposes the tax the change in price relative to the tax will be relatively large and the change in land rents relative to tax collections will be relatively small. If the smaller community (the 30-percent community) imposes the same rate of tax, price in the nation changes by less and rents in the taxing jurisdiction will fall by a relatively large portion of the revenue. If the tax jurisdiction is relatively small, then within the taxing jurisdiction the fall in land rents relative to taxes collected will be large. This distinction between large and small regions may narrow whatever differences in interpretation that remain.

The allowance of regions of unequal size provides a basis for interpreting incidence in terms of what will happen within the region or of what will happen in the nation as a whole. Analysis of what will happen nationwide not only is a better approach but also it is what the policymaker will want to know. McLure has not persuaded me that analysis within a region is a more appropriate approach.

Comments

Mason Gaffney

Two economists stood on a platform with two politicians in Louisville in 1977, addressing the National Tax Association. The subject was inter-governmental competition for energy revenues. The politicians were Byron Dorgan, now senator from North Dakota, and Sidney Goodman, Michigan commissioner of taxation. The economists, Warren Samuels and I, held very different views. Yet we both sized up the question much as Charles McLure has in his careful chapter.

The economist sees tax exporting mainly as a transfer of rents (and therefore of land values) among jurisdictions. He does not wax moralistic or righteous on either side, for the interstate distribution of rent sources was initially arbitrary and is subject to constant windfalls and a few wipeouts as shifting world markets give some here and take from there.

Nor does the economist see much scope for states to export taxes any-way. Most taxes, whatever the nominal base, come out of the taxing state's own rents. That follows simply from the interstate mobility of national pools of labor and capital: migration and arbitrage operate to equalize after-tax returns. But land cannot move among tax jurisdictions that are defined as fixed areas of land. John Locke, Francois Quesnay, and Adam Smith had this rather well thought out over two centuries ago. It is often called the physiocratic doctrine of tax incidence, after Quesnay, but it is by no means peculiar to Physiocrats.

The politicians speak from different perspectives. In addressing the National Tax Association much was made of "a fair shake for the homeowner" (farmer, consumer, worker, pensioner, and so on). Both politicians assumed full forward-shifting: prices are based on cost plus tax. All costs to them are lean and hard and ineluctable; all needs are fixed, with survival at stake. There is no slack or fat in the system. Put another way, they see highly elastic supplies and inelastic demands, with the latter based not on consumer affluence but on consumer desperation. Thus there is no give, no cushion, everything is marginal, and every adjustment is calamitous. These are, of course, strong initial bargaining positions from a certain world view, but it is weaker than the view that each state is taxing primarily the rent of lands under its undisputed sovereignty.

Both politicians seemed to accept a ground rule that North Dakota had to justify its taxes by benefits delivered to miners or by costs that miners impose on the state. Monetary expenses and environmental damages were acceptable chips in this game. It was not enough merely to note that each state enjoys a sovereign power of taxation not limited by benefits (at least in the usual narrow construction). Some economists seem prone to this view as well, and lawyer Henry Monaghan, speaking at this conference, has a firm impression that we are all like that, faithful copies of Frank Knight and Milton Friedman. Charles McLure, with his emphasis on benefit taxation, may be fortifying the impression.

If it be true that land value is a social product, then an *ad-valorem* tax on land is a benefit tax. But today the usual benefit doctrine is more narrowly construed. It is more like the old joke whose end line goes "Yes, but what have you done for me lately?" One lawyer referred to a railway protesting a tax with the plea "What is the state doing for us, keeping the Indians away?" How easily we forget that Custer died for our sins—sovereignty over land comes from power; power costs lives and money and creates a continuing obligation in the landholder to support the sovereign from whom he holds title. That was the feudal law, the feudal law shaped the common law, and the common law is our law.

More generally, Alfred Marshall described land value as a "public value" resulting from public spending (including that which establishes and maintains sovereignty) and spillover benefits from the use of complementary lands. Since not one of these benefits is created by the holder of land, they must be received as a consequence of holding title. The logical upper limit of benefit, therefore, is value; the supposed excess of value over benefit received is an illusion, and *ad-valorem* taxes on land are benefit taxes.

The only moot question is from which sovereign are the benefits derived, the original federal grantor or the state? This question seems largely answered by federal abandonment of direct property taxation to the states.

Beyond that, I agree with the main lines of McLure's analysis and content myself both with trying to fill some gaps that strike me as too important to leave empty and with registering in one respect, a disappointment.

The disappointment is on the spiritual level. A correct analysis like McLure's is inherently a positive contribution, but what is the message for suffering mankind? Such great technical skill and virtuosity as McLure displays should not be spent on small purposes, yet the chapter suffers from a certain aimlessness. This is a cautious *caveat* chapter, carefully disclaiming most aims. The only avowed aim is to show that incidence can be complicated. We already knew that.

It is as though one went to a surgeon with abdominal aches and he said "I could cut out your appendix, but let me first tell you how many things could go wrong. Let us begin by noting that the city power supply could fail. . . ." The style calls to mind what Knut Wicksell said of Eugen von Böhm-Bawerk: "He delights in piling up difficulties, in order that he may remove them later." Wicksell greatly admired the Austrian, recall, just as I admire McLure. We only seek improvement because what is there is already valuable.

Thus McLure's message is muted and uninspiring when it could be constructive and seminal. He could, for example, use his tools to show that a severance tax imposes excess burdens and that there are better ways to tap rent for the fisc. In a way he does lay such a message between the lines, when he indicates that income taxation is a better way to tap rents. But this is too easy. If the income tax really were aimed right to the rent bull's-eye, marvelous. Let us move from the spiritual to the substantive and fill in the gaps left when income taxes are equated with taxes on rent.

Income, in normal usage, refers to returns imputable to all equity assets. These include capital used to develop land. On marginal land such taxes are not on rent at all, as there is none. They simply sterilize the land, as a severance tax does (and thus they lend what credence there is to the tax-exporting hypothesis).

Debt capital is deductible and therefore excludable from taxable income. A highly leveraged corporation then presents virtually no tax base at all, however much valuable coal it controls.

The income tax, personal or corporate, is not *in rem* but *in personam*. For individuals, the base includes value added by personal service. For individuals and corporations both, it invites use of world income, with arbitrary and contestable apportionment formulae; tax avoidance by cute transfer pricing; allocation of out-state costs to local profits; transfer of tax credits; and so on, ad infinitum. After all that is done, the base is not much related to local land rents as the tax base.

In this chapter, and in all the chapters here, I miss any recognition of this vital distinction of *in rem* and *in personam*. When we say "rent" we are talking of an *in-rem* concept—the income imputable to land, regardless of who owns it, of his personal circumstances and shelters and dodges and residence and citizenship and partners and wives and debts and medical bills and deductions and exemptions. Rent is an objective fact, peculiar to a parcel of land sited unequivocally in a given tax jurisdiction. The use of "income" changes all that to the *in-personam* mode, and it is grossly misleading to equate income and rent, or to suggest any analogy.[1]

There do exist taxes on land income that are *in rem*. They are net-proceeds taxes and are found in Nevada, Idaho, South Dakota, and a very few other states. The taxable unit is the parcel of mining land. The tax base is gross receipts less expenses on the specific parcel.[2] Another tax of the same genus is that levied on copper in Papua-New Guinea. This tax is conceived and defined as a tax on pure rent. It was drafted by economists Ross Garnaut and Anthony Clunies-Ross. It is central to the subject of McLure's chapter that such taxes do exist and are understood to be taxes that hit the bull's-eye of rent, free of most excess burdens other than those of an administrative nature.[3]

There is yet another vital concept that eludes this chapter: what A.C. Pigou called "the announcement effect."[4] This effect is the one that causes excess burdens. It comprises the taxpayer's avoidance maneuvering when it is announced to him that he is subject to a tax that, like most taxes, "shoots anything that moves" but spares what stands still. Income taxes, severance taxes, and net-proceeds taxes are on a unit-of-production basis: no production, no tax. They only tax rent ex post, that is, as realized.

Very different in this respect is the property tax. Here, the taxable event is not production but the arrival of an anniversary on the calendar. The incentive effect of such an announcement is the reverse of most tax announcements. Here the taxpayer is not like a share tenant of the state but a cash tenant. He pays for the privilege of tenure, and then does what he pleases. As Pigou observed, the property tax on bare land has zero announcement effect, unlike other taxes. He counted this in its favor.[5]

In effect, the property tax makes rent a first claim on production. The entrepreneur gets the residual. Others have noted that this tax therefore works to increase production, especially if levied on land alone, exempting capital. The implications for our subject are profound. This tax could never be exported, could never obstruct interstate commerce. If anything it benefits consumers by increasing supply. Consuming states could never claim injury from such a tax.

Absentee owners might claim injury, however, and this is probably what all this foofaraw about tax export is really about. States like North Dakota and Montana are basically colonies, their coal mainly owned by foreign corporations. When these states tax coal, they are taxing these absentees. But the latter are rich, organized, and influential. It is they, I surmise, who stir up the rabble with all this outcry about tax export. It is they whom James Madison set out to protect with his checks and balances calculated to break up and abort factions who might want to tax property. It is they alone who always have standing in court because they own property and who therefore inevitably become the major focus of lawyers' concerns. At the same time it is they who lack any ultimate defense against taxation because our common law makes them tenants of their sovereign, who may assert his overriding ownership of land as "he"—that is, we—please(s). So they plant myths about tax export and then seek to enjoin these mythical effects. I do wish that McLure had explored this side of his subject.

My last point is that interstate collusion to restrain trade, as envisioned by McLure, is most unlikely. States simply are not organized that way. I dwell in the most suspect of states, California, with its many farm specialty crops with national monopolies, its farm prorates, and its producer coops. What do we do with these dangerous powers? Now and again we burn some oranges and knock down green peaches, but we never block the entry of new lands into producing these things. On the contrary, we habitually subsidize and promote this, to the extent that many of our older producers are ruined by oversupply and low prices. The simple force behind this behavior is that our richest, most politically effective people know that the way to prosper is to buy cheap dry land ahead of settlement and then get the state to water it, road it, and so on.

Economists' traditional concern with monopolies and artifical scarcities misses the mark here. I do not question that there are monopolies: Vermont marble may be a good one. But our states' high propensity to subsidize the development of submarginal land creates a problem of artificial abundance in the things subsidized. The scarcity that ensues then is a general shortage of capital for all other things. If we eat the seed corn to sustain us while building roads into the wilderness, how then shall we plant the new land? Compared to this outcome, mere monopoly seems relatively benign. It is this pattern, I suggest, that has set us up for a long time of troubles ahead, to mend which economists should now turn their major efforts.

Notes

1. Compare Mason Gaffney, "Objectives of Government Policy in Leasing Mineral Lands," in A. Thompson and M. Crommelin (eds.), *Mineral Leasing as an Instrument of Public Policy* (Vancouver: University of British Columbia Press, 1977), pp. 3-26.

2. Robert Paschall, "A Comparison of Minerals Tax Systems," *The Assessors' Journal* 11 (December 1977):221-237.

3. Ross Garnaut and Anothony Clunies-Ross, "A New Tax for Natural Resources Projects," in Thompson and Crommelin, *Mineral Leasing*.

4. A.C. Pigou, *A Study in Public Finance*, 3d rev. ed. (London: MacMillan, 1949).

5. Ibid., pp. 147-153.

6 A Constitutional Perspective on Federal-Provincial Sharing of Revenues from Natural Resources

John D. Whyte

Even the most casual observer of Canadian political life has been able to discern that over the last five years political cleavages within Canada not only have been deep but until recently were effective in frustrating the development of needed national policies. Although there is nothing unique about a country experiencing conflict over competing and irreconcilable views about its policies for the future, what made the heart beat faster, at least for constitutional lawyers, was that the Canadian conflict was rooted in different conceptions of the basic constitutional order.

On both major political fronts—constitutional reform and resource-revenue sharing—truces, or partial truces, have been reached. However, the area of conflict with which this chapter is concerned—the problem of dividing the revenues from nonrenewable resources—is one in which none of the constitutional issues have been finally resolved. The Canada-Alberta Energy Agreement,[1] signed on 1 September 1981, and the subsequent British Columbia and Saskatchewan agreements,[2] will quiet some aspects of the debate for some years, but the basic question of the constitutional limits of provincial resource-revenue taking remains.

There are three methods by which governments may obtain direct fiscal benefit from resource extraction. First, they may tax the benefits derived from mining the resources. Second, to the extent they own the resources, they may exact a rent from enterprises to which they give the right to extract the resource. Third, they may assume an entrepreneurial role and engage in the production and marketing of resources for their own account.

There are, of course, other indirect benefits that governments may seek to gain from resource extraction within the boundaries of the province, state, or country. Attempts to acquire these benefits (or reduce the economic and social costs that accompany this so-called blessing) are also subject to constitutional constraints. In fact, the single biggest blow to provincial constitutional economic regulatory powers in recent years came in a

The views expressed in this chapter are my own and are not necessarily those of the Government of Saskatchewan. I am grateful to George V. Peacock, of the Department of the Attorney General, Saskatchewan, for his many helpful comments.

1978 Supreme Court of Canada decision in which a provincial attempt to compensate for overproduction in the potash industry through a prorationing and price-stabilization scheme was struck down as being a law interfering with the federal trade-and-commerce power.[3] The constitutional dispute over the limitation on provinces to regulate the structure of an industry, its rate of growth, and ancillary features (such as the composition of the work force) of an industry, the commodity of which moves largely in extraprovincial trade, is a problem of major proportions in the years ahead.[4] Nevertheless, I shall restrict my analysis to constitutional problems relating to taxation, ownership, and state entrepreneurial activity.

Taxation

The provincial and federal powers to tax are included in the two lists by which legislative powers are assigned to the two levels of government in the British North America Act of 1867 (BNAA) Canada's major constitutional document. Under the BNAA, provinces are limited in section 92(2) to the power to levy "Direct Taxation within the Province in order to the raising of a Revenue for Provincial Purposes." Canada's taxation power under section 91(3) is plenary: "The raising of Money by any Mode or System of Taxation." Constitutional interpretation most frequently entails assigning mutually compatible meanings to classes of activity that have been described so as to produce a vast area of overlap between competing heads of power. Only to a limited extent has this been the process of giving meaning to the provincial power. In general, the competing federal head has not been the taxation power found in section 91(3) but rather the federal Parliament's power under section 91(2) to regulate trade and commerce, which is a classification less formal, and more functional, than the federal-taxation head. The scant history of attempts to reconcile the two taxation powers in the courts[5] bears out William Lederman's observation: "There is no constitutional prohibition against killing geese that lay golden eggs. Federal and provincial governments can be severally or collectively foolish about this."[6] (As we shall see, this view may not go unchallenged much longer, but the claim against rapaciousness will not be based on the view that one taxation power carries an implicit limitation of the other but rather that excessive taxation is colorably regulatory.)

   The general pattern of constitutional interpretation is further deviated from in the sense that the provincial taxation power contains clear but indefinite textual limitations, requiring exegesis. The most obvious limitation is the exclusion of indirect taxes. This exception is not as considerable as one used to economic taxonomy would expect. In the leading case in the area, *Bank of Toronto* v. *Lambe,*[7] the Judicial Committee of the Privy

Council, adopting the views of John Stuart Mill, defined *direct* and *indirect* in this way: "A direct tax is one which is demanded from the very person who it is intended or desired should pay it. Indirect taxes are those which are demanded from one person in the expectation and intention that he shall indemnify himself at the expense of another; such are the excise or customs."[8]

This completely unstartling starting point has been rendered more startling (and more reasonably generous to provinces) in operation. The only passing on of tax costs, inherent in the tax, that creates indirection, for the purposes of section 92(2), is that which is recovered in precisely recognizable form. In other words, if the recoupment is circuitous the tax will nevertheless be counted as direct. For example, Justice Rand in *C.P.R.* v. *Attorney General of Saskatchewan* offered this test for indirect taxes: "If the tax is related or relatable, directly, or indirectly to a unit of the commodity or its price, imposed when the commodity is in course of being manufactured or marketed, then the tax tends to cling as a burden to the unit or the transaction presented to the market."[9]

Furthermore, the courts have recognized that there is a received wisdom abut the character of certain taxes; despite their economic incidence some taxes will be accepted as falling historically within, or without, the category of direct tax. Net-income and net-profit taxes and real property taxes are historical categories of direct tax, and import and export taxes, taxes on gross income or on production, and commodity taxes are recongized categories of indirect tax. If a tax fits a recognized category, it is classified as direct or indirect accordingly. If it does not fit, the court will resort to the general test.

The other textual limitations of provincial taxation are that the taxation must be within the province and must be for "the raising of a revenue." Both these limitations have been hypothetically put forward to strike down resource taxes.[10] But in respect of both phrases, when the argument, which would be advanced by a taxpayer challenger, is considered it is seen to be based less on section 92(2) than on the claim that the tax entrenches on the federal power to regulate trade and commerce. The lesson to be learned, therefore, is that exercises of the provincial power to tax revenues from resources, unless constructed mindlessly, should not overrun the basic grant of provincial taxing power. On the other hand, the effect produced by such taxes can produce a different constitutional result; if taxes substantially interfere with interprovincial and international trade they may be struck down as invading the federal power. Therefore, taxes directed specifically at oil and gas revenues will inevitably be under a constitutional cloud, since the three Canadian producing provinces produce overwhelmingly for out-of-province markets. This problem is highlighted by the November 1977 decision of the Supreme Court of Canada in the *CIGOL* case.[11]

Following the jump in oil prices in the autumn of 1973, the government of Saskatchewan moved quickly to capture what were perceived to be the windfall profits of oil producers.[12] By a complex set of legislation and regulations, Saskatchewan moved on three fronts. First, revenues from oil produced from lands held in freehold were subjected to a mineral-income tax. The tax was 100 percent of the difference between the price received at the well-head (normally the new, rising, world price) and the statutorily defined "basic well-head price" which was established at approximately the same level as the price per barrel received by producers prior to the oil embargo and price escalation. The tax scheme allowed some deductions, under approval of the minister of Mineral Resources, for increases in production costs and extraordinary transportation costs. As a device to counter tax avoidance the minister was given power to determine the well-head value of the oil when he was of the opinion that oil had been disposed of at less than its fair value.

Second, freehold rights in about one half of the 40 percent of the producing tracts in the province not held by the province as crown lands were expropriated. Third, a royalty surcharge was imposed on oil whether it came from existing crown lands or from newly expropriated lands. The royalty surcharge was generally calculated on the same basis as the mineral-income tax.

The Saskatchewan Court of Queen's Bench and the Saskatchewan Court of Appeal both upheld this scheme as a valid taxation measure.[13] The law did not, however, survive review by the Supreme Court of Canada, which, in a 7 to 2 decision, found the tax to be invalid both because it was considered to be a form of indirect taxation and because it was thought to interfere with international and interprovincial trade to such a degree that it constituted an invalid encroachment on a federal head of power.

The Court did not declare the expropriation of freehold interests to be unconstitutional. Beyond that, however, the provincial scheme was found to be unsupportable. The Court considered the royalty scheme to be not an exercise of the province's proprietary rights but rather in substance, if not in form, taxation. Neither conclusion need concern us except to say that it does not seem unwarranted for the Court to conclude that the statutory imposition of contractual terms requiring payment during the life of a contract is indistinguishable from taxation (unless, of course, the capacity to inflict statutory changes has been agreed on as a term of the contract).

The majority decision was written by Justice Martland. He found the tax to be *ultra vires* the province, since its effect was to regulate the export price of oil. Two critical comments may be made. First, it is not true that the effect of this taxation measure was to set the export price. In fact the scheme had, in most cases, no impact on price. Second, although the scheme touched on goods moving in international trade, Canadian jurisprudence is clear in sustaining the proposition that provincial schemes that affect price, supply, or quality of goods moving largely in extraprovincial

trade are not for that reason invalid. Invalidity results when it is imperative
to see the design of the legislation as being in relation to the regulation of
the terms of such trade. When the design is credibly to achieve a valid provincial purpose, and that purpose does not directly produce such an altera-
tion in the terms of trade so that that effect becomes a putative legislative
aim, then the provincial legislation is allowed to stand.[14] Interestingly,
Martland did not directly disagree with this test for provincial validity.
Rather he concluded that the taxation so closely controlled the price of
goods in the export market that there was no doubt about the character of
the law. Martland's views of the operational effect of the tax is found in
these passages:

> In considering this issue the important fact is, of course, that practically all
> of the oil to which the mineral income tax or the royalty surcharge becomes
> applicable is destined for interprovincial or international trade. . . . The
> producer must, if he is to avoid pecuniary loss, sell at the well-head at the
> well-head value established. The company which has its own oil production
> transported from the Province must, if it is to avoid pecuniary loss, ulti-
> mately dispose of the refined product at a price which will recoup the
> amount of the levy. Thus, the effect of the legislation is to set a floor price
> for Saskatchewan oil purchased for export by the appropriation of its po-
> tential incremental value in interprovincial and international markets, or to
> ensure that the incremental value is not appropriated by persons outside the
> province.[15]

> [The] Minister is empowered to determine the well-head value of the oil
> which is produced which will govern the price at which the producer is com-
> pelled to sell the oil which he produces. In an effort to obtain for the pro-
> vincial treasury the increases in the value of oil exported from Saskat-
> chewan which began in 1973, in the form of a tax upon the production of
> oil in Saskatchewan, the legislation gave power to the Minister to fix the
> price receivable by Saskatchewan oil producers on their export sales of a
> commodity that has almost no local market in Saskatchewan. Provincial
> legislative authority does not extend to fixing the price to be charged or re-
> ceived in respect of the sale of goods in the export market. It involves the
> regulation of interprovincial trade and trenches upon ss. 91(2) of the *British
> North America Act, 1967.*[16]

The crux of Martland's error, therefore, lies in his view of the function
of the commonplace antiavoidance provisions. At one point of the decision,
he gives these provisions an uninflated significance (". . . it enabled the
Minister to prevent a reduction of the tax payable by reason of a sale at less
than what he considered to be fair value of the oil"[17]), but when he comes
finally to attributing the leading constitutional aspect to the taxation
scheme the minister's power is seen as compulsion to sell the product "at a
price equivalent to what the Minister considers to be its fair value."[18] Arne
Paus-Jenssen has observed that "the Minister of Mineral Resources of Sas-

katchewan must indeed have been very surprised to discover the immense power to set prices in export markets which was attributed to him by the Supreme Court of Canada, power which in fact he does not possess and never did possess.''[19] In passing it should be observed that this attribution to the minister of price-control powers was also the basis of the majority's finding that the tax was indirect and, accordingly, on that basis alone, invalid.

It was pointed out by Justice Dickson, writing in dissent for himself and one other justice, that the price of Saskatchewan oil was not affected in any way by the provincial tax; it simply could not be claimed that the price was altered to allow the producers to recoup the tax cost.[20] Martland's response to this incontrovertible observation was this:

> It is contended that the imposition of these taxes will not result in an increase in the price paid by oil purchasers, who would have been required to pay the same market price even if the taxes had not been imposed, and so there could be no passing on. . . . This, however, overlooks the all important fact that the scheme of the legislation under consideration involves the fixing of the maximum return of the Saskatchewan producers at the basic well-head price per barrel, while at the same time compelling him to sell at a higher price. There are two components in the sale price, first the basic well-head price and second the tax imposed. Both are intended by the legislation to be incorporated into the price payable by the purchaser. The purchaser pays the amount of the tax as a part of the purchase price.[21]

Thus Martland has confused the fact of economic recoupment with the test of whether the taxpayer has, through pricing, passed on the tax burden to a third party.

In dealing with the question of the character of the tax Martland also employed the "categories test." He labelled the tax an export tax which, by definition, is not only indirect, but is not "for Provincial Purposes" as required by section 92(2).[22] This was a highly suspect line of reasoning, since the tax applied to all production whether or not the oil left Saskatchewan. The only basis on which the Court would have been warranted in ignoring this fundamental aspect of the tax is if it had been willing to impute subterfugeous intent to the Saskatchewan legislature. Clearly it could not do so, since the universality of the tax accorded with the reasonable, or constitutional, aim of the tax—the raising of revenue. In other words, extending the application of the tax to oil destined for out-of-province markets is consistent with the tax motives of the law.

The result of the *CIGOL* case has been to cast a cloud over provincial taxes directed at oil and gas revenues. The mere fact that the tax affects the value of a produced commodity moving largely in interprovincial and international trade is sufficient to raise the spectre of a "Trade and Commerce" classification.

Saskatchewan, daunted but not resigned, enacted the Oil Well Income Tax Act (Bill 47) with retroactive provisions that allowed the retention of the $500 million collected under the invalid law.[23] However, the legislative history of Bill 47 and the fact of the *CIGOL* decision present substantial concerns about whether any tax on provincial resources might be challenged at some time. For one thing, it would appear, perhaps illogically, that provincial legislation designed to remedy the constitutional defects of earlier legislation is especially vulnerable.

Part of the aftermath of *CIGOL* has been provincial determination to remove this constitutional cloud through constitutional amendment. It is clear that *CIGOL*'s impact on resource taxes is so uncertain that that decision alone would not have provided the impetus for constitutional change. There are other causes for Canada's engagement, since the fall of 1978, in broadly based constitutional reform. The chief motives include the need to patriate the Constitution and develop a procedure under which the Constitution of Canada may be amended by a procedure that is wholly domestic rather than one requiring resort to the Westminster Parliament for implementation. Another motive was the widespread desire to respond to the threat posed by the election of the Parti Quebecois in Quebec in November 1976. However, western provinces, notably Saskatchewan and Alberta, have pushed for changes that respond directly to the West's constitutional needs. As a result, during the negotiating processes in 1978-1979 and the summer of 1980 resources and taxation of resources were "on the table."

When eleven-sided negotiations broke down at the First Ministers' Conference of September 1980, the federal government chose to proceed with unilateral constitutional amendment. As a condition of support for the constitutional package, and the unilateral process, the federal New Democratic Party (NDP) took up the western interest in constitutional reform of the resources and taxation area. Although the draft text agreed to by the federal NDP seemed to reveal that Party's unfamiliarity with the constitutional needs of provinces with significant energy resources, it did contain a provision for provincial taxation powers in respect of nonrenewable natural resources. It was hoped this would solve, in part, the so-called *CIGOL* problem. Subsequently, the federal government's plans for unilateral constitutional reform were challenged in the courts by some provinces. On 28 September 1981, the Supreme Court of Canada handed down its decision holding, in part, that a federal request to the United Kingdom Parliament for amendment to the British North America Act, over the opposition of most of the provinces, was contrary to constitutional convention in respect of amendment.[24] Following that decision the prime minister and provincial premiers met in November 1981 to see if a general agreement on constitutional change between most, or all, governments could not be reached. The meetings were successful to the extent that the federal government and the governments of nine of the ten provinces (Quebec being the dissenting province) agreed on the terms of a resolution to be sent to the United Kingdom. The accord reached in November radically altered some of the elements of the constitutional text but left intact the provisions relating to jurisdiction over nonrenewable natural resources. Consequently new provincial-taxation powers over natural resources will soon be included in the Constitution.

The new powers will be contained in section 92A of the BNAA, which includes this power:

> (4) In each province, the legislature may make laws in relation to the raising of money by any mode or system of taxation in respect of
> (a) non-renewable natural resources and forestry resources in the province and the primary production therefrom, and
> (b) sites and facilities in the province for the generation of electrical energy and the production therefrom,
> whether or not such production is exported in whole or in part from the province, but such laws may not authorize or provide for taxation that differentiates between production exported to another part of Canada and production not exported from the province.[25]

In other clauses of the new section 92A provinces are granted exclusive legislative authority over development, conservation, and management of natural resources.[26] These provisions may be not so much a novel grant of powers as an amplification of powers already enjoyed by provinces under existing provisions of the BNAA.[27] In any event, this constitutional grant, or recognition, could conceivably have the effect of immunizing resource-specific taxes from the attack based on the overwhelmingly extraprovincial trade in the subject matter of the tax. This argument, however, would be only makeweight in light of the specific taxation provisions in the Constitution. Furthermore, the recognition of a nonrenewable-resources jurisdiction logically does nothing to diminish the scope of the federal trade and commerce power, which can be advanced as a limitation on provincial powers no matter in what terms those powers are cast. Likewise, this may be the chink in the *CIGOL* solution; the provincial-taxation measure or its anti-avoidance provisions can at some point be classified as an extraprovincial-trade regulatory mechanism and not as a tax or a measure necessary to enforce the tax. This would clearly occur when the taxation measure is colorable in that it is unambiguously directed at regulating that trade without significant revenue-raising objects. This result would not be unreasonable; constitutional powers are meant to be exercised in good faith and, when they are not, constitutional integrity requires a finding of invalidity. However, in light of *CIGOL,* it remains a possibility that, when the tax, regardless of legislative motive, affects the cost of goods moving largely extra-provincially, the courts will simply label the leading aspect of the legislation to be trade and commerce. This possible outcome causes concern about the real benefit of section 92A(4). The legacy of *CIGOL* seems to be that when the process of characterizing challenged laws does not treat competing heads as equally important, there may be no means, through altering the constitutional text, to get around the characterization problem.

Earlier I advanced the view that the provincial taxing power created no implicit limitation on the federal power to tax but stated that, nevertheless, the apparently unlimited federal power might be subject to a restriction. This possibility is raised in the Statement of Claim of the City of Medicine Hat in its application for a Declaration against the attorney general of Canada and the minister of National Revenue that the two taxes announced in the federal government's National Energy Program are unconstitutional as applied to that city.[28] Medicine Hat is making the predictable claim that it, as an instrumentality of the provincial government, is entitled to the constitutional immunization from taxes on crown property. However, Medicine Hat's claim is also that the rate of tax on natural gas is, compared to its pretax cost, so high and that the effect on the cost of gas for consumers is so drastic, that the city's constitutionally recognized local-government function has been impaired. In other words, Medicine Hat is advancing a version of the colorability argument. The federal Energy Program taxes, although possessing the form of taxes, impact so heavily on a provincial head of power ("Municipal Institutions in the Province") that the proper characterization of the tax, at least as applied to Medicine Hat, is that it is a law in relation to a provincial head.

Ownership

The majority of lands in the western provinces from which oil and gas are being produced is public land, that is, land owned by the crown in the right of the province.[29] The implication of provincial crown ownership of resource-producing tracts is that the provinces are able to extract a royalty payment in respect to each unit of production. The obligation of producers to pay the royalty arises out of a contract between the producer and the province as owner of the producing tract. In exercising the rights of an owner, as opposed to legislative powers constitutionally granted, there are no constitutional limits on what contractual terms can be set. This is not to say that a province exercising its ownership powers need fear no overriding constraints, since it is always possible for valid federal law to be passed that would limit the province in the terms that it imposed in its leases. Such overriding federal legislation would not, of course, be common or easily found to be constitutional, since *ex hypothesi,* such legislation would be interfering with the constitutionally recognized ownership rights of the province.

However, it is possible to conceive of circumstances in which valid federal overriding legislation could be enacted. Federal jurisdiction over the regulation of trade and commerce [section 91(2) of the BNAA] could support legislation respecting international or interprovincial trade in resources that limited, in some way, the scope of contractual freedom for the province, so long as this limitation was purely incidental, or ancillary, to a legitimate trade regulatory scheme. Likewise the power of the federal government to make laws for "the Peace, Order and Good Government of Canada," a power found in the opening words of section 91 of the BNAA, has been held to support legislation enacted to meet emergency situations. It is entirely conceivable that Canada could experience an energy-supply emergency that would justify a comprehensive federal policy of resource extraction, distribution, and revenue sharing that overrode the royalty pattern put in place by a provincial government.[30]

In addition, it should be noted that section 121 of the BNAA may place a limitation on the rights of the province in the exercise of its proprietary powers.[31] That section states: "All Articles of the Growth, Produce, or Manufacture of any one of the Provinces shall, from and after the Union, be admitted free into each of the other Provinces." The effect of this proscription might be to foreclose a royalty-rate structure that contained differentials based on whether the production was destined for intraprovincial use or extraprovincial use. This distinction would result if a province were to use the royalty structure to provide cheap energy to its residents or, alternatively, if the province were to encourage, through the reduction of royalties, a domestic secondary-energy industry.[32]

It should be noted that this interpretation of section 121 is arguable. The section states that goods shall "be admitted free into each of the other Provinces." The proscription, therefore, may simply be against levies on imports and may not address the question of export levies. The federal government's belief that the Canadian Economic Union does not enjoy sufficient constitutional buttressing is an indication that the wider reading of the section might not be sustained in the courts.[33] On the other hand, there is the suggestion in the opinion of Justice Rand in *Murphy* v. *C.P.R. and Attorney General of Canada*[34] that section 121's purpose is to create a general prohibition on restraints on the movement of products.[35] And elsewhere in the same opinion he implicitly identifies section 121 as being concerned with "interference with the free current of trade across provincial lines."[36] Under this view of the section there is a potential limitation on the provinces' contracting powers.

The power to make laws in relation to crown minerals is conferred on provinces by section 92(5) of the BNAA, which gives provinces exclusive jurisdiction over "the Management and Sale of the Public Lands belonging to the Province and of the Timber and Wood thereon." The primary nature of this jurisdiction over crown lands is not limited by the reference to timber rights.

Provincial ownership of public lands is conferred under section 109 of the BNAA, which states:

> All Lands, Mines, Minerals, and Royalties belonging to the several Provinces of Canada, Nova Scotia, and New Brunswick at the Union, and all Sums then due or payable for such Lands, Mines, Minerals, or Royalties, shall belong to the several provinces of Ontario, Quebec, Nova Scotia, and New Brunswick in which the same are situate or arise, subject to any Trusts existing in respect thereof, and to any Interest other than that of the Province in the same.

This section refers only to the original provinces, but, with the exception of Alberta, Saskatchewan, and Manitoba, parallel sections were enacted at the time new provinces joined confederation. When the three Prairie provinces were created, Manitoba in 1870 and Alberta and Saskatchewan in 1905, the lands, mines, minerals, and royalties incident thereto were retained by the dominion. This situation, which was a constant irritant to those provinces, persisted until 1930, when Canada entered into an agreement with Manitoba, Saskatchewan, and Alberta under which they were placed on an equal footing with the other provinces; provincial rights under section 109 of the BNAA were extended to those provinces. The opening section in each of the agreements states: "In order that the Province may be in the same position as the original Provinces of Confederation are in by virtue of section one hundred and nine of the British North America Act, 1867, the interest of the Crown in all Crown lands and all sums due or payable for such lands, mines, minerals or royalties . . . belong to the Province. . . ."[37]

There is a degree of uncertainty about the extent to which public-land ownership confers on the provinces the right to regulate the exploitation of resources on those lands. It is altogether likely that the province enjoys broader powers in respect to regulating exploitation of these lands than they have by virtue of the legislative powers under section 92. For instance, in the early case of *Smylie v. The Queen*, the Ontario Court of Appeal held that Ontario could validly require, as a condition of granting a license to cut timber from crown lands, that all cut timber must be processed within Canada.[38] Likewise, in *Brooks-Bidlake and Whittall Limited* v. *Attorney General of B.C.*, the Judicial Committee of the Privy Council allowed a provincial prohibition against employing Chinese or Japanese labor to be inserted as a condition of a crown timber license.[39] These results prevailed, notwithstanding federal jurisdiction over trade and commerce and over aliens. As indicated, had there been valid federal law with which these conditions conflicted, the results would likely have been different. In any event, this form of exercise of proprietary powers does not relate directly to resource revenues; ambiguity about either the propriety or current significance of these decisions need not cast doubt on the central point that true royalty provisions are clearly valid.

A final point about this power is that provinces not only may contract for whatever royalty rate they are able to obtain but also they may contract for the inclusion of a provision under which lessees agree to comply with all relevant provincial legislation in force from time to time. In this way, ownership is used to bring about a prospective adoption by reference of provincial laws, as a term of the lease, with attendant contractual remedies for their breach. In other words, provincial control over resource revenues includes the ability to change the terms of the contract whenever the province chooses. Under Alberta law, all crown leases are subject to two significant features: the first is that the lessee agrees to deliver his oil to the Alberta Petroleum Marketing Commission, which acts as his exclusive agent for marketing the oil,[40] and the second is that there is a prospective adoption of all royalty rates, which may be set from time to time by regulation.[41]

State Firms

General Issues

To the extent that a province wishes to become an entrepreneur in the oil and gas industry it is, of course, able to exert a considerable influence over the province's share of resource revenues. This is true whether the provincial enterprises derive revenue from crown lands, freehold lands acquired since confederation (or in the case of the Prairie provinces, since 1930), or from lands worked under mineral leases. There seems to be no constitutional limitation on a province's capacity to create crown corporations through which provincial monies are dedicated to the acquisition or creation of commercial enterprises. It is true that the provincial taxation power is limited to "raising of a Revenue for Provincial Purposes" and that the provincial incorporating power is limited to "the Incorporation of Companies with Provincial Objects," but neither of these provisions has been read to impose a constraint on the provincial-policy objectives that are achievable through the creation of crown corporations. It would appear that what a provincial legislature determines is of benefit to the province, either by way of spending or by way of incorporation, will satisfy the tests of "Provincial Purposes" and "Provincial Objects."

A related issue is the extent to which the province is constitutionally permitted to expropriate existing energy enterprises as a means of becoming involved in the industry. This is an issue of purely academic relevance at this time, since there seems to be an adequate capacity for provinces to become engaged in the field through contractually based activity. In fact, the only circumstance under which expropriation would be a necessity is if a province were to set, as its policy, state ownership of the entire industry within the province. Twice in the last two decades British Columbia has passed legislation designed to nationalize an industry (that is, establish a state monopoly for either the whole province or a part of the province). The courts disallowed the first attempt, the *B.C. Power Corporation* case,[42] and permitted the second, the *Insurance* case.[43] The first attempt failed because the expropriation was of a single company that was the sole asset of its federally incorporated parent. It was held that British Columbia's compulsory purchase of the company impaired the federal incorporating power as exercised in the incorporation of the purchased company's parent. In the second case, where nationalization entailed the creation of a state monopoly in automobile insurance to the detriment of a large number of companies conducting business in an area subject to provincial legislation, the state monopoly was permissible.

The reasoning in the *B.C. Power Corporation* case would not apply to a strategy of expropriating all the companies in the energy-resources area. On the other hand, the *Insurance* case could also not be relied on. In the first place, it did not deal with expropriation. In the second place, it is not clear that provincial legislation allowing expropriation of oil and gas businesses, because of their extraprovincial character, could be said to be passed in relation to a provincial head of power, namely, property and civil rights, as opposed to a federal head, namely, the regulation of trade and commerce. The recent Quebec Court of Appeal decision in the *Asbestos Corporation* case upheld the right of the Province of Quebec to expropriate the assets of Asbestos Corporation. This decision lends support to the view that the nationalization of an industrial sector is a permissible provincial policy notwithstanding the largely interprovincial and international trading of the products of that sector.[44]

The Section-125 Problem

The major constitutional issue bearing on the operation of state firms is the extent to which the revenues, or income, of those firms are subject to federal revenue taxes, or federal corporate-income taxes. At first blush it appears that the BNAA provides an easy answer to this question. Section 125 states simply "No Lands or Property belonging to Canada or any Province shall be liable to Taxation."

Case law on this section has not been plentiful, and, indeed, it is only recently that the so-called 125 problem has gained widespread attention. The significance of section 125 to sharing resource revenues arose on the introduction of the National Energy Program at the end of October 1980. That program introduced two new taxes. The first was an excise tax of 30 cents per thousand cubic feet (mcf) (the Natural Gas and Gas Liquids Tax, or NGGLT). The second was an 8-percent Petroleum and Gas Revenue Tax (PGRT). The legislation in respect to both taxes makes explicit that the taxes are to be leviable against the crown in the right of the province.[45] The three major producing provinces of Canada (British Columbia, Alberta, and Saskatchewan) all responded by challenging the validity of imposing the new energy taxes on the provincial crown. Alberta directed questions to the Alberta Court of Appeal to obtain a judicial ruling on the constitutional validity of applying the NGGLT to gas produced by the Province of Alberta and sold by the province to purchasers in the United States. The Alberta Court of Appeal handed down its decision in the spring of 1981, holding that the application of that tax to export transactions of its own gas by the province is unconstitutional.[46] The Government of Canada appealed that decision to the Supreme Court of Canada, and argument of the case was heard in late June 1981. Both British Columbia and Saskatchewan, which, unlike Alberta, have crown corporations operating in the oil and gas production and distribution business and, therefore, attract these taxes, refused to make payment of them to the Government of Canada. The Government of Saskatchewan passed an Order in Council referring questions as to the validity of the application of these taxes to two of its crown corporations—Saskatchewan Power Corporation and Saskatchewan Oil and Gas Corporation—to the Saskatchewan Court of Appeal.[47]

However, before the matter was set down for hearing discussions were held between the governments of Canada and Saskatchewan, and an agreement over oil and gas prices and taxation of revenues was reached.[48] The parties to these negotiations had realized that the issue of the liability of the provincial crown for federal taxes was one that had to be resolved in the context of the pricing and taxation agreement. Since the purpose of the agreement is to allocate projected oil and gas revenues between the industry, the provincial government, and the federal government, it was imperative that the two governments know whether the federal share included tax revenues in respect to resources either produced by or, in the case of some taxes, marketed by, provincial crown corporations. In other words, if agreement were reached on the assumption that section 125 immunized the production of the Saskatchewan Oil and Gas Corporation from federal taxes and if the courts later concluded that this production should bear federal tax, the revenue "splits" between the federal and provincial governments, worked out in the agreement, would be disrupted. Consequently, the pricing and taxation agreement contains clauses under which the monies payable under the various federal taxes by the provincial crown are paid in the form of grants and the Government of Canada agrees not to collect the taxes. The agreement is stated to be without prejudice to the positions of each government.[49] A similar arrangement was reached in the British Columbia-Canada Agreement.[50]

Although these agreements, and the fact that Alberta has little, if any, crown production, mean that Canadian courts will not be as burdened with questions concerning the meaning and scope of the section-125 tax immunity, the recent confrontation has underscored the growing importance of this issue. Federal ambitions to subject all nonrenewable-resource revenues to a uniform federal-tax regime will not have evaporated with the signing of the energy-pricing agreements. The question has only been postponed, and only in respect to oil and gas. There are other major resources exploited under crown ownership that produce revenues of which the federal government is not a beneficiary.

There are three interpretative questions posed by section 125. The first is to determine whether the new energy taxes are taxation within the meaning of the section. The second is to determine whether imposing tax liability on crown corporations, performing an entrepreneurial role in the oil and gas industry, is tantamount to making the province liable to taxation. The third is to define exactly which tax bases count as imposing liability on the property of the province.

What Is Taxation? An examination of the legislative history behind section 125 of the BNAA suggests that the motive for its inclusion was to constitutionalize the crown-prerogative immunity from taxation.[51] This suggests that the language of section 125, particularly the word *taxation*, should not be construed very narrowly. On the other hand it should not be construed to immunize the provincial crown from regulatory burdens not primarily concerned with the raising of money, that are placed on provincial property through valid federal legislation. In fact, the case law dealing with the reach of federal regulation vis-à-vis provincial governmental agencies suggests that the tax immunity in section 125 has not been considered a source of broad immunity from regulatory levies.

The major analytical issue in applying the tax immunity has been the extent to which federal imposts could avoid the constitutional immunity for provinces on the basis that the impost, although in the form of a tax or duty, was in fact an instrument of federal legislation allowable under a head of section 91 other than section 91(3)—the taxation power.

In *Attorney General of British Columbia* v. *Attorney General of Canada* (the *Johnny Walker* case) the Judicial Committee of the Privy Council held that section 125 did not apply to exempt the Province of British Columbia from liability to pay federal-customs duty on the importation by the province of a case of scotch whiskey intended for sale in the province's crown-owned liquor stores.[52] The best reading of the Privy Council decision is that the law imposing the customs duty was primarily a law in relation to trade and commerce under section 91(2) and not a law primarily in relation to taxation. Lord Buckmaster in a somewhat obscure judgment states:

> The imposition of customs duties upon goods imported into any country may have many objects; it may be designed to raise revenue or to regulate trade and commerce by protecting native industries, or it may have the two-fold purpose of attempting to secure both ends; in either case it is a power reserved to the Dominion. . . . [S.125] is to be found in a series of sections which, beginning with s. 102, distribute as between the Dominion and the Province certain distinct classes of property, and confer control upon the Province with regard to the part allocated to them. But this does not exclude the operation of Dominion laws made in exercise of the authority conferred by s. 91. The Dominion have the power to regulate trade and commerce throughout the Dominion, and, to the extent to which this power applies, there is no partiality in its operation. Sect. 125 must, therefore, be so considered as to prevent the paramount purpose thus declared from being defeated.[53]

This passage seems to indicate a finding that the customs duty imposed in this case had as its paramount purpose the regulation of international trade and, therefore, the *ratio* of the case would be that when a taxing statute is enacted in relation to trade and commerce and not in relation to taxation it will not be subject to the limitation found in section 125. The Supreme Court of Canada decision,[54] from which British Columbia appealed, does not give forth any clear principle, but it too proceeds on the assumption that section 125 was drafted to protect government property only from taxation and not from regulation—even though regulation can in some instances amount to a deprivation of property as in the *Johnny Walker* case or in expropriation cases.

Although the point was not made in either the Supreme Court of Canada judgment or the Privy Council judgment, it is worth noting that the act imposed in the *Johnny Walker* case contains the following clause: ". . . provided, however, that nothing herein contained is intended to impose or to declare the imposition of any tax upon, or to make or to declare liable to taxation, any property belonging to His Majesty either in the right of Canada or of a province."[55] This indicates that the federal government, in that case, clearly viewed its customs duty as a device not to raise revenue but to control importation. This goal may be distinguished from the explicitly stated purposes of the National Energy Program taxes. The document announcing that program states: "Another source of revenue is needed. The Government of Canada will, therefore, impose a new natural gas and gas liquids tax."[56]

Although in the Alberta case the federal government attempted to apply the *Johnny Walker* decision to the National Energy Program taxes, it is likely that this attempt will fail, on the facts of the *Alberta Reference*, in the Supreme Court of Canada. The federal government stated that the challenged tax was a tax on exports (this is semantically true), that a tax on exports is an export tax, that an export tax is equivalent to an import duty, than an import duty is designed to regulate international trade, and that, therefore, the tax on exports did not fall under section 125. There are clear logical fallacies in this line of reasoning but, apart from these, the argument in any event is not available in a general challenge to the application of these taxes to provincial government operations, since in such a case all aspects of the National Energy Program taxes would be subject to consideration and not merely the export aspect. An attempt by the federal government to support the energy taxes under the trade-and-commerce power, using arguments similar to those used in the *Johnny Walker* case, would not likely succeed. Although these taxes are levied on commodities that enter the flow of international and interprovincial trade and commerce and, therefore, incidentally affect trade and commerce, it can hardly be said that the purpose of the taxes is to regulate trade and commerce. As has been noted, the federal government, both in the National Energy Program and in the budget papers, labelled the taxes as taxation and identified their purpose as raising sufficient revenues to support the Canadianization program outlined in those papers. It is clearly valid for the federal government to pursue the Canadianization purpose, but it does not follow that the raising of monies to promote that valid objective transforms taxation into regulation. The test can only be the purpose of the levy itself and not the purpose to which the funds raised by it are part. If the latter were the test then all federal taxes could be imposed on provinces so long as the funds produced were dedicated to federal purposes.

In addition, since neither the taxes nor the other legislative goals pursued treat differently the oil and gas kept within the producing province from the oil and gas taken out of the province, the scheme arguably does not meet the test for valid federal trade-and-commerce regulations. In other words, the National Energy Program is probably best sustained under Parliament's taxation and spending powers, and it is self-defeating for the federal government to deny its reliance on the former head. In any event, the federal government already has in existence ample legislative and regulatory controls over the production, distribution, pricing, and sale of gas and oil. To superimpose a tax on this regulatory framework with the excuse that the tax is an integral part of the regulatory scheme appears specious.

What Is Included within a "Province"? The main issue under this aspect of section 125 seems to be whether provincial crown corporations can be considered an integral part of the government of a province. There seems to be little doubt about the answer; it is clear that a crown corporation that is controlled by the crown is entitled to the same rights and privileges as the crown itself, whether those rights and privileges derive from common law, from statute, or from the Constitution. Furthermore, there are a number of cases that have confirmed this principle in relation to the application of section 125.[57] Property belonging to the following crown corporations has been held to belong to the crown for the purposes of section 125: Canada Mortgage and Housing Corporation,[58] British Columbia Power Commission,[59] the Canadian Broadcasting Corporation,[60] and the Halifax Harbour Commissioners.[61]

The two Saskatchewan crown corporations that under the terms of the National Energy Program would have been liable for taxes have been legislatively identified as agents of the crown. For example, the Saskatchewan Oil and Gas Corporation Act provides that:

> 2(4) The corporation is for all purposes an agent of Her Majesty in right of Saskatchewan, and its powers under this Act may be exercised only as an agent of Her Majesty.

> (5) The corporation may, on behalf of Her Majesty, contract in its corporate name without specific reference to the Crown or Her Majesty.

> (6) All property whether real or personal, and all money acquired, administered, possessed or received by the corporation is the property of Her Majesty in right of Saskatchewan and shall for all purposes be deemed to be the property of Her Majesty.[62]

The matter becomes more complicated when considered with the question of the tax liability of subsidiaries of crown corporations. It is possible that a court would find that the subsidiaries are not crown agents and not entitled to the protection of section 125. The subsidiaries, for example, of both the Saskatchewan crown corporations to which the energy taxes purportedly apply are not creations of the provincial crown nor are their assets the property of the provincial crown. Even if the degree of control actually exercised by the provincial government over the subsidiaries were as great as that exercised over the parent corporations, the courts would likely fasten on the separate legal existence of the subsidiaries as distinct corporations. Likewise, the statutory designation of these subsidiaries as agents of the crown may not be effective in immunizing them from federal taxes. The subsidiaries would remain as privately incorporated companies, in most cases created under the laws of other jurisdictions and not operating within the province. It would be hard to maintain that extraprovincial subsidiaries are agents of a crown the constitutional jurisdiction of which is limited to governmental activity "within the province."

A more difficult aspect of the question of section 125's scope of protection is whether that section protects provincial property acquired through commercial activity as opposed to forming part of the province's conventional government operation. For some years the federal government has maintained that section 125 should be considered a shield for provincial crown corporations engaged competitively in commercial activities. The most recent manifestation of federal anxiety on this score is found in the report of the parliamentary taskforce on federal-provincial fiscal arrangements, entitled *Fiscal Federalism in Canada*, issued on 31 August 1981:

> [S. 125] means that provincial hydro electric utilities and firms such as the Potash Corporation of Saskatchewan pay no income taxes. Combined with the complicit backing of the provincial governments, the advantageous tax treatment available to some provincial Crown corporations could make them formidable competitors. In addition, tax exemption for Crown corporations provides an incentive to convert profitable private industry firms to this status. The real issue is the extent to which a large portion of what is now private property may become immune from federal taxation.
>
> It has been suggested that if the provinces' position *vis-á-vis* section 125 is fully supported by the courts (including the Supreme Court of Canada), the producing provinces could turn major portions of their oil and gas industries into Crown corporations. This would enable these provinces to shelter a large part of their oil and gas revenues from federal taxation. Since all property of provinces is immune from federal taxation, it may be worthwhile for the provinces generally to "nationalize" other industries so as to pre-empt the federal government from deriving revenues it believes it is justified in collecting.[63]

There may be a certain appeal to the proposition that when a province embarks on a commercial enterprise it should be treated as having accepted the same tax regime as that imposed on a privately owned enterprise. And, as is pointed out in the last extract, if tax exemptions are extended to all activities carried out by provinces the expansion of state capitalism would be encouraged, and this could erode seriously the federal tax base.

On the other hand there is no satisfactory principle, either as a matter of constitutional law or as a matter of economic discernment, that characterizes an activity of a crown corporation as commercial. It might be said that once a government decides to embark on an enterprise this indicates that a governmental interest has been identified. Which undertakings would a court feel comfortable in labelling as without legitimate government purpose or as the result of pure commercial motives? W.H. McConnell in his *Commentary on the British North America Act* states: "Rarely does a government launch a commercial undertaking or Crown corporation purely in an effort to compete for private profit."[64] No doubt there are public-policy (that is, governmental) considerations that have drawn Saskatchewan so deeply into the oil and gas industry.

Furthermore, section 125 gives no textual support for such a distinction. It might be argued that had the distinction been appropriate for applying section 125 it would have been picked up in the *Johnny Walker* case, since in that case the province's liquor-retailing activity was motivated, at least in part, by a desire to capture the profits of that business. Furthermore, it cannot be argued that the distinction was not thought of in that case, since Justice Idington, in the Supreme Court of Canada, noted that the province's activity could not have been within the contemplation of the framers of the BNAA.[65] No other justice in that Court or in the Privy Council adopted this point of analysis.

The distinction is, however, not unknown in U.S. constitutional jurisprudence. The limitation on state tax immunity based on the commercial activity of the state was first articulated in *South Carolina* v. *United States* in which it was held that a state was liable to pay a federal tax, in the form of a license fee, on the sale of liquor in state liquor stores.[66] The court said that the exemption of the state was limited to functions "of a strictly governmental character" and did not extend to "the carrying on of an ordinary business." In *New York* v. *United States* (the *Mineral Waters* case), in which a federal tax on the sale of mineral waters was held applicable to the sale by New York State of mineral waters taken from state-owned springs at Saratoga, it appears that the governmental/commercial distinction is in operation.[67] Although all judges rejected the distinction as untenable, the majority then held that the tax was allowable, since it did not "curtail the business of the state government more than it does the like business of the citizen," thereby implicitly perpetuating the distinction.[68] However, it should be noted that there is no provision of the U.S. constitution explicitly creating intergovernmental tax immunity and that difference between the U.S. and Canadian constitutional texts makes the U.S. jurisprudence of only marginal interest.

We are, nevertheless, left with the problem of defining a limit on the operation of section 125 that would forestall massive disruption of federal taxation policies through high levels of provincial nationalization. Perhaps the answer might be found in the suggestion from the *Mineral Waters* case that when the activities of the state are paralleled by "the like business of the citizen" (or, in other words, when the crown corporation acts in competition with the private sector in a particular market) intergovernmental tax immunization should not be available. This would not be because of the unfair advantage given to crown corporations, since it is difficult to discern competitive fairness as a constitutionalized value. Rather it would be because the governmental decision not to create a state monopoly is an indication that the economic and social function is being performed adequately under the normal competitive model. In other words, in these situations it is not possible to discover governmental objectives that override the social welfare produced by normal market activity; there are no special policies that the government has in relation to the delivery of those goods and services that are not capable of being met through the operation of the market. This is not to say that there are no governmental objectives behind the creation of the state firm, such as obtaining access to an industry or capturing a share of a lucrative market for the public benefit, but rather that those objectives do not meet the threshold test of governmental interest.

The major difficulty with such a test is that it would provide a powerful inducement to provinces, when initiating governmental participation in a particular sector of economic activity, to enter it through the removal of all private activity. Of course, the creation of a government monopoly in this way is often precisely what the government wants. For instance, provincial automobile-insurance schemes designed to implement efficient indemnification schemes logically require a government insurance monopoly, at least to the minimum level of protection established as government policy. On the other hand there are times when governmental economic goals are satisfied through merely being a participant. The effect of the proposed test might be to induce provinces to exclude all private actors, merely as a tax-avoidance measure, each time the province became involved for whatever reason. If this happened the purpose of the test or distinction (that is, to prevent broad erosion of the federal tax base) would be defeated. In turn the result of this could well be that courts would begin to determine which provincial monopolies were "valid" and which were "invalid." Courts would undertake assessments of the legitimacy of creating provincial crown monopolies. This is not an appropriate function for a court, since nationalization policies are totally political—that is, they are a product of distinct ideological views concerning the role of the state.

A further test by which crown market activity could be judged as being governmental is whether the activity is conducted through the instrumentality of a government department or a crown corporation. This test, which appears overly formal, can be justified as responsive to a rational governmental/commercial distinction on the basis that, if the activity is able to be carried on in a department, governmental objectives would seem to be satisfied by less free-wheeling and entrepreneurial activity. If it must be carried out through a corporation, that is, under an organization acting under less severe jurisdictional and rule-of-law constraints, it would appear that the governmental objectives are more purely competitive or entrepreneurial. However, this test, like the former one, might lead to the use of inefficient structures (and even false and arbitrary structures) to obtain the benefit of the tax immunity.

On balance both attempts to give content to the governmental/commercial distinction lead to tests that, although they contain some rational elements, would likely produce inefficient tax-avoidance behavior. Once that happened courts would have to undertake a second-generation enquiry of whether the apparent satisfaction of the test for immunity should not be recognized because the governmental structure and behavior is the product of no rational motive other than tax avoidance. The potential for intrusive economic judgment by the judiciary under the second-generation enquiry is high and unfortunate.

Property under Section 125. There are two aspects to the question of what is property under section 125. The first aspect is to discover the nature of the property that is mentioned in the section and the second is to determine whether some tax bases may be considered not to amount to a tax on property.

With respect to the first of these questions, it has been argued that, since section 125 appears in part 8 of BNAA, entitled ''Revenues; Debts; Assets; Taxation,'' the immunity created by that section is limited to taxation on property that is otherwise identified in that part of the act. In particular, it is suggested that the tax immunity refers only to what is known as section-109 property. But there is nothing within the text of section 125 to suggest this limitation apart from its location within the same part of the BNAA. Furthermore, it is not altogether clear that part 8 is not a pot pourri of provisions, the sections of which do not necessarily interrelate. The title of the part does not suggest any interconnection between the various sections. Although there is clearly a fiscal tone to the part, the fact of a common theme does not make it evident that the section dealing with tax immunity should be bound by the section dealing with land ownership. Indeed, the rather unusual punctuation in the title suggests that the part is not all ''of a piece.''

If section 125 were seen to be limited to section-109 property, the result would be that only crown property or the revenues produced by the use of crown property would be exempt from taxation. Crown property in this context refers simply to that property owned by the province by virtue of either section 109 or, in the case of Prairie provinces, the Natural Resources Transfer Agreement—that is, property that was crown property at the time a province entered confederation or at the time of the public-property transfer. Section 109 refers only to property held by the crown at the time of confederation or the transfer from one crown to another, since that section simply states that lands belonging to the preconfederation provinces shall belong to the postconfederation provinces. In this way, the section identifies specific lands and constitutionalizes ownership of them. Its basic function is not to delineate the concept of ownership but to confer a specific ownership. The result is that if the property referred to in section 125 is restricted to section-109 property, section 125's immunity relates only to those specific lands.

There is a further potential test for classifying property under section 125. It could be that property in that section refers to any property held by the province—whether or not it is section-109 property—so long as the property is held as a provincial asset. But if the property is held by the province merely in trade, it would not be protected by section 125. Applying this point to the National Energy Program taxes, the NGGLT would be payable by the Saskatchewan Power Corporation in respect to natural gas purchased for distribution to consumers. There is no textual support for this distinction. Furthermore, no previous case on section 125 has made a distinction between various pedigrees of property whether preconfederation, postconfederation, or inventory property. Nor is there a great deal of textual support for the distinction between conduit or inventory property on the one hand and provincial assets on the other. Nevertheless, such a distinction does allow for a break point so that there would be protection for the tax base if a province were to create a crown corporation that performs a conduit role in respect to virtually all commodities. On the other hand the ability of the federal government to recover commodity taxes through a retail-sales tax or consumption tax under which the province would not be the taxpayer is such that there is no real need for this sort of break point.

The last issue in connection with the concept of property is whether federal taxes are payable by provincial crown corporations if the taxes are on persons, transactions, or income, so long as they are not on commodities (or property). Although there is support for classifying taxes as not imposing a liability on property, in the recent federal-court decision of *Snow* v. *The Queen,* it would seem that the possibility of providing a rational test whereby the tax could be seen as not burdening property but only burdening, say, a transaction, is not high.[69] In the *Alberta Reference,* the Alberta Court of Appeal rejected the attempt to classify taxes in this way:

> Section 125 refers only to lands or property. It does not expressly relate to taxes on persons, or on transactions, or on the exercise of property rights such as use or movement of the property. But the practical effect of a tax on the transaction by which a government disposes of its property, or a tax on the person of the proprietor of that property, differs little from a tax on the property itself. We do not agree that the plain purpose of section 125 can be avoided by so simple a device. The immunity extends not only to the property of a Province but to a Province with respect to its property.[70]

The true flaw in the attempt to distinguish taxes on property from taxes on persons or transactions is that if it were to succeed it would render section 125 meaningless. Small drafting changes could easily change the classification of any federal tax. The tax on property could be transferred easily into a tax on a person or transaction, with the property being used to measure the amount of the tax. Also, changes in the basic tax scheme could effect a different constitutional result. A tax on net income could be changed to a tax on production at a lower rate. It is not likely that the Supreme Court of Canada would accept a distinction that enables section 125 to be so easily evaded.

Conclusion

It will be seen that, in respect to interjurisdictional tax immunity, the courts have barely begun to address the problems of interpretation and delineation. Governmental activity and economic conditions that have permitted these issues to go unresolved for so long are quickly changing; section-125 jurisprudence will be an important factor in the sharing of resource revenues by governments.

The other forms of governmental capture of revenues pose less diverse juridical speculation. But even here the imminent introduction of section 92A and especially section 92A(4), the new provincial taxing power, will produce a slightly new configuration of competing powers. Judicial interpretation of the powers to tax and to regulate through the exercise of crown ownership rights is not complete; the tensions in these areas are not purely historic.

At a very general level provincial powers in this area—the wide power to tax, the control of resource development and revenue that flows from ownership of crown land, and the immunity, of uncertain scope, of the provincial crown from federal taxes—are considerable. In a federal state the central government can always, if it chooses to make inroads on provincial activity, generate a centripetal force.[71] There is evidence that central economic regulation has been alluring to the federal government over the past decade. This is not surprising; activist governments, such as Canada has had, normally proceed through equal parts of self-confidence and ambition. The question that remains is whether the considerable provincial-resource powers will serve to keep the tension alive, to hold up the present balance between the center and the regions. If so, resources may be serving a double duty in Canadian development: enhancing its economic growth and, through federal-provincial conflict over resources, producing long-term political stability.

Notes

1. Memorandum of Agreement between the Government of Canada and the Government of Alberta relating to Energy Pricing and Taxation, 1 September 1981. Paragraph 14 of the agreement states: "The Government of Canada and the Government of Alberta do not intend to introduce any tax, royalty or levy specific to the oil and gas producing industry, other than those set out in this Agreement." Similar undertakings are given severally by the parties in paragraphs 9 and 10.

2. The British Columbia Agreement took the form of a letter from the Hon. Marc Lalonde, federal minister of Energy Mines and Resources to the

Hon. Robert H. McClelland, British Columbia's minister of Energy Mines and Petroleum Resources, dated 24 September 1981. The terms of the Saskatchewan agreement are contained in a letter of Understanding and Appendix between the Government of Canada and the Government of Saskatchewan relating to Energy Pricing and Taxation, dated 26 October 1981.

    3. Central Canada Potash v. Government of Saskatchewan, [1978] 88 D.L.R.3d 609 (S.C.C.).

    4. A new factor in this dispute will be the newly expressed grant of power to the provinces under section 92A of the BNAA. (Section 92A is contained in section 50 of the Constitution Act, presently in the form of a Resolution adopted by the Parliament of Canada, December 1981). This section states, in part:

> 92A. (1) In each province, the legislature may exclusively make laws in relation to
> (a) exploration for non-renewable natural resources in the province;
> (b) development, conservation and management of non-renewable natural resources and forestry resources in the province, including laws in relation to the rate of primary production therefrom; and
> (c) development, conservation and management of sites and facilities in the province for the generation and production of electrical energy.

    This new section may not significantly improve the constitutional position of provinces, since provincial laws respecting "development, conservation and management" may so markedly affect international trade that courts will ascribe a federal character to them rather than a section-92A character.

    5. In Caron v. R., [1924] A.C. 999 (J.C.P.C.) Lord Phillimore stated that Parliament could not levy direct taxation to raise revenue for provincial purposes. This is an instance of reading and placing limits on the federal power in light of the provincial power. See, G. LaForest, The Allocation of Taxing Power under the Canadian Constitution 51-53 (2d ed. 1981) for a discussion of the relation of federal to provincial taxing power.

    6. Lederman, *The Constitution: A Basis for Bargaining,* in Natural Resources Revenues: A Test of Federalism 57 (A. Scott ed. 1976).

    7. [1887] 12 App. Cas. 575 (J.C.P.C.).

    8. *Id.* at 582.

    9. [1952] 2 S.C.R. 231 at 252. This test has been expressly adopted and applied in the recent Supreme Court of Canada judgment in Minister of Finance v. Simpsons Sears (decision of 26 January 1982). In this case Chief Justice Laskin, speaking for the Court, said: "The fact that the company may, competitive and other factors permitting, recoup the tax in its overall pricing structure, is no ground for classifying it as an indirect tax" (at 18).

10. These limitations are discussed in Moull, *Natural Resources: The Other Crisis in Canadian Federalism,* 18 Osgoode Hall L. J. 1 at 6 (1980).

11. Canadian Industrial Gas & Oil Ltd. v. Government of Saskatchewan [1977] 80 D.L.R.3d 449 (S.C.C.).

12. For descriptions of the problems created in Canada by the cartelization of Middle Eastern oil in 1973-1974, see Breton, *The Federal-Provincial Dimensions of the 1973-74 Energy Crisis in Canada* in *The Political Economy of Fiscal Federalism* 105-113 (W. Oates ed. 1977); Moull, *supra* note 10, at 11-12; Smiley, *The Political Context of Resource Development in Canada* in *Natural Resource Revenues: A Test of Federalism* 61-73 (A. Scott ed. 1976).

13. Queen's Bench decision: [1975] 2 W.W.R. 481; Court of Appeal decision: [1975] 65 D.L.R.3d 79, [1976] 2 W.W.R. 356.

14. Extraprovincial effect was rejected as a controlling criterion in Carnation Co. v. Quebec Agricultural Marketing Board, [1968] S.C.R. 238.

15. *Supra* note 11, at 463.

16. *Id.* at 464.

17. *Id.* at 461.

18. *Id.* at 462.

19. Paus-Jenssen, *Resource Taxation and the Supreme Court of Canada: The CIGOL Case,* (1979), 5 Can. Pub. Pol'y 45 at 53; also quoted in Moull, *supra* note 10, at 24-25.

20. *Supra* note 11, at 481.

21. *Id.* at 463.

22. *Id.* at 461. Justice Martland stated: "The tax under consideration is essentially an export tax imposed upon oil production. In the past a tax of this nature has been considered to be an indirect tax."

23. Enacted as S.S. 1977-78, c. 26; now cited as R.S.S. 1978, c. 0-3.I.

24. *Reference re Amendment of the Constitution of Canada* [1981] 125 D.L.R.3d 1 (S.C.C.).

25. Contained in section 50 Constitution Act, 1981, presently in the form of a Resolution of Parliament adopted December 1981.

26. See *supra* note 4.

27. Provincial powers over resource management, apart from section 92A, flow from heads 5, 13, 16 of section 92 of the BNAA. These state:

In each Province the Legislature may exclusively make laws in relation to matters coming with the classes of subjects next hereinafter enumerated; that is to say . . .

5. The Management and Sale of the Public Lands belonging to the Province and of the Timber and Wood thereon.

13. Property and Civil Rights within the Province.

16. Generally all matters of a merely local or private nature in the Province.

In addition head 10 giving provinces exclusive jurisdiction over "Local Works and Undertakings" supports provincial regulation of resource management.

28. City of Medicine Hat v. Attorney General of Canada, Statement of Claim, filed in Court of Queen's Bench of Alberta, Judicial District of Calgary, 25 August 1981.

29. See Moull, *supra* note 10, at 6-8 for a discussion of provincial ownership rights. More detailed discussions of constitutional ownership and its effect on provincial resource-regulation power are found in Crommelin, *Jurisdiction over Onshore Oil and Gas in Canada,* 10 U.B.C. L. Rev. 86 at 88-115 (1975-1976) and Milen and Savino, "Nationalization or Regulation? Constitutional Aspects of the Control of the Saskatchewan Oil Industry," 39 Sask. L. Rev. 23 at 38-47 (1974-1975).

30. In fact the federal Parliament has already enacted such legislation. It first enacted the Energy Supplies Emergency Act, S.C. 1973-74, c. 52. The substantive portions of this act expired 30 June 1976. Second, Parliament enacted the Energy Supplies Emergency Act, 1979, S.C. 1978-79, c. 17. This latter act contains provisions relating to the mandatory allocation of supplies and the rationing of controlled products.

31. This line of argument is suggested, without elaboration, in Moull, *supra* note 10, at 8.

32. The new provincial tax power under section 92A(4) contains an express prohibition of this sort of discrimination (see text accompanying note 25, *supra*). However, this limitation on legislative power would not apply to provincial royalty schemes unless, of course, the royalty schemes were legislatively altered without a prior contractual term contemplating such changes. In this situation new royalty rates would be viewed, for constitutional purposes, as a tax.

33. See J. Chretien, Securing the Canadian Economic Union in the Constitution 19-20 (1980).

34. [1958] S.C.R. 626.

35. *Id.* at 637-643. For example, at 642 he states: "I take s.121 . . . to be aimed against trade regulation which is designed to place fetters upon or raise impediments to or otherwise restrict or limit the free flow of commerce across the Dominion as if provincial boundaries did not exist."

36. *Id.* at 638.

37. *See, e.g.,* sec. 1 Memorandum of [Natural Resources Transfer] Agreement between the Government of Canada and the Government of Saskatchewan, 20 March 1930. This agreement and the agreements with Manitoba and Alberta (and British Columbia in which a transfer of the Railway Belt and Peace River Block, held back in 1871, was made) were constitutionalized by the BNAA, 1930, 21 Geo. V, c. 26 (Imp.). For a

discussion of this history see G. LaForest, *Natural Resources and Public Property under the Canadian Constitution* 27-47 (1969).

38. [1900] 27 O.A.R. 172. (Ont. C.A.).

39. [1923] A.C. 450 (J.C.P.C.).

40. The Mines and Minerals Act, R.S.A. 1970, c. 238, as amended by the Mines and Minerals Amendment Act, 1973, S.A. 1973, C.94, s.5, which enacted sec. 170.1 of the main Act.

41. *Id.* sec. 4, which enacted s.142.1 of the main act. This section voids any royalty form that sets a maximum rate.

42. British Columbia Power Corporation v. Attorney General of British Columbia [1963] 47 D.L.R.2d 633 (B.C.Sup.Ct.).

43. Canadian Indemnity Co. v. Attorney General of British Columbia [1976] 63 D.L.R.3d 468 (S.C.C.).

44. Societe Asbestos Ltee. v. La Societe Nationale de L'Amiante and le Procureur General de Quebec (decision of Quebec Court of Appeal, 4 March 1981).

45. See, Excise Tax, Excise and Petroleum and Gas Revenue Tax, S.C. 1980-81, c. 68, sec. 25.12, which states: "This Part [Natural Gas and Gas Liquids Tax] binds Her Majesty in right of Canada or a province and every person acting for or on behalf of Her Majesty in right of Canada or a province." See, also, in the same statute, sec. 80, which states: "This Part [Petroleum and Gas Revenue Tax Act] is binding on Her Majesty in right of Canada and in right of any province."

46. *Reference re Proposed Federal Tax on Exported Natural Gas* [1981] 122 D.L.R.3d 48 (Alberta Court of Appeal).

47. Saskatchewan Order in Council 809/81, referring certain questions to the Saskatchewan Court of Appeal, passed under authority of the Constitutional Questions Act, R.S.S. 1978, c. C-29.

48. *Supra* note 2.

49. This arrangement is expressed in the Canada-Saskatchewan Energy Pricing and Taxation Agreement in the following paragraphs:

7. *Payment of Natural Gas and Gas Liquids Tax (NGGLT) and of the Canadian Ownership Special Charge (COSC)* The Government of Saskatchewan takes the position that the Crown in right of Saskatchewan, its agents, and every person acting for or on behalf of the Crown in right of Saskatchewan, are not liable to pay taxes under the NGGLT and COSC and the Government of Canada takes the position that it has the right to levy such taxes on the Crown in right of Saskatchewan, its agents, and every person acting for or on behalf of the Crown in right of Saskatchewan. The Government of Canada and the Government of Saskatchewan have agreed, however, to set aside those differences of position without prejudice to them in order to achieve the general purposes of this letter of understanding. Therefore:

The Government of Canada agrees to remit for the term of this agreement, effective November 1, 1980, the NGGLT and the COSC insofar as they apply or purport to apply to the Crown in the right of Saskatchewan, its agents, and every person acting for or on behalf of the Crown in right of Saskatchewan. The Government of Saskatchewan agrees to cause to be paid to the Government of Canada grants in lieu of the NGGLT and COSC in the amounts and at the times that are equivalent to those that would have been obtained under the NGGLT and COSC in respect of the Crown in right of Saskatchewan, its agents, and every person acting for or on behalf of the Crown in right of Saskatchewan. The grants shall include a payment forthwith to the Government of Canada of a grant in lieu equivalent to all amounts (including interest thereon as calculated by Revenue Canada) that would have been payable to date from November 1, 1980 under the provisions of the NGGLT and COSC by the Crown in right of Saskatchewan, its agents, and every person acting for or on behalf of the Crown in right of Saskatchewan.

The Government of Saskatchewan agrees to provide to the Government of Canada all the information and other material that would have been required under the provisions of the NGGLT and COSC.

8. *Payment of the Petroleum and Gas Revenue Tax (PGRT) and the Incremental Oil Revenue Tax (IORT)* The Government of Saskatchewan takes the position that the Crown in right of Saskatchewan, its agents, and every person acting for or on behalf of the Crown in right of Saskatchewan are not liable to pay taxes under the PGRT and IORT and the government of Canada takes the position that it has the right to levy such taxes on the Crown in right of Saskatchewan, its agents and every person acting for or on behalf of the Crown in right of Saskatchewan. The Government of Canada and the Government of Saskatchewan have agreed to set aside those differences of position without prejudice to them in order to achieve the general purposes of this letter of understanding.
Therefore:

The Government of Canada agrees to remit for the term of this letter of understanding, effective January 1, 1981, the taxes under the PGRT and IORT insofar as they apply or purport to apply to the Crown in right of Saskatchewan, its agents and every person acting for or on behalf of the Crown in right of Saskatchewan.

The Government of Saskatchewan agrees to cause to be paid to the Government of Canada grants in lieu of the PGRT and IORT in the amounts and at the times that are equivalent to those that would have obtained under the PGRT and IORT in respect of the Crown in right of Saskatchewan, its agents, and every person acting for or on behalf of the Crown in right of Saskatchewan. The grants shall include a payment forthwith to the Government of Canada of a grant in lieu equivalent to all amounts (including interest thereon as calculated by Revenue Canada) that would have been payable to date from January 1, 1981 by the Crown in right of Saskatchewan, its agents and every person acting for or on behalf of the Crown in right of Saskatchewan.

The Government of Saskatchewan agrees to provide to the Government of Canada all the information and other material that would have been required under the provisions of the PGRT and IORT.

50. The British Columbia-Canada arrangement is expressed in paragraph 1 of the letter of 24 September 1981, *supra* note 2:

> 1. I understand that the Government of British Columbia has agreed to
> cause its emanations to remit immediately to the Government of Canada all
> amounts owing (including interest owing thereon as determined by
> Revenue Canada) with respect to the Natural Gas and Gas Liquids Tax
> (NGGLT) and the Canadian Ownership Charge (COSC). Further, it is my
> understanding that the Government of British Columbia agrees to cause its
> emanations to pay those taxes for the period up to December 31, 1986 or in
> the event that the Government of British Columbia or its emanations are
> determined not to be liable for these taxes, the Government of British Co-
> lumbia or its emanations will cause to be paid to the Government of
> Canada an amount equivalent to these taxes and interest owing for the
> period November 1, 1980 to December 31, 1986.

It is interesting that this paragraph does not make any mention of the two
federal energy taxes (the Petroleum and Gas Revenue Tax and the Incremental Oil Revenue Tax). It is assumed that the agreement in respect to
the paying of these taxes by the provincial crown is contained in a further
letter that has not been made public. It is also interesting to note that British
Columbia agreed to remit the taxes for the duration of this agreement. It is
unclear whether the frank concession by British Columbia to pay federal
taxes will weaken any argument based on section 125 that it may wish to
make at the expiration of the agreement or in respect to some other sectors
of provincial-government activity.

51. Section 125 was given no recorded attention at the constitutional
debates in Charlottetown (1864) and little attention in Quebec (1864). It also
received little attention in the Parliament of the Province of Canada (1865)
or in London (1866-1867). The only plausible reason for this is that the idea
it embraced was ordinary and self-evident: the crown enjoys a general
prerogative immunity from taxation. That principle was simply that before
tax can be levied on the crown it must be clear that the crown has consented
to be taxed. The fact that the leading English cases on the scope of crown
immunity *Mersey Docks* v. *Jones* and *Mersey Docks* v. *Cameron,* 11
H.L.C. 443 (1865) were under appeal to the House of Lords from Court of
Exchequer Chamber at the time of the Quebec Conference may be the
reason why the principle was expressly included in the BNAA. Alternately,
it may have been recognized that with the division of the crown brought
about by the creation of a federal state the general rule needed to be expressed
in adapted form.

52. [1924] A.C. 222 (J.C.P.C.).

53. *Id.* at 225.

54. [1922] 64 S.C.R. 377.

55. An act to amend the Customs Act, S.C. 1917, c. 15, sec. 1.

56. Government of Canada, The National Energy Program, 1980 35 (1980).

57. For a discussion of the scope of "belonging to Canada or any Province" found in section 125 see LaForest, *supra* note 5, at 186-187.

58. Societe Centrale d'Hypotheques v. Cite de Quebec, [1961] Que. K.B. 661.

59. British Columbia Power Commission v. Victoria, [1951] 2 D.L.R. 480.

60. Re Canadian Broadcasting Corp. Assessment, [1938] 4 D.L.R. 591; Recorder's Court v. Canadian Broadcasting Corp. [1941] 2 D.L.R. 551.

61. City of Halifax v. Halifax Harbour Commissioners, [1935] S.C.R. 215.

62. The Saskatchewan Oil and Gas Corporation Act, R.S.S. 1978, c. S-32.

63. Report of the Parliamentary Task Force on Federal-Provincial Fiscal Arrangements, Fiscal Federalism in Canada 191 (1981).

64. W. McConnell, *Commentary on the British North America Act* 369 (1977).

65. *Supra* note 54, at 380. Brodeur, in the same case, however, did refer to Idington's distinction between governmental and commercial functions. He did not reject the distinction but said that the direct sale of liquor was the final step in the evolution of a public policy relating to liquor consumption (at 391).

66. 199 U.S. 261 (1905).

67. 326 U.S. 572 (1946).

68. *Id.* at 588-589.

69. [1979] 102 D.L.R.3d 191 (Federal Court of Appeal), affirming [1979] 92 D.L.R.3d 71 (Federal Court Trial Division).

70. *Supra* note 46, at 16.

71. See J. Corry, My Life and Work: A Happy Partnership 226-236 (1981) for an exposition on the inevitability of centralizing drifts in democratic states.

Comments

Thomas J. Courchene

I believe this to be an excellent survey of the constitutional underpinnings of federal-provincial actions in the natural resource sector. Indeed, it is much more than this. John Whyte, when dealing with Section 125 of our Constitution,[1] goes well beyond the realm of survey and precedent and offers some insightful projections about the potential limits of applicability of this increasingly important provision.

The first point I want to make relates to Whyte's quote from Lederman: "There is no constitutional prohibition against killing geese that lay golden eggs. Federal and provincial governments can severally or collectively be foolish about this." At a practical level, this is probably an apt description of what has happened to the Canadian energy sector. Low domestic energy prices, high provincial royalty rates, preferential tax treatment for Canadian-owned firms, the "back-in" or expropriation provision for energy finds in the so-called Canada Lands, and the nationalization of some energy firms have all contributed to the situation where activity in Canada's energy sector has been brought to a relative standstill compared to a few years ago. Obviously this is a comment on policy and not on the underlying constitutional issues that motivate Whyte's paper. But Lederman's observation has to be taken seriously, because it touches on a feature of the BNAA that may be peculiar to parliamentary systems. The role of the Canadian courts when addressing constitutional issues was not so much to decide whether a particular piece of legislation was *intra vires*.[2] Parliament was supreme: there was always one level of government that could enact any measure. Rather, the issue before the courts was which level of government had the right to enact such legislation. An example may drive home the point that the federal and provincial governments can collectively fleece the private sector. In the 1950s the Supreme Court struck down the operations of a provincial marketing board on the grounds that it was engaging in interprovincial trade. The response of the federal government, under pressure from various provinces, was to amend the Agricultural Products Marketing Act in 1957, which thereby enabled provincial marketing boards to engage in interprovincial trade. By 1970, fifty-nine such boards had their provincial powers extended to interprovincial and export trade.

Under the new Canadian Charter of Rights and Freedoms (which is part of the Constitution Act, 1982), all levels of government will be constrained to abide by its provisions. In terms of economic rights, however, the new charter does not go very far. There is a freedom-of-labor-mobility clause, but it is watered down considerably by a provision whereby any province with an above-average unemployment rate can enact affirmative-action programs directed toward its socially or economically disadvantaged citizens. I wish that Whyte would have addressed the issue of whether this or any other provision in the new constitution provides the market sector with any degree of immunity from government action. Or is it still the case, as I suspect, that there is always one level of government that can enact any and every measure?

Executive Federalism

Pursuing further Lederman's comment that governments can "severally and collectively" conspire, as it were, against the market sector, it is instructive to focus on another area where this principle comes into play (and another area where Canadian and U.S. political systems probably differ). This relates to the practice of so-called executive federalism—conferences of executives from federal and provincial governments. Fast approaching 1,000 such meetings annually, this innovation may well be Canada's "contribution to the art of federalism."[3] However valuable executive federalism may be to lending the needed flexibility to the BNAA in the political sphere, this so-called third level of government has not had a positive influence in the economic sphere and more particularly in the energy sphere. Indeed, it is usurping the role of the courts in ironing out federal-provincial jurisdictional disputes. Consider the recent (1981) federal-provincial energy agreements. In the Ottawa-Alberta Agreement there was an arrangement whereby both parties agreed not to go to the Supreme Court to test the legality of Ottawa's export tax on oil to the United States. In the Ottawa-Saskatchewan Agreement, both parties recognized that some of Ottawa's revenues under the agreement were coming from the operations of crown corporations, but again they agreed that neither party would bring this issue (section 125) before the courts. And in the proposed Ottawa-Newfoundland agreement there was a clause suggesting that the issue of who has jurisdiction over offshore oil would not be brought before the Supreme Court. Executive federalism may work to the combined advantage of the two levels of government, but by maintaining the cloud of uncertainty associated with not knowing who has ultimate control it is clear that it is not working to the advantage of the energy industry.

Why Go to the Supreme Court

Finally, it seems that often not much is gained by challenging government legislation in the Canadian courts. I already proferred the marketing-board example. The *Cigol* case, which Whyte treats in great detail, provides another example. I agree with Whyte that the Court's decision in this case borders on the absurd. With the federal government fixing the domestic market price, it is a trifle far-fetched to view Saskatchewan's tax measures as either falling into the indirect category (under the original BNAA the provinces could levy only direct taxes) or interfering with interprovincial trade.[4] For present purposes, the interesting aspect is that after the Supreme Court ruled against Saskatchewan, the province enacted the Oil Well Income Tax Act in 1978 with retroactive provisions that allowed the retention of the $500 million collected under the invalid law. As I understand the situation in the United States, the courts would have seen through the new legislation and most likely deemed it to also be *ultra vires*. This may or may not be so in Canada (it is probably less likely in my opinion). At any rate, after nearly four years this new legislation has not been challenged. Perhaps this is a reflection of the fact that when all is said and done, parliaments are still supreme, and as long as provincial and federal goals in any area are coincident some way will be found to enact the desired legislation.

The Trade-and-Commerce Clause

Whyte argues that as a result of recent court decisions the federal trade-and-commerce power appears to be on the rise. He also notes that this may be tempered by the recent provisions embodied in section 50 of the Constitution Act, 1982, which allows the provinces to raise money by any mode of taxation (including indirect taxes) in respect to nonrenewable resources. I have no problems with his analysis. Two observations are appropriate, however. First, the trade-and-commerce power did not always play this important role. Writing on the interaction between the trade-and-commerce power and the control over natural resources, S.I. Bushnell notes:

> The legislative authority given by the Constitution to the Dominion to regulate trade and commerce has always been recognized to be expansive due to the extremely wide terms used—"trade and commerce." Indeed the Supreme Court of Canada in its early decisions saw this power to be just what it appeared to be from the words used—the full, complete, and unrestricted power to regulate business.[5] But this wide view of Dominion authority was short lived and in 1881 the Judicial Committee of the Privy Council made the decision to restrict the power in order to preserve the autonomy of the provinces.[6] This rationale for the curtailment of the potential Dominion legislative power inherent in the constitutional provision has never been doubted, and as late as 1951 the Judicial Committee could assert that "trade and commerce" had to be limited "in order to preserve from serious curtailment, if not virtual extinction, the degree of autonomy which, as appears from the scheme of the act as a whole, the provinces were intended to possess."[7]

In *Citizens' Insurance Company v. Parsons,* the 1881 decision of the Judicial Committee in which the power was first restricted, the Dominion authority over trade and commerce was said to extend to the regulation of international and interprovincial trade, and as well, possibly the general
regulation of trade affecting the whole Dominion. This latter part, that is,
the general regulation, remains to this day in great measure a phantom.
Whatever was the actual extent of the restriction of the power envisaged by
the Privy Council in *Parsons*, the case did begin a trend towards restriction,
which reached its climax in the 1920s when the Judicial Committee reduced
the specific grant of power to regulate trade and commerce to that of an
auxiliary status within the Constitution,[8] meaning it could only be used in
aid of Dominion power found elsewhere in the Constitution. Lord Haldane
termed the trade and commerce power "merely ancillary,"[9] and in addition
spoke of it as needing some paramount Dominion purpose, some excep-
tional situation before it could be utilized, in other words, an emergency
situation.[10]

Second, even if the role of the trade-and-commerce clause is in the
ascendancy, it is inconceivable that it would ever attain the dominance and
power that the interstate-commerce clause has in the United States.

It has [the U.S. commerce clause] by means of the Shreveport doctrine
been interpreted to allow Congress to legislate with respect to intrastate activities that affect interstate commerce. Thus, when there is some connection to interstate trade, Congress may legislate with respect to labour relations and cognate matters, hours of work, labour arbitration, retirement
pensions, unemployment, local as well as interstate marketing including the
fixing of prices, the production of commodities and, generally, every phase
of industrial production organized on a multi-state basis.[11]

This degree of power accruing to the Canadian equivalent of the interstate-
commerce clause exists only in the wildest dreams of our centralist man-
darins.[12] Nonetheless, Whyte is probably correct in hinting that we have not
yet seen the full extension of the trade-and-commerce clause.

Supply Limitation

Whyte organizes his analysis around three issues: taxation; ownership, and
state firms (entrepreneurship). The last one of these will be dealt with in the
final section. In this section I want to focus on ownership and, more
specifically, on an aspect on which Whyte did not touch. Throughout the
first three quarters of 1981 the Alberta government turned down the taps, as
it were, and reduced the supply of oil to the rest of Canada. Was this constitutional? Ottawa did not challenge the move in the courts, thereby lending
some tacit support to the proposition that Alberta was within its rights in
restricting output.

This would, I think, be the way in which an economist would view the issue. If ownership means anything it means that the owner can hold output from the market. For example, I own my own labor. If I sell it to someone and as a result earn income I will be subject to the various income taxes. Thus, ownership in this sense does not mean the ability to alienate the entire proceeds from the selling of the output. But I do have the right to withdraw my services. In much the same sense it seems to me that Alberta has the right to withhold oil from the market. If it does not, then I do not understand what it means to say that the provinces "own" the resource.

There is, of course, the possibility that the federal government could invoke some draconian measure (such as the "peace, order and good government" clause) to forbid this sort of supply restriction. Perhaps it is even the case that the trade-and-commerce power could be brought into play here. In any event, this episode was certainly a fascinating one from a constitutional perspective. Hopefully, Whyte will in some other context turn his capable analytical powers to addressing this issue of the rights of a province in restricting supply.

Section 125

Whyte is truly to be commended for devoting so much effort to wrestling with the issues related to section 125 of the Constitution. This issue is going to surface in a major way in the near future because it touches on so many facets of the economic and institutional fabric of Canada. For example, with assets now approaching $12 billion, the Alberta Heritage Fund should be earning interest somewhere in the neighborhood of $1.5 billion per year (or roughly $700 per Albertan). Under Section 125, the federal government cannot tax these interest earnings, or at least it has not challenged this in the courts. The various hydro companies operated by the provinces are beginning to make tremendous profits: these too are currently going untaxed by the federal level. What this provision amounts to is a tremendous incentive for government to nationalize private enterprises. Saskatchewan has already done this with respect to much of its potash industry.

Whyte has focused on some of the complex legal issues that may arise when this provision is tested in the courts; for example, what is taxation, what is a province, and what consitutes property under section 125. To my knowledge (admittedly limited) he is breaking virgin territory here and has indeed provided valuable insights for the future.

From an economics vantage point, I find section 125 particularly inimical to the future of private enterprise in Canada. No doubt this reflects my free-market inclinations. Nevertheless, the underlying issue would appear to be whether or not factor incomes (rents, profit, interest) accruing in the public sector ought to be taxed preferentially compared with factor incomes accruing in the private sector. This is putting the issue a bit differently than Whyte does in his analysis. To be sure, Whyte's analysis of "what is taxation" does come close to the heart of the matter, since the line between what is a tax and what is a factor income is on occasion a very fine one. It is of some interest to note that for purposes of the Canadian equalization formula the profits of government enterprises are treated in the same way as private-sector profits (and lumped together in the revenue source entitled "business-income revenues"). Obviously, this has no legal status before the courts but it does suggest that there is an increasing awareness that the present situation is anomalous. Indeed, in the recent report of the Parliamentary Task Force on Federal Provincial Fiscal Arrangements the all-party committee went as far as to suggest that consideration be given to reviewing the privileged tax status existing under section 125.[13] Thus it is possible (although not vary likely) that this issue may be resolved or at least clarified by a process of bargaining in the context of the operations of executive federalism. Whyte's insightful analysis on the probable current limits of the applicability of section 125 is a valuable contribution no matter how this issue is eventually tackled.

Notes

1. Section 125 reads:

"No Lands or Property belonging to Canada or any Province shall be liable to Taxation."

In more common language, it is often referred to as the provision whereby the "Crown cannot tax the Crown."

2. I am speaking in the past tense, since the new Constitution Act, 1982, when it takes effect, will alter what follows at least as far as civil rights and freedoms are concerned.

3. A.E. Safarian, *Ten Markets or One? Regional Barriers to Economic Activity in Canada,* Ontario Economic Council Discussion Paper 18 (1980).

4. The fact that this was a confiscatory tax (essentially 100-percent tax on increments to rent) would, as I understand it, be a factor under U.S. law but appeared not to be an issue in this case.

5. Severn v. The Queen [1878] 2 S.C.R. 70; City of Fredericton v. The Queen, [1880] 3 S.C.R. 505.

6. Citizens Insurance Co. of Canada v. Parsons [1881] 7 App. Cas. 96.

7. Canadian Federation of Agriculture v. A.G. for Quebec (1951), A.C. 179.

8. Toronto Electric Commissioners v. Snider, [1925] A.C. 396.

9. Re the Board of Commerce Act, 1919 and the Combines and Fair Prices Act, 1919, [1922] A.C. 191.

10. Bushnell, *The Control of Natural Resources through the Trade and Commerce Power and Proprietary Rights,* 6 *Canadian Public Policy/ Analyse de Politiques* 315 (1980).

11. J. Chretien, Securing the Canadian Economic Union in the Constitution (1980).

12. One critical difference between our constitutions on this issue is that section 92 explicitly spells out provincial powers.

13. Hours of Commons, Fiscal Federalism in Canada (1981).

Index

About the Contributors

Roy Bahl is professor of economics and director of the Metropolitan Studies Program in the Maxwell School at Syracuse University. He was previously an economist in the Fiscal Affairs Department of the International Monetary Fund and an assistant professor of economics at West Virginia University. He has been a consultant to various public and private agencies including Standard & Poor's Corporation, the Committee for Economic Development, and the State of New York. He is or has been a member of the editorial board of the *National Tax Journal,* member of the Board of Directors of the National Tax Association, and an elected member of the Committee on Taxation, Resources and Economic Development. He is the author of numerous books, monographs, and scholarly papers about urban-regional economics and finance. Dr. Bahl received the B.A. from Greenville College in Greenville, Illinois, in 1961, and the Ph.D. in economics from the University of Kentucky in 1965.

Robin Boadway studied at the Royal Military College of Canada and at Oxford University before receiving the Ph.D. in economics from Queen's University in Kingston, Ontario. He was a postdoctoral Fellow at the University of Chicago. Dr. Boadway taught at the Royal Military College and is now professor and head of the Department of Economics at Queen's University. His publications include *Public Sector Economics* (1979); *Canadian Tax Policy* (1980) and *Intergovernmental Transfers in Canada* (1980), both for the Canadian Tax Foundation; and a recently completed study for the Economic Council of Canada. He has also written several articles in economics journals.

Albert M. Church received the B.A. from Colorado College in 1963 and the Ph.D. from Claremont Graduate School in 1971. He has taught at Middlebury College and is currently a professor at the University of New Mexico. Dr. Church has written numerous publications in professional journals and is the author or coauthor of *Computers and Statistics in the Appraisal Process, The Sophisticated Investor,* and *Taxation of Nonrenewable Natural Resources.*

Thomas J. Courchene received his undergraduate education at the University of Saskatchewan and his Ph.D. from Princeton University. He is currently a professor of economics at the University of Western Ontario. Dr. Courchene has written several books on Canadian monetary policy and frequently writes about fiscal-federalism policy issues. He is a member of the Royal Society of Canada and has recently been appointed chairman of the Ontario Economic Council.

Peggy Cuciti is a senior research associate at the Center for Public-Private Sector Cooperation, University of Colorado-Denver. At the time of the TRED conference she was on the staff of the Advisory Commission on Intergovernmental Relations. Previously she was a policy analyst with the Congressional Budget Office. Dr. Cuciti received the Ph.D. from the Department of Political Science, University of Chicago.

Frank Flatters received the Ph.D. in international trade and public finance from The Johns Hopkins University. He is now associate professor of economics at Queen's University in Kingston, Ontario. His recent studies on regional economics include *The Economics of Equalization* (1982) and *Productivity, Transfers and Employment: Government Policies and the Newfoundland Economy* (1981), both for the Economic Council of Canada. He has also published articles in the *Canadian Journal of Economics.*

Mason Gaffney is professor of economics, University of California at Riverside. He received the B.A. from Reed College in 1948 and the Ph.D. from the University of California at Berkeley in 1956. He has previously been affiliated with the University of Oregon, North Carolina State University, University of Missouri, and the University of Wisconsin at Milwaukee. He has also worked at Resources for the Future, Inc., and the British Columbia Institute for Economic Policy Analysis. Dr. Gaffney has written numerous articles on the economics of land use and is the author of *Concepts of Financial Maturity* (1957), *Extractive Resources and Taxation* (1967), and *Oil and Gas Leasing Policy: Alternatives for Alaska* (1977).

Harvey Galper is currently a senior public finance resident on the staff of the Advisory Commission on Intergovernmental Relations. He previously was director of the Office of Tax Analysis in the U.S. Treasury Department, a senior research staff member of the Urban Institute, and a staff economist with the Board of Governors of the Federal Reserve System. He has taught at Dartmouth College and the University of California, Berkeley, and is currently adjunct professor at the Georgetown University Law Center. He received the B.A. from Dartmouth College and the M.A. and Ph.D. from Yale University. Dr. Galper has published primarily in the areas of public finance and taxation and is coauthor of "State and Local Government Fiscal Behavior and Federal Grant Policy," *Brookings Paper on Economic Activity,* no. 1, 1973; "Preferential Taxation and Portfolio Choice: Some Empirical Evidence," *National Tax Journal,* December 1977; "Modelling the Allocation and Revenue Effects of the Use of Tax-Exempt Bonds for Private Purposes" in *Efficiency in the Municipal Bond Market: The Use of Tax-Exempt Financing for "Private" Purposes,* George G. Kaufman, ed., 1981.

Walter Hellerstein is associate professor at the University of Georgia School of Law, where he has taught since 1978. Previously he taught at the University of Chicago Law School and practiced law at Covington & Burling in Washington, D.C. He is coauthor of *State and Local Taxation, Cases and Materials,* (1978), and has published numerous articles on state taxation in legal periodicals. He graduated from Harvard College in 1967 and from the University of Chicago Law School in 1970.

Robert Lucke received the A.B. in economics from the University of California at Berkeley in 1977. He received the M.A. from the Humphrey Institute of Public Affairs at the University of Minnesota in 1980. He is the author of the Advisory Commission on Intergovernmental Relation's most recent study on the representative-tax system, *Tax Capacity of the Fifty States: Methodology and Estimates,* 1982.

Oliver Oldman is Learned Hand Professor of Law at the Harvard Law School and director of the school's International Tax Program. He has been a consultant on tax law and policy to national, state, and city governments in the United States and abroad. He was a member of the Shoup Commission to Venezuela in 1958 and the Musgrave Commission to Colombia in 1968. Mr. Oldman is coauthor of *State and Local Taxes and Finance* (1974) and *Financing Urban Development in Mexico City* (1967), and is coeditor of *Readings on Taxation in Developing Countries* (1964) and *Readings on Income Tax Administration* (1973). He has also written numerous articles in scholarly journals.

Eric J. Toder is currently a financial economist on the staff of the Office of Tax Analysis, U.S. Department of the Treasury. His previous positions were director, Office of Finance and Tax Analysis, U.S. Department of Energy; senior research associate, Charles River Associates; and assistant professor of Economics, Tufts University. Dr. Toder received the Ph.D. in economics from the University of Rochester. His previous publications include a major study of the U.S. automobile industry and several articles on the taxation of income from capital.

John D. Whyte was educated at the University of Toronto; Queen's University at Kingston, Ontario; and Harvard University. He joined the law faculty of Queen's University in 1969 and is now professor of law. He is currently the director of constitutional law in the Department of the Attorney General of the Government of Saskatchewan. He is coauthor of *Canadian Constitutional Law*, a casebook widely used in Canadian law faculties.

Martin B. Zimmerman is associate professor of management at the Massachusetts Institute of Technology from which he received the Ph.D. in economics. He has written extensively about energy economics and the economics of the coal industry. His recent publications include *The U.S. Coal Industry: The Economics of Policy Choice* (1981).

About the Editors

Charles E. McLure, Jr., is a senior Fellow at the Hoover Institution at Stanford University. He has previously been vice-president of the National Bureau of Economic Research, professor of economics at Rice University, and a member of the senior staff of the Council of Economic Advisers. He has been an adviser on tax policy to various U.S. government agencies, foreign governments and international organizations.

Peter Mieszkowski is professor of economics at Rice University. He studied at McGill University in Quebec and received the Ph.D. from The Johns Hopkins University in 1963. Dr. Mieszkowski has taught at Yale University, Queen's University in Kingston, Ontario, and the University of Houston. He was a postdoctoral Fellow at the University of Chicago. Dr. Mieszkowski has written on the theory of tax incidence and related problems of income distribution. He has also worked on urban issues, regional development, and problems of intergovernmental relations. His current research interest is the taxation of natural resources and energy.

DATE DUE

Sloan 9-4-85	SEP 18 85	
Sloan 9-27-85	OCT 23 85	
DEC 1 6 1987		
DEC 1 0 87		

DEMCO 38-297